THE LAW OF PROPERTY

By

CHRISTOPHER SERKIN

Professor of Law

Brooklyn Law School

CONCEPTS AND INSIGHTS SERIES®

FOUNDATION PRESS

2013

THOMSON REUTERS™

© 2013 By THOMSON REUTERS/FOUNDATION PRESS

    1 New York Plaza, 34th Floor

    New York, NY 10004

    Phone Toll Free 1–877–888–1330

    Fax 646–424–5201

    foundation–press.com

Printed in the United States of America

ISBN 978–1–60930–062–3

Mat #41187091

For Kim and Amalia

ACKNOWLEDGMENTS

I owe an enormous intellectual debt to Jim Krier, who has directly and indirectly taught me much of what I know about property. Likewise, Michael Heller introduced me to property law and shaped how I think about the topic. The insights of Greg Alexander, Vicki Been, Hanoch Dagan, Bob Ellickson, Rick Hills, Tom Merrill, Michael Schill, Joe Singer, and Henry Smith—from their casebooks, teaching, and scholarship—give this book much of its content. I am grateful to the property faculty at Brooklyn Law School, and in particular to Gregg Macey, Dana Brakman Reiser, and Brian Lee for comments and reactions. This book would not have been possible without the support of Brooklyn Law School, and in particular my colleagues Michael Cahill, Fred Bloom and Nelson Tebbe. I would especially like to thank John Serkin for his invaluable comments and advice.

TABLE OF CONTENTS

THE LAW OF
PROPERTY

INTRODUCTION

Why have property? This sensible question can be divided in two. Why is property one of the staples of the legal curriculum? And why do we have a system of property rights, anyway? The second question is more substantive and, by some measure, this entire book is an attempt at an answer. But the first question usefully frames the general enterprise.

Property has long been a required course in the first year of law school. At first blush, its inclusion is not obvious. Property does not order our system of government, like constitutional law. It does not govern our commercial interactions, like contracts, nor justify the power of the state to impose punishment, like criminal law. But property is just as fundamental as those other subjects. It is, at its core, about the nature of ownership and the rights that ownership confers.

Property is one of three sources of private rights in the common law, along with contracts and torts. In many ways, it is the foundational source of private rights. Contracts, after all, typically involve exchanges of property (especially if property is defined broadly enough to include labor). And torts usually arise from injuries to property (especially if property includes one's body). Property and property rights are therefore building blocks for the rest of the private law.

The property curriculum also undergirds other more advanced legal subjects. Wills and trusts and family law involve the transfer of property at death and divorce. Intellectual property, whether patents, copyright, trademark, or common law doctrines like trade secrets, is about the creation of rights in intangible property. Real estate transactions involve conveyances of real property, and land use explores the forms and limits of government regulation of real property. Other less-obvious courses also rely on property's central insights. Bankruptcy and secured transactions require courts and parties (and law students!) to identify property interests, while many other subjects, from employment law, to tax, bioethics and environmental law all borrow heavily from property categories and concepts. While the introductory study of property law can seem at times anachronistic and out of date, it is key to understanding much of the legal system and many of its cutting-edge topics.

Perhaps even more importantly, property is a useful lens for examining different modes and methods of legal analysis. Philosophy, law and economics, and history offer important lessons for understanding property, and vice-versa. Fluency in the law of property means developing a command over various analytical approaches to law. As much as anything, the goal of studying property is to develop proficiency in these different vocabularies.

To the extent possible, this book is methodologically agnostic and presents the leading arguments relating to each topic regardless of the animating discipline. This tracks the pedagogical decision that many property professors make when teaching a property class. But different courses will undoubtedly weight the relative disciplines differently—and some may even focus exclusively on, say, a historical account and leave law and economics entirely aside. By offering as broad a treatment of property as possible, this book seeks to be useful to students approaching the topic from a wide variety of perspectives.

This book is therefore different from many other secondary property texts. While it presents the black-letter law and provides a firm foundation for straightforward doctrinal analysis, its emphasis is on those important concepts and insights that make sense of the doctrine from a variety of theoretical perspectives. For most property students, command of the doctrine is necessary but not sufficient for mastering the subject, because one central purpose of studying property is to develop the ability to see beyond the doctrine and to articulate and argue about its animating principles. To put it bluntly, if you want to know the statute of limitations for adverse possession in various states, read a different book. But if you want to understand why there is a doctrine of adverse possession in the first place, and how it relates to property law's otherwise firm protection of prior possessors, then keep reading.

The book is organized into three main themes: acquiring property, dividing property, and limiting rights in property. Although not keyed to any particular property text, this book most closely tracks the organization of DUKEMINIER, KRIER, ALEXANDER & SCHILL, PROPERTY (7th edition). It discusses cases presented in that book, as well as cases from MERRILL & SMITH, PROPERTY: PRINCIPLES & POLICIES (2nd edition), and SINGER, PROPERTY LAW: RULES, POLICIES & PRACTICES (5th edition). Cases are keyed to the page numbers in those textbooks in the following format: [DKA & S]; [MS]; and [S], respectively.

In addition to working methodically through the core subjects within each theme, this book also highlights and explores some cutting-edge property topics. These detours are important for two reasons. First, they permit exploration of traditional property concepts in new and emerging controversies. Second, and more prosaically, they may be where the real action is in many property classes today. Although not every property course will cover all the topics discussed in this book, chances are good that the newer and more speculative topics will be the focus of extra attention precisely because so many interesting questions remain unresolved.

There are many different ways to teach and to learn property. No single text, just like no single class, can cover all topics and offer all perspectives. This book certainly does not try. But what it does offer is a coherent, clear, and careful path through the standard property course, while including enough fresh insights and analysis to provide even property veterans with new and helpful perspectives on property.

Part I
THE ORIGINS OF PRIVATE PROPERTY

Chapter 1

FUNDAMENTALS

On first encounter, property can have the feel of a foreign language. It is governed by seemingly byzantine rules, and described in a vocabulary that dates to feudal times. Terms like "subinfeudation" or "livery of seisin"—among many others—convey no obvious meaning to the beleaguered property student.

But property is much more than a linguistic challenge, and the project and promise of studying it is more than just comprehension. Keeping a clear eye on the role of property reveals the stakes of the enterprise: Property is fundamental to how we order our lives and relate to one another. The study of property is no less than the study of society, the State, and the very underpinnings of law. To see why this is so, and to set a proper frame around the doctrinal material in the chapters that follow, it is important to wrestle first with some of the basic questions: What is property? Why (and how) does the legal system recognize property rights? What are the goals of a property system, and what are its costs?

These questions turn out to be not so basic after all. This chapter offers some preliminary answers and, in the process, identifies ongoing themes and inquiries that carry through the rest of the book.

A. What Is Property?

The work of defining property seems like a natural place to begin exploring the subject. But merely framing the question can be misleading. Property, in its legal sense, does not only refer to things in the world. The study of property, after all, is not the study of your house, your clothes, or any of your physical possessions. What is property, anyway? This fundamental definitional challenge has spanned centuries and continues to this day.

In William Blackstone's canonical eighteenth century formulation, property is "that sole and despotic dominion which one man claims and exercises over the external things of the world, in total exclusion of the right of any other individual in the universe."[1] Property, in this view, is characterized by total dominion. It defines a sphere of protected liberty. People are free to do with their

---

1. 2 WILLIAM BLACKSTONE, COMMENTARIES ON THE LAWS OF ENGLAND *2 (1766).

property whatever they want, free from any one else's competing interests. It is also an *in rem* right; it is a right to a thing (the property) that is good against the world.

By the early twentieth century, however, this absolutist conception of property gave way to a new view of rights generally. The prominent legal theorist Wesley Hohfeld argued that people do not have rights to an object in the world; they have rights against each other.[2] Property's *in rem* rights are nothing more (and nothing less) than relationships *between people*. In a strong form of this claim, property is not about things in the world at all, but instead consists of a loosely organized bundle of rights that people have against one another.[3]

Today, this "bundle of rights" conception predominates property law and scholarship. From this view, property is not a single right. No single attribute determines whether property exists. Instead, property is a more-or-less loose collection of separately specifiable rights, which typically includes the rights to exclude, to possess or use, and to transfer (and subcategories within each).[4] One or more sticks in this bundle can be limited or removed and still leave property, depending on the constellation of rights that remain. For example, you cannot sell or otherwise transfer your law degree, but you may still have a protectable property interest in it if the government, or your spouse, or a creditor tries to take it away.

More recently, the "bundle" metaphor itself has come under attack. Some "bundle critics," most notably Professors Thomas Merrill and Henry Smith, have sought to reclaim, at least in part, the *in rem* nature of property.[5] They argue that property, at its core, is the right to exclude others from a specific resource. Their claim amounts roughly to an argument that property is what most people think it is: the exclusive right to a resource in the world. Moreover, it may be possible to derive all of the other rights from exclusion, by manipulating its contours and selectively excluding others for different purposes. Exclusion, then, may be *the* foundational right—the right from which all others spring.

To oversimplify the debate, some—call them Hohfeldians— view property as a collection of rights that can be reconfigured in

---

2. See WESLEY N. HOHFELD, FUNDAMENTAL LEGAL CONCEPTIONS AS APPLIED IN JUDICIAL REASONING AND OTHER LEGAL ESSAYS (1923).

3. For further exploration and critique of this view, see J.E. Penner, *The "Bundle of Rights" Picture of Property*, 43 UCLA L. REV. 711 (1996) [M & S, p. 17].

4. A.H. Honeré, *Ownership,* in OXFORD ESSAYS IN JURISPRUDENCE 197 (1961).

5. See, e.g., Thomas W. Merrill & Henry E. Smith, *The Morality of Property,* 48 WM. & MARY L. REV. 1849 (2007); *see also* JAMES E. PENNER, THE IDEA OF PROPERTY IN LAW (1997).

various ways. Others—Blackstonians, for short—view property in more categorical terms as consisting of a more-or-less exclusive right to a resource. Not surprisingly, modern proponents of these competing visions offer sophisticated and subtle variations and defenses of their views. Theirs is simultaneously an abstract disagreement and one with real teeth, as we will see throughout this book. But it also demonstrates that the definition of property is contested—that even the *project* of defining property is contested. At the edges of difficult property disputes, where black letter law provides no clear resolution, these disagreements again emerge and competing answers may hinge on fundamental disagreements about what property is.

Consider *Jacque v. Steenberg Homes, Inc.*,[6] in which the defendant sought to deliver one of its mobile homes to a customer. The shortest and easiest route for delivery was across property belonging to the Jacques, who refused to grant permission. Steenberg Homes crossed their land anyway, and the Jacques sued. Despite the absence of any damage to their property, a jury awarded $100,000 in punitive damages for the intentional trespass over the Jacques' land. The State Supreme Court upheld the award, reasoning that "both the private landowner and society have much more than a nominal interest in excluding others from private land."

This case serves as a useful introduction to the nature of the right to exclude—and is the first case in the Merrill & Smith casebook—precisely because it does not involve any physical harm or economic loss. It is only one right—the right to exclude—that Steenberg Homes "took" from the plaintiffs. For the *Jacque* court, that was enough. Owning property means being able to deny permission to someone to enter, even for idiosyncratic reasons, and the law should vindicate this fundamental right regardless of other injuries. For our Blackstonians, the case is an elegant articulation of the primacy of the right to exclude.

Hohfeldians can embrace the case, too. In the bundle of rights, the right to exclude is of course extremely important. But exclusion is not necessary for property, and indeed must sometimes give way because property, after all, consists of rights between people that can vary depending on context. *Jacque* is therefore usefully contrasted with *State v. Shack*.[7] There, the owner of a farm sought to

---

6. 563 N.W.2d 154 (Wis. 1997) [DKA & S, p. 89]; [M & S, p. 1]. But see Hinman v. Pacific Air Transport, 84 F.2d 755 (9th Cir. 1936) [M & S, p. 10] (requiring showing of damages before allowing trespass action based on airplane overflights).

7. 277 A.2d 369 (N.J. 1971) [DKA & S, p. 90]; [M & S, p. 409]; [S, p. 3]; see also Ploof v. Putnam, 71 A. 188 (Vt. 1908) [M & S, p. 400]; [S, p. 32] (recognizing limit of right to exclude a ship in a storm, especially where human life is at stake).

prohibit farmworker representatives from entering his property to meet with, and provide services to, the migrant workers he employed. Defendants entered anyway and were charged with trespass. They claimed they had a right to enter the property. In essence, they called for balancing the owner's right to exclude against the workers' right to access services. The New Jersey Supreme Court agreed with the defendants, eloquently writing: "Property rights serve human values. They are recognized to that end, and are limited by it. Title to real property cannot include dominion over the destiny of persons the owner permits to come upon the premises." This is a more contingent right to exclude than the *Jacque* court articulated.

To appreciate what is at stake in these somewhat abstract debates, consider our second question: Why does our legal system recognize rights in property, anyway?

B. Why Have Property?

Examining why we have a system of property rights goes a long way to understanding what the content of those rights are and should be. As property's doctrinal contours emerge over the coming chapters, its outer boundaries will frequently require returning to this fundamental question. Philosophy, history, and law and economics, provide different kinds of answers. Each is motivated by very different underlying goals and rationales, which together contribute to an overall sense of the purpose of a property regime in our legal system.

These three lenses recur explicitly and implicitly throughout the study of property as well as this book. The following descriptions frame the basic approaches of these three disciplines, laying a foundation for their later application to particular property doctrines.

Philosophy

One set of answers about the purpose of property comes from core philosophical insights. John Locke is among the best known philosophers in the property literature. He argued, in essence, that property rights arise out of human labor. Since "every man has a property in his own person," people acquire property by adding labor to resources in the world.[8] Property, in this view, is the natural result of human toil—whether tilling fields, building houses, or writing books. Why have property? Because, Locke would reply, it is the result of human endeavor.

---

8. John Locke, Two Treatises of Government, Book II, Ch. V (1690).

There are caveats. Where a resource is scarce, contributing labor does not necessarily justify removing it from the common pool and converting it to private property. Moreover, Locke's labor theory, as it is known, raises complicated questions about how much and what kind of labor should count. If one person lays a thin string around a field, and then someone else comes along later and tills the field by hand, who can claim it? What labor is required to establish a property claim? Locke's theory provides a powerful way of thinking about the problem of property, but it raises as many questions as it answers.

Locke's labor theory nevertheless occupies a dominant place in American conceptions of property. It is also closely associated with individualistic and libertarian attitudes towards property because it does not explicitly rely on the State—or at least on any particular conception of the State—to generate property rights. Private property comes from the individual, toiling alone, to transform wild nature into productive, domesticated resources.

David Hume provided a competing State-centered account of private property. Hume argued that "Our property is nothing but those goods, whose constant possession is establish'd by the laws of society; that is, by the laws of justice."[9] In other words, without the State, we merely have possession—and ephemeral possession at that. It is only with the State that we can have the social rules, and the just laws, that create property rights that others have a moral duty to respect. Thomas Hobbes, too, saw property as the product of sovereign or State authority. Indeed, he derived the authority of the State from the need for stable property rights.[10]

Many other philosophers have focused on the problem of property, from Plato and Aristotle to Hegel and Kant. Each has contemporary proponents as well, so that the works of Locke, Hume and the others return again in modern guise throughout the later chapters of this book. But in answering the initial question here, why property exists, philosophy provides both individual and State-focused answers. Property exists because people work for it, or because the State recognizes it. These justifications are in constant tension throughout the study of property.

There is a more purposive philosophical account of property as well. In a leading view, property is essential for human liberty.[11] It

---

9. David Hume, A Treatise of Human Nature [1739] 488 (L.A. Selby–Bigge & P. H. Nidditch eds., 1978).

10. Thomas Hobbes, De Ceve: The English Version [1647] 26–27 (Howard Warrender, ed. 1983).

11. See, e.g., James W. Ely, Jr., The Guardian of Every Other Right: A Constitutional History of Property Rights (3d ed. 2008).

defines a sphere that is safe from governmental intrusion. It gives people the means to be self-sufficient without the State, and so is a necessary precondition for genuine political participation. This view generates a different kind of explanation for the existence of property. It is not derived *a priori* from the nature of the relationship between people and the State or the world, but is instead an instrumentally important tool for securing other goods: security, freedom, and human flourishing.

Philosophical debates about property are, of course, ongoing. It is enough for now to recognize that they exist, and to see, in general terms, how they frame the study of property law.

History

History provides a different kind of account of the existence of property. At the most general level—addressing the very existence of property as a concept—history has little to say. Indeed, the history of property would presumably need to trace back to the origins of human civilization. But history can be tremendously illuminating about the emergence and shape of property rights in particular contexts.

Economists, philosophers, and law professors have offered various kinds of genealogical accounts of property, finding in its rise and evolution confirmation of one overarching theory or another. Whether it is Harold Demsetz's account of Indian fur traders and the rise of land ownership,[12] or Robert Ellickson's detailed description of the community norms around property rights among ranchers in Shasta County,[13] history is often pressed into service for some conceptual account of property.

History also has its own explanatory power, although it is descriptive and not prescriptive. Understanding the occasionally anachronistic contours of many modern property doctrines requires tracing their evolution from feudal origins—a project taken up at various times throughout this book.

Viewing property through a historical lens also reveals how its content is determined in no small measure by social, political, and technological change. As conceptions of the family change, so, too, do the laws governing the division of property at divorce or death. As the State's role in consumer protection expanded in the 1950s and 1960s, property rules governing the relationship between landlords and tenants shifted in favor of the latter. And, with the rise of

---

12. Harold Demsetz, *Toward a Theory of Property Rights,* 57 AM. ECON. REV. 347 (1967) [DKA & S, p. 39]; [M & S, p. 275].

13. ROBERT C. ELLICKSON, ORDER WITHOUT LAW: HOW NEIGHBORS SETTLE DISPUTES (1991).

the telegraph—and, more recently, its modern analogue in Facebook—the rules of ownership and dissemination change to keep up.

Why have property, then? Or why, at least, have *our* property system? Because of, historians would argue, how the world has developed. Property is historically contingent, and history therefore shapes—and is itself shaped by—its content.

Law and Economics

Still another prominent set of answers comes from the consequentialist reasoning of law and economics. In fact, this mode of analysis dominates modern property discourse and provides a powerful set of justifications for property rights. Why have property? Because it makes people better off. In particular, it allows (or forces) people to bear the costs of their actions, solves certain collective-action problems, and makes it easier for people to engage in welfare-maximizing transactions.

The underlying goal of a law and economics approach to law is to facilitate, as much as possible, the movement of resources into the hands of the highest-valued user. In these terms, the justification for property is that it increases overall societal wellbeing by minimizing conflict and creating the conditions for voluntary transactions. This is a simple but central insight in the law of property.

If transactions were entirely frictionless, then, from an economic perspective, everything could be made private property and voluntary market transactions would ensure that every resource wound up with the person who valued it the most. If I had something—a book, jewelry, food, a kidney[14]—that you valued more than I did, you should be willing to offer me enough money that I will sell it to you. Or, viewed from another perspective, if you cannot offer me enough money to get me to sell it to you, then—by definition!—I value it more than you do. What's more, the initial allocation of resources (or rights to resources) will not affect their ultimate distribution. In a world without transaction costs, as the economist Ronald Coase hypothesized in his famous thought experiment, a person who values property more will always be able to acquire it from a lower-valued user.[15]

Of course, we do not live in a frictionless world. Transaction costs are everywhere and will often prevent exchanges that would otherwise have made both parties better off. Search costs, coordination costs, bargaining costs, and the like, mean that resources will

---

14. The moral dimension of treating everything like property—even babies and body parts—is addressed below. See *infra* Part C; see also Chapter 2(D).

15. See Ronald Coase, *The Problem of Social Costs*, 3 J. L. & Econ. 1 (1960) [M & S, p. 31].

often stay in the hands of lower-valued users. From an economic perspective, then, property is justified to the extent that it maximizes the value of resources, and minimizes the costs of transacting for them. An overarching theme of studying property from an economic perspective is to ask when and how protecting private rights will result in a more efficient allocation of resources than some other alternative, like communal ownership or regulation.

This idea is on stark display in Harold Demsetz's account of property.[16] He argued that property rights arise "to internalize externalities when the gains of internalization become larger than the cost of internalization." This is a profound albeit cryptic insight, and it requires understanding the concept of an "externality" (a core concept in any law and economics account of property, and an important one to understand).

An externality, in economics parlance, is a cost (or benefit) imposed on someone else that the cost-maker does not have to bear. The idea is at once straightforward and slippery. It is easy enough to recognize that people impose costs on each other all the time. When someone smokes a cigarette in a crowded room she is imposing costs on surrounding non-smokers. When someone talks loudly on a cell phone, uses a laptop in distracting ways in class, or eats the limited free pizza in the student lounge, she imposes costs on those around her (smoke, distraction, reduction in available pizza). Conversely, when Trader Joe's opens in an under-served neighborhood, when someone keeps a lovely garden in the front of her house, or provides some otherwise pleasurable experience to passersby, positive benefits flow to others.

These costs and benefits are not necessarily externalities, however. They are only externalities to the extent that the person creating them does not internalize them. To make this intuition concrete, imagine someone using a laptop during class to watch a movie. Depending on the movie (and the class), this activity is likely to impose a cost on people sitting behind her. She is, in other words, creating a negative externality, because she is imposing a cost on others that she does not bear. What does she care of the harm to the people behind her? She may not even be aware of it. But the distracted neighbors have a potential response. One or more of them could offer to pay the laptop user to stop using her laptop for movies and to concentrate instead on taking notes. If the irritated neighbors offer enough, the laptop user will presumably stop. That is, there is a price at which the laptop user would be

---

16. Demsetz, *supra,* [DKA & S, p. 39]; [M & S, p. 275].

willing to pay attention in class instead of watching Star Wars Episode I.

But—and this is the crucial point!—the laptop user does not have to stop watching the movie for the externality to end. This is why an externality does not simply mean a cost imposed on someone else. If a neighbor offers, say, $10 to stop, and the movie-watcher *continues*, she has now internalized $10 of the cost she is imposing on her neighbor, even if she does not accept the money. That is, she declined a cash offer, which amounts to "spending" $10 to keep watching Jar Jar Binks. She may well be imposing additional costs to additional neighbors. And the $10 offer may not fully reflect the extent of the harm her movie watching created. Any other costs, in excess of the $10 offer, remain externalities. But, again, the laptop user is no longer externalizing the full costs of her actions once she rejects an offer to stop, even though she continues to impose the same quantity of harm.

Why is this so important? It might seem to be emphasizing an awfully fine distinction. In fact, a lot turns on the concept, because the presence of externalities is likely to produce either too much or too little of an activity. Take a more serious example than laptops in class: air pollution. A noxious polluting factory imposes costs on neighbors. If the factory does not have to bear those costs, it may over-pollute, that is, emit more pollution than it otherwise would if it in fact had to pay the full costs of its actions. Perhaps it would make fewer widgets, or adopt other pollution-mitigation strategies, if it had to internalize the costs of widget production. Or perhaps its activity is valuable enough, and mitigation expensive enough, that it would prefer simply to pay and not otherwise change its conduct. But forcing the factory to compensate puts it to the test and forces it to consider—and price in to its decisionmaking and its widgets—the costs it is imposing on others.

Return, then to Demsetz's claim that property serves "to internalize externalities when the gains of internalization become larger than the cost of internalization," but in the context of a specific example. Imagine that Harold maintains a beautiful community garden on public land next to his house. He takes great pleasure from it, as do all of his neighbors who like to sit on a little iron bench in the shade and smell the flowers. However, the garden requires time and money to maintain—burdens that presently fall only on Harold. He may well become unwilling to maintain the garden anymore, despite the fact that it provides more pleasure to many people than it actually costs Harold in time and money. The problem is that he has no mechanism for capturing the benefit that the garden confers on his neighbors. If he did, he would continue to

14

maintain it. Adding some stylized numbers makes the point even clearer.[17]

Imagine that the garden is worth $1,000 to Harold (meaning that he would be willing to pay up to $1,000 to maintain it), but costs him $1,500 to maintain. It also generates pleasure for others on the block as well—say ten people who each receive $100 worth of pleasure from the garden. With these numbers, Harold will stop maintaining the garden, even though it creates $2,000 worth of benefits and costs Harold only $1,500. The problem is that $1,000 of the benefits comes in the form of positive externalities. The aggregate wellbeing of society will increase if Harold maintains the garden, but because it is not in his personal self-interest, Harold may not. If he could capture even $501 worth of that externalized benefit, though, he would continue tending the garden.

Consider the potential solutions. The ten neighbors may voluntarily get together, each chip in $100, and pay Harold to keep maintaining the garden. But this is unlikely. Each neighbor has an incentive to free-ride, that is, to rely on the other neighbors giving money, allowing her to enjoy the benefit for free. But if everyone thinks this way, no one will pay (or everyone will pay less than her fair share), and the garden will again disappear. Also, as the numbers go up—if there were one hundred or one thousand neighbors instead of ten—the costs of coordination among the neighbors may become prohibitive. Where that is true, some other kind of solution is needed.

The government could intervene, using its taxing power to collect money from the neighbors and distributing it to Harold to maintain the garden (or the government could maintain the garden itself). Mandatory taxes avoid the free-rider problem, but raise serious pricing concerns. The government may not be particularly good at assessing the extent to which each neighbor values the garden, and therefore may end up either taxing too much, or subsidizing "benefits" that are not, in fact, worth their cost. Furthermore, the government might not reach the efficient outcome even if it perfectly represents the interests of its constituents. In this example, the $1,500 maintenance costs would be spread evenly among eleven people (because once the government takes over, there is no need for Harold to pay a disproportionate share), meaning that the government would need to charge approximately $136 per person in taxes. But ten of the eleven people would not be

---

17. These kinds of hypothetical scenarios, with fictional numbers attached, are a staple of property analysis. The point is not to find the actual values to assign, but is instead to observe, in numerical form, the effect of different rules on the distribution and use of resources.

willing to pay that much for the garden—they value it at $100, each—and would vote against the tax.

Finally, then, property provides a potential solution. If Harold had the capacity to exclude others from the garden, then he could charge people to enter. That is, by turning the public park into a private one, Harold could contract with his neighbors to capture some of the garden's value to them, and he might again be willing to maintain it.

Notice, though, that property is not always a solution. As Demsetz frames the calculus, it depends both on the available gains from internalizing externalities, and the costs of doing so. Here, the costs are obvious. They include the costs of creating the ticketing system: a gate, a turnstile, a pricing system, and the like. And they also include the costs of monitoring to make sure that people are, in fact, paying as required. If these costs—the costs of internalization—exceed the amount that Harold could capture through tickets—the gains of internalization—then creating private property rights will still not allow Harold to collect enough money to maintain the garden.

Property, in this view, is a mechanism to allow or force people to internalize externalities, and it applies widely. Creating pollution credits so that factories have to pay to pollute forces them to bear some of the costs of their actions. Protecting patents allows inventors to capture some of the value of their useful inventions from would-be copiers. Whether it is the best solution, or even an appropriate one, depends on its relative advantages over voluntary coordination, government regulation, or some other institutional arrangement—an issue of relative competence that will reappear throughout this book.

Under this conception, property's appeal comes from giving owners the power to decide how to manage resources and maximize their own wellbeing. If someone wants to invest in developing her land or take meticulous care of her car, she bears the costs but also reaps the benefits. Property allows people to decide for themselves how to value those costs and benefits. Preferences are likely to be idiosyncratic, and will depend, for example, on aesthetic values, risk aversion, cash flow, and the like. The range and content of preferences is truly limitless. And this is precisely why property generally protects owners' autonomy to weigh those costs and benefits however they want and to manage their resources however they think best, so long as they are internalizing (bearing) the full costs of their decisions.

16

From an economic perspective, this kind of decisionmaking authority can maximize societal wellbeing. The underlying assumption is that people's voluntary decisions necessarily increase their wellbeing. That is, people will not make decisions—whether to invest in property, sell an asset, read a book, go to school, allow fields to lie fallow—unless doing so makes them better off in some way. It may be that the decision imposes a short-term cost but with the promise of a long-term gain. Or the opposite. But property, by allowing people to set their own values for a resource, ensures that people make decisions that make them better off, however they define that for themselves. This includes deciding to buy or sell property, and the assumption in any voluntary exchange is that both parties are made better off (or at least, no party is made worse off, and at least one party benefits). Therefore, facilitating property transactions increases societal wellbeing by encouraging transfers of resources to people who value them more.

A constraint on owners' authority over property comes from the possibility that individual decisions will impose costs—externalities—on others. While you can choose for yourself how much to invest in maintaining your car, if you spend too little your brakes might fail and you might cause an accident. You internalize some of those costs; you don't want to be in an accident either. But you do not internalize all of them. Likewise, your decision to develop property may consume important wildlife habitats, interfere with others' views, or impose any of a number of specific or general harms on neighbors and the community as a whole. Some specific property doctrines seek to mediate these conflicts,[18] but they speak to a broader principle: the existence of externalities can motivate different approaches to private property.

This is on stark display in Garrett Hardin's famous account of the tragedy of the commons.[19] Anyone who has ever attended a school-sponsored pizza party has probably experienced a tragedy of the commons at work. Imagine the following scenario. You are moderately hungry and walk into a crowded student lounge with boxes of free pizzas at one end. If you had your way, and were alone in your house or apartment, you would probably have a single slice, wait a little while, and then, perhaps, have another one or two over the course of the evening. But that is not, in fact, the approach you are likely to take in the student lounge. Instead, after jockeying your way to the front of the room, you will probably grab two slices immediately—or however many will fit on your plate—eat them as

---

18. The most obvious examples are nuisance, discussed in Chapter 11, and land use regulations, discussed in Chapter 12.

19. Garrett Hardin, *The Tragedy of the Commons*, 162 SCIENCE 1243 (1968).

quickly as possible, and perhaps even return for a third (or fourth) just as quickly as you can. But if this is not your preferred pattern for pizza consumption—if, left to your own devices, you would likely eat less, and certainly eat more slowly—why the change in behavior in the student lounge?

The answer is not temporary insanity or loss of self-control. The problem, instead, is the anticipated behavior of everyone else around you. If you hold off on eating an additional slice, knowing that you would prefer it more an hour from now, you have no guarantee that there will be any pizza left when you eventually want it. If you don't eat it now, it might be gone! What's worse, everyone around you is worried about the same thing. The result: everyone has an incentive to over-consume the pizza, eating it more quickly than he actually wants, and no one has an incentive to act as a responsible steward for the pizza, to ensure that it is allocated efficiently.

Step back and analyze the problem formally and by adding some numbers to the example. Imagine that there are 50 students in the student lounge, and 100 pieces of pizza. There is, then, enough for each student to have two slices. But if your friend Garrett takes 2 slices of pizza, there are now only 98 pieces of pizza left for everyone, or enough for everyone to have 1.96 slices of pizza (98 divided by 50). Measuring people's "wealth" in terms of pizza, look at what has happened: Garrett's "wealth" has increased from 2 slices (his 1/50th share in the original pool of pizzas) to 3.96 (because he already captured two slices, but still has his share of the rest). Meanwhile, everyone else's wealth has decreased, from 2 to 1.96. Anyone who takes a slice of pizza out of the common pool captures the full value of that slice, and externalizes the cost on everyone else by reducing the amount of pizza left over. Therefore, each person has an incentive to capture as many slices of pizza, and as quickly, as possible (setting aside the diminishing marginal utility of pizza).

If everyone feels the same way, why don't all the students agree simply to pace themselves? The problem is transaction costs. Even if everyone would be better off with slower consumption, the cost of reaching that agreement, of getting all 50 people to slow down their eating, is likely to be prohibitively high. In order to be assured that there will be pizza left over an hour from now, everyone would have to agree not to eat too quickly.

This, then, is the tragedy of the commons in a nutshell. When too many people have the right to use or consume a sufficiently valuable expendable resource, every individual has an incentive to over-consume and high transaction costs can keep people from bargaining to a more efficient outcome (i.e., an outcome that maximizes the value of the resource). The problem exists far beyond the school pizza party. It includes over-foresting and over-fishing, which are, in Hardin's words, "tragic" because they are the predictable outcomes of individual incentives in the absence of collective management of a resource. Even air pollution can be described in these terms, where the expendable resource is clean air, and polluters over-consume it with their emissions. Indeed, having identified the phenomenon, the tragedy of the commons begins to turn up everywhere.

Creating private property rights, and allowing "owners" to control consumption of the resource, can be a solution. Return to the pizza. If, instead of an unrestricted right to eat as much pizza as possible everyone were given an entitlement to two pieces of pizza, then you could eat one slice now and save your second for later. That is, by creating private property rights in the pizza, you would be given control over your allocation in the future, and could then choose when to consume it to maximize the value of the pizza to you.

Furthermore, the existence of private property can make coordination easier. If someone wants to acquire additional pizza, she can more easily identify rights holders and can negotiate for an extra slice without needing to obtain consent or forbearance from everyone else. Private property, when well implemented, can have the effect of reducing coordination or transaction costs.

Of course, private property is not the only solution to a tragedy of the commons. Regulation can work, too. Instead of creating private property in a resource—whether pizza, fish, or trees—the State can regulate the amount of the resource that anyone is allowed to capture or consume. Fishing quotas, limits on logging, or rules governing pizza consumption could each substitute for private property rights to prevent over-consumption of the underlying resource.

Community norms, and social sanctions, might work as well. Going out for pizza with close friends, the problem is often not over-consumption but under-consumption. The last piece of pizza may stay on the tray unclaimed because no one wants to incur the social costs of polishing off the last of the pie. This, of course, is highly contingent on the strength of the social bonds and the norms (social rules) around the table. But it is at least important to recognize that a tragedy of the commons is not the inevitable result of communal ownership, and that solutions other than private property rights exist. When it comes to choosing among these various kinds of solutions, careful attention must be paid to their relative costs and benefits.

This kind of law of economics analysis appears throughout modern understandings of property, and familiarity with its concepts is essential. But for now the more general point is the important one: Basic economic principles provide both a positive and normative account of property. Property exists, in this view, to make people better off, by aligning incentives around the production and consumption of resources. Property can prevent people from over-consuming, can minimize transaction costs, and can encourage industry by ensuring that individuals can capture the benefits of their work—to reap where they have sown. As a descriptive matter, property has developed where these benefits are sufficiently important. As a normative matter, this is desirable because it makes society as a whole better off, even if not every person within it will benefit. But it is always important to ask about alternatives. If the goal is to maximize societal wellbeing, the question is whether property will do it better than likely alternatives. From the perspective of law and economics, property is justified when the answer is, "yes."

There are still other accounts of property that can modify or substitute for the philosophical, economic, and historical ones. These arise in the context of various property doctrines, discussed in subsequent chapters. For now, it is enough to situate the study of property within these three broader analytic frameworks.

C. Why Not Have Property?

For all the reasons to embrace property, there are countervailing considerations. As mentioned above, property regimes can be expensive to set up and to administer. The costs may not justify the benefits in some situations. But there are other kinds of concerns as well that sound a cautionary note about property.

The first is a concern that it is somehow inappropriate—perhaps even immoral—to treat certain relationships as "property." The most obvious example is slavery. While it is possible to analyze slavery through the lens of law and economics, and to situate it historically in this country's property tradition, it is morally outrageous to view people as property. In fact, even applying a property framework to people seems an affront to their dignity and autonomy. This point can be extended and refined, suggesting limits to property discourse for organs and body parts, babies, and sex. These are all explored below, in the material on acquisition. But it is important to recognize that the very label of property can be controversial and even harmful.

Second, the "right to exclude" that property generally confers on its owners comes with a corollary limitation on others' interests in being included. That is, protecting one person's claim to a resource means that others are excluded from it. While that seems harmless enough—of course owning a house means your neighbors cannot use it for tea!—it can entrench inequitable distributions. What if, instead a house, someone owns thousands upon thousands of acres of fallow agricultural land? Protecting her property rights might mean that you—a poor, hungry, subsistence farmer—have no land for a vegetable garden to feed yourself and your family. Or, to take a more contemporary example, what of drug companies that possess treatments for otherwise fatal diseases like AIDS, but yet price them out of reach for many of the world's poor? There may well be strong reasons for protecting the land baron or drug company in these situation—reasons considered in the chapters that follow—but it is important to recognize the costs of doing so. Converting a resource to private property may impoverish others, or entrench interests in ways that we find inequitable or even immoral.

A third concern about property comes squarely from the law and economics tradition: the tragedy of the anti-commons. The tragedy of the commons, recall, arises when too many people have the right to use an exhaustible and sufficiently valuable resource. The result is inefficient over-consumption and private property is one possible solution. According to Professor Michael Heller, and his enormously influential work on the topic, the tragedy of the anti-commons is just the opposite.[20] It occurs when too many people have the right to exclude others, leading to inefficient under-consumption of a resource. His principle example is a good one. Why, in post-Soviet Russia, were Moscow storefronts empty, while a robust trade by street vendors occurred in the cold just in front of empty buildings? Everyone would have been better off if the street trade had simply moved inside. Professor Heller identified the root of the problem: too many people needed to be bribed or legitimately paid off to take possession of any of the vacant shops. In other words, too many people had the right to exclude.

This is, again, a problem of coordination and transaction costs. Assuming that a business would, in fact, be more valuable inside

---

20. See Michael A. Heller, *The Tragedy of the Anticommons: Property in the Transition from Marx to Markets*, 111 Harv. L. Rev. 621 (1998).

than out, and that an empty storefront is not generating rents, there should be gains from allowing the business to occupy the store. Everyone should be made better off from the move. But it still might not happen if the excluders each demand an excessive portion of the surplus value. Adding some stylized numbers is again revealing.

Imagine that moving a business inside generates an increase in value of $100. The business owner should therefore be willing to pay up to $99 to make the move. Imagine further that ten different people (various government ministers and officials for example) need to consent before the move can happen. Collectively, those ten people can charge anywhere from $1 to $99 dollars and everyone will be made better off. But if each person knows that the economic surplus from the transaction is $99, each may try to capture a disproportionate share of the gains from the transaction. If each person demands $15, for example, then the deal will not happen (because the total demand will be $150, and the business owner will be willing to pay a maximum of $99). Collectively, everyone will be made worse off and, in the absence of transaction costs, the government officials should agree amongst themselves not to demand more than $99 as a group. But as transaction costs and coordination costs increase, they may not reach an agreement, and several may demand too much, causing the deal to fail.

Having identified this phenomenon in the storefronts of Moscow, it begins to appear everywhere. The tragedy of the anticommons occurs wherever fractionated ownership makes it difficult to assemble property into usable (or at least beneficially usable) bundles. This is sometimes the case with medical research, which can require individual agreements with many different owners of individual gene patents.[21] Or it can occur with land, when a large new development requires buying up the interests of many different parcel owners. Even the recent mortgage crisis is potentially an example. Interests in mortgages have been sold to so many different banks and investors that it can be difficult to reassemble the economic interests to work out the loans. These are all examples taken up again below, but it is important to see the general contours of the problem: too much property—or at least ownership of certain kinds of resources divided among too many different people—can lead to the inefficient under-use of valuable resources.

Property, then, can raise moral, distributional, and efficiency concerns, each of which recurs throughout this book.

---

21. See MICHAEL HELLER, THE GRIDLOCK ECONOMY xiii (2008) (discussing this and the following examples).

D. Reasoning Through Property Problems

These broad questions about property—where it comes from, why we have it—do not generate specific or predetermined answers for different property doctrines. But they helpfully set the stage for evaluating what we want from the law of property and how we should think about it. Likewise, the modes of analysis introduced here—philosophy, history, and law and economics—do not definitively resolve the many property disputes that follow. But they are all important tools in the common law toolkit. Each one can be taken out and deployed individually to reason towards a specific conclusion.

Of course, not every property problem calls for economic (or philosophical, or historical) analysis. Practical-minded judges (or lawyers or law professors) are unlikely to care, in particular, what Kant (or Locke, or Hume) thought about a problem. But it is a mistake to view these modes of analysis as abstract theory, divorced from the meat-and-potatoes of legal reasoning. The following, then, serves as something of a roadmap for property analysis and a way of reasoning through a new case or set of facts.

Much of property law—as with all common law—begins with judge-made doctrine. The first part of any legal analysis should therefore include a careful consideration of judicial rulings and statements, and, of course, statutes if any. But more often than not, past precedent is at least potentially distinguishable from new cases and new facts.

History can be important for sealing such gaps, revealing meaningful comparisons with cases that came before. Rules can be called anachronistic if they were based on claims or assumptions about the world that are no longer true, or the opposite. Where cases are not on all fours, doctrine cannot be mechanically applied and earlier case law is more or less indeterminate; other modes of analysis then step in to fill the gaps and push existing doctrine to incorporate a new situation.

Law and economics reasoning is often a good place to start. Its focus is on effects, specifically the consequences that different legal outcomes will have on present and future parties. Giving property rights to inventors, for example, encourages creation in the first place. But law and economics also seeks to minimize impediments to voluntary market transactions on the assumption that private parties should be allowed to price their preferences for themselves. Law and economics therefore generally favors rules that minimize transaction costs, or that allocate resources to parties in the best position to place property into the stream of commerce. There can be a lot of room for disagreement about what the content of such rules should be—disagreement that often relies on empirical claims about the world and that plays out differently in different cases— but these goals provide a framework for evaluating legal rules. Therefore, argue first: the world will be better off if the legal rule is "X".

Law and economics often has little to say about distributive justice, however. It may be that some property rules will maximize overall societal welfare but unfairly, for example at the expense of society's very poorest. Some might embrace this outcome, but others might look for principled grounds to object. Philosophy, then, can provide a sophisticated vocabulary for articulating moral and other normative intuitions. For example, property sometimes boils down to base fights over who deserves something more:

"It's mine," says the plaintiff, "because I made it."

"Not so," says the defendant, "for I found it and used it for years before you asserted a claim."

Who is right? Neither, obviously, but philosophy can help capture the competing claims. Even without invoking Locke by name, one might argue that property does *and should* belong to the person who made it, or that rights *should* transfer to the subsequent possessor after she owns it long enough. Philosophy, then, offers normative prescriptions, accounts of how property law *ought* to work in the interests of fairness and justice.

Properly equipped with the tools of property analysis, it is now possible to look closely at the law of property, at its doctrines, its functions, and its normative commitments. There is no better place to begin than with the rules of acquisition. It is one thing to have decided why we have property; it is something else entirely to decide how to get it.

Chapter 2

FIRST IN TIME

Intuitions about property are fundamental and develop early. A two-year-old can articulate a coherent claim, "Mine!" Every homeowner views the threshold of her house as a border, a gateway that others can cross only with permission. Even butterflies appear to recognize entitlements to the spots of dappled sunlight that other butterflies lighted on first.[22] But what generates these reactions? What is the source of these asserted rights?

Contracts and Torts, the other sources of private rights, raise similar questions, but theirs are easier to answer. Contracts create rights based on mutual assent, real or inferred. People should be allowed to order their lives in voluntary arrangements. Torts create rights based on duties and our obligations to treat each other with reasonable care. But property? Where does it come from?

The base intuition is undoubtedly rooted in a claim of "first in time." Property belongs to the person who got it first, whether it is a seat in a classroom or an undiscovered island. But this basis for property claims, as intuitive as it seems, may be a shaky foundation to support so looming an edifice as private ownership. Think of the many rights and resources that are routinely divvied up. How many would be fairly or justly apportioned through first-in-time? Imagine if slots to a school—whether a law school or a university—were allocated based solely on application date. Or imagine if all jobs were given first-come first-served instead of with an eye to the quality of the applicant. Some resources are appropriately distributed to the first in time, but not all. It can be difficult to give any moral footing to assigning rights based simply on the fact that someone got there first.

There is a lot at stake in the legitimacy of first-in-time. When people acquire property through contract, or any of the other mechanisms discussed in Chapter 3, they acquire rights from the previous possessor. But what gave that person rights to convey? Presumably, that prior owner acquired the property from someone else, who acquired it from someone else, who acquired it from someone else, back to some (mythological?) original acquisition. The legitimacy of the present distribution of property and property rights therefore depends, in no small measure, on the legitimacy of

---

22. Herbert Gintis, *The Evolution of Private Property*, 64 J. ECON. BEHAV. & ORG. 1 (2007).

the original allocation of property rights—on the claim, in other words, of first-in-time.

Before turning to the difficult conceptual task of justifying first-in-time, however, there is an analytically prior question to consider: how to decide who got there first. And it is this most basic of property questions that animates the law of acquisition and original creation, conceptually and temporally the first important doctrines in the study of property. Exploring these surprisingly difficult issues also begins to suggest some of the underlying justifications for first-in-time.

A. Capture

Capture is one of the most obvious contexts for asserting a first-in-time claim. Capture is at issue whenever someone seeks to take possession of an unowned and fugitive resource, like a wild animal, water, or even a homerun baseball hit into the stands. Capture is often uncontroversial. But competing claims to capture a resource, or one person's interference with another's efforts to capture a resource, give rise to some of the most colorful cases in the common law. Capture also appropriately frames the complexity of the property inquiry.

The law of capture is easy to state but hard to apply. An unowned, fugitive resource belongs to the person who captures it first. Now, this is only true in the absence of competing claims, based on even more fundamental rights. For example, the owner of the land on which the resource was taken may have better rights than any capturer *ratione soli* ("by reason of the soil"), when owning land confers rights to the resources found on the land. But that is not the difficult conceptual problem raised by the law of capture. The real challenge is to decide, as between two pursuers, who got there first?

Pierson v. Post[23] reveals the central problem. This old favorite—a staple of the first-year property curriculum, and something of a rite of passage for law students—involves two competing claims of capture. Lodowick (really!) Post was on a foxhunt and had flushed a fox. With his hounds in pursuit, Post followed on his horse. Suddenly, and in sight of Post, Pierson (that "saucy intruder") grabbed the fox and beat it to death. He carried the fox carcass away with him, and Post sued for its recovery. Who should win? Pierson does, but the outcome of the case is far less important than deciding how to go about answering the question. As amazing as it

---

23. 3 Cai. R. 175 (N.Y.Sup. 1805) [DKA & S, p. 18]; [M & S, p. 82]; [S, p. 152].

seems, a dead fox turns out to be a perfect lens for seeing many of the central threads that weave together the law of property.

Both Pierson and Post claimed the fox because each believed he got it first, Post because he was the first to flush and pursue the fox, Pierson because he was the first to grab it and kill it. Neither one is obviously right. And, if nothing else, the case reveals this central insight: first-in-time is a legal conclusion. It is not the basis for a property claim, but the result of one. The reason Pierson wins is not because he was the first to capture the fox. He was "first" because the court determined that actual capture, not mere pursuit, counts as first-in-time when it comes to fox hunting. But in a case like *Pierson v. Post*, and indeed in many property disputes, the content of first-in-time is not self-evident.

One approach to deciding the rule of capture is to rely upon longstanding doctrinal categories. Indeed, the majority in *Pierson* looks at some of the most venerable sources in the common law and concludes that pursuit without wounding that deprives the animal of its natural liberty is insufficient to establish possession. But this reasoning is simply not illuminating. Indeed, the dissent examines similarly august early commentators and concludes—perhaps facetiously—that the law of capture varies if the pursuit is by large dogs and hounds as opposed to "beagles only" and if the pursuit is "with lance or sword as opposed to dart, sling, or bow." The majority and dissent can therefore discern very different rules, reaching contradictory results, from the same set of authorities.

The interpretive challenge is even more intractable than it seems. Is the right answer even to be found in ancient common law doctrines? The dissent argues that the question would have been better submitted "to the arbitration of sportsmen." Superficially, this is a dig at the stakes of the case; rights in the carcass of a dead fox should not be litigated to the highest court in the state. But it is also raises a serious question about the source of property rights. Sportsmen may, indeed, have been able to resolve the case easily. They may have well-settled norms governing the capture of their game. But can community norms provide the rules of acquisition or the content of property rights? They might reflect the reasonable expectations of a particular community more accurately than any judge, but they may miss the interests of society as a whole. Give the case to the sportsmen to decide, and one strongly suspects the sportsman—Lodowick Post—will win. This relationship between community norms and formal property rules recurs throughout the study of property. There are times when norms provide the content of property rights, and others where they make property rights superfluous or only marginally important. Application of sportsmen's norms might have quickly resolved the conflict here, but with the relevant community at least somewhat up for grabs, it would not necessarily have been for the best.

A more promising analysis requires looking beyond formal categories to the underlying goals of the law of acquisition—indeed, to the goals of property law itself. Here, again, the majority and dissent disagree about the content of the goals and about how best to achieve them, but the analysis is more revealing.

In a casual line at the end of the opinion, the majority concludes that its preferred rule of capture—actual capture and not "mere pursuit"—is motivated by a desire for certainty and the preservation of peace and order in society. How can that be? The majority's rule protects the rights of the saucy intruder to grab and beat a fox to death in plain sight of the hunter in hot pursuit. That seems quite unlikely to promote "peace and order in society." But at a higher level of generality, removed from the possible pugilistic outcomes on the ground, the majority's rule has the benefit of being easier to administer, and perhaps that *will* lead to greater certainty, and therefore peace and order in the long run. At least when it comes to foxes, physical possession is easy to see and easy to protect. Pursuit, on the other hand, is a much fuzzier line to police. The same may not be true of all kinds of fugitive resources, but an advantage of the majority's rule in this case is its apparent ease of application.

Of course, ease of application cannot be the highest goal for any legal rule. Otherwise, a rule that allocates property based on the alphabetical order of the parties' names would seem positively enlightened. Administrability may be a consideration, but other interests steer the law. And it is here that the dissent is so powerful, at least when taken at face value. According to the dissent, "our decision should have in view the greatest possible encouragement to the destruction of an animal, so cunning and ruthless in its career." Or, to put the point more bluntly: the goal of the rule of acquisition should be more dead foxes. This reasoning has a decidedly modern cast, focusing on the functional outcome of the legal rule instead of doctrinal categories—worrying about the incentives the rule will create, instead of reasoning from abstruse first principles. But it is also here that more modern legal analysis can interrogate the dissent's intuitions, because it is not at all clear that the dissent's preferred rule, leaving the fox with the huntsman instead of the saucy intruder, would actually lead to more dead foxes.

28

The dissent suggests, quite eloquently, that awarding the fox to Pierson (the actual capturer) instead of Post (the pursuer) will discourage people from investing in fox hunting. "[W]hat gentlemen, at the sound of the horn and at peep of day, would mount his steed and for hours together, '*sub jove frigido*,' or in vertical sun, pursue the windings of this wily quadruped, if . . . a saucy intruder . . . were permitted to come in at the death and bear away in triumph the object of pursuit?" The point goes far beyond fox hunting and to the core of property law. Indeed, under leading law and economics accounts, the purpose of a property regime is to encourage people to invest in the productive use of property. To recast the dissent's question in more general terms: who will invest in acquiring property without some assurance of being able to reap the rewards?

There is, however, a contrary intuition consistent with the same goal of more dead foxes. Instead of discouraging people from investing in fox hunting, protecting the actual capturer might encourage investments in more effective capture technology. In fact, protecting mere pursuit might reduce the need to develop tools any more effective than lances or swords. Why bother improving on the steed and hounds if the fox ultimately belongs to the pursuer, no matter how anemic or ineffective the chase?

But there is a deeper question lurking here, too, behind the fight over a single dead fox. Who gets to decide the normative goal to pursue? For the majority, it is certainty, peace and order in society. For the dissent, it is more dead foxes. But there are surely other options as well. Today, basing a rule of capture on the goal of more dead foxes would seem bizarre if not downright offensive. Environmentalists would surely object. How should courts go about deciding the goal of the property regime? When and how do those goals change over time, and what should courts do then? Rules of capture based on outmoded objectives can cast long shadows into the future unless the underlying purpose of the rule is apparent and amenable to change as conditions change.

That very dynamic, including a fight over goals, might even be at the heart of *Pierson v. Post* itself. In a revisionist account, two recent commentators pointed out that the goal of fox hunting, even at the time of the case, was most decidedly not "more dead foxes."[24]

---

24. Bethany R. Berger, *It's Not About the Fox: The Untold History of* Pierson v. Post, 55 DUKE L. J. 1089, 1131–32 (2006) ("At the time of Lodowick's hunt, foxhunting was not instrumental, but was established as a leisure activity of wealthy men. In fact, the goal of the hunt in America was not even necessarily to kill the fox, as a previously hunted fox might lead a better chase."); *see also* Andrea McDowell,

Justice Livingston, the dissenter, surely knew that. Perhaps *Pierson v. Post* is not a case presenting competing rules for the efficient capture of fugitive resources. Instead, it is about a culture clash. The Piersons as a family were educated Presbyterian farmers of high standing in the community, and Pierson was himself a local schoolteacher. He was perhaps guarding his family's livestock both from foxes and from the hunters who destructively chase them through cultivated land. The Posts, by contrast, were both newly rich and newly educated. Their money came from commerce and the war, and they appeared eager to show their newfound wealth.[25] Post was engaged in that most flamboyant of leisure activities: foxhunting. For Justice Livingston, the goal was never more dead foxes. The goal was to protect the interests of an emerging American wealthy elite against meddlesome interference by farmers. If that is true, both the stakes of the case and the resulting rule take on a decidedly different cast.

This may all be well and good, but where are the answers? For all its interesting questions, what, if anything, does this case tell us about property, and the source and nature of property rights? More than it might seem. Look, for a moment, at the breadth of analysis implicated by the death of a simple fox. It spans straightforward (if un-illuminating) doctrine in the guise of the ancient common law theorists; the role of community norms and institutional competence to resolve the competing claims; law and economics in the concern for incentives created by competing outcomes; and law and society in the newly-revealed power dynamics lurking beneath the facts of the case. And the story of the fox does not end there. Indeed, these various vocabularies—these lenses for discerning the meaning of first-in-time—offer an interpretive frame for the entire law of original acquisition and, indeed, for much of property!

When, in *Ghen v. Rich*,[26] someone finds and claims the carcass of a whale on shore, killed by the bomb lance of a commercial whaling ship, who should win? Is the case distinguishable from *Pierson v. Post*? If not, the actual capturer (the person wandering the beach) should win against the mere pursuers (the whalers). But the whalers win. Is that because firing a bomb lance is somehow different from flushing a fox? Is it so clear that the latter comes closer to capturing the beast? Are bomb lances more like mastiffs or beagles, and why should it matter? Again, something different, something more substantial seems to distinguish the two cases.

Legal Fictions in Pierson v. Post, 105 Mich. L. Rev. 735 (2007) (describing the history of foxhunting, and the factual context of *Person v. Post*).

25. See *id.*

26. 8 Fed. 159 (D. Mass. 1881) [DKA & S, p. 26]; [M & S, p. 90].

If the goal in *Pierson v. Post* was more dead foxes, the goal in *Ghen v. Rich,* according to the court, was more dead whales. And few people would engage in the incredibly dangerous enterprise of hunting finback whales if someone else could claim a whale carcass once it washed ashore, especially since finback whales were simply too fast and too strong to be secured to the ship that struck the fatal blow. But who gets to decide that the goal really is, or should be, more dead whales? Today, most people would refuse to let the whaling industry set the goals for the rule of capture. Moreover, whaling technology has changed so much that it is now possible to capture whales—indeed, ships can swallow them whole—in ways that were unimaginable in the nineteenth century. As much as anything, then, *Ghen v. Rich* reveals the important lesson that definitions of property rights are always situated in a specific time and context. But the bottom line is this: there is an uneasy tension between *Pierson v. Post* and *Ghen v. Rich.* In the former, mere pursuit was not enough and actual capture was required to establish a first-in-time claim. In the latter, mere pursuit (or at least something short of actual physical possession) was enough, and the person who actually ends up with the carcass loses. There are, of course, many differences between the two cases, but the challenge is to decide which are the important differences when it comes to extending these cases to other fugitive resources.

Since legal reasoning relies on analogy, extending *Pierson v. Post* and *Ghen v. Rich* requires deciding whether and how new cases are like the earlier ones. If someone fires off guns to scare ducks from Minott's Meadow, should the pond-owner have a claim? In *Keeble v. Hickeringill,*[27] Keeble had built a duck decoy pond. Hickeringill stood nearby the pond—but not on Keeble's property—and fired guns to scare off the birds. The court ruled that this impermissibly interfered with Keeble's property. But why? The ducks had not yet been captured by Keeble; they had merely landed temporarily on his pond. If Hickeringill had simply lured them away with a better decoy pond, Keeble would have had no claim.

Reason from *Pierson* and *Ghen.* Are ducks more like foxes or whales? They are more like foxes because they can be captured. But the pursuer may be more like the whalers in *Ghen* who are engaged in an occupation or trade instead of mere sport. Perhaps, then, the property at issue was not the ducks at all but was instead Keeble's interest in pursuing his trade without interference—or at least, free from some kinds of unproductive interference, like scaring away the birds instead of building a better trap.

---

27. 11 East 574, 103 Eng. Rep. 1127 (Queen's Bench, 1707) [DKA & S, p. 30]; [M & S, p. 93].

Or, to take another example, if someone in the stands makes a grab for Barry Bonds' famous homerun baseball, only to have it dislodged and end up in someone else's hands, is that case similar to or different from these others?[28] Does it matter whether baseballs are more like foxes, ducks, or whales? They fly like ducks, are capable of being captured like foxes, and bear little resemblance to whales. But that inquiry seems entirely beside the point. Once again, a more productive inquiry is to ask what underlying purpose the rule of capture is meant to serve in this particular context. Maybe society does not care if people invest in catching baseballs. Indeed, there is no suggestion of any kind of interference with a productive trade or business. So what should be the goal of the rule of acquisition when we have no particular interest in encouraging capture? Perhaps the goal should be preserving peace in the stands, although it is not clear what legal rule could actually alter behavior on the ground (or in the bleachers, as the case may be). As much as anything, then, this example again raises the institutional question: who should decide the content of the rule? Where there are no real societal interests at stake in the underlying resource—no public concern about more captured baseballs—it makes more sense to defer to community norms and so the law should perhaps be led by the expectations of baseball fans.

Of course, it is possible that the formal declaration of property rights might also shape norms. Property law does not have to be a passive recipient of community expectations, but can also lead or determine them, in which case the rule should protect the rights of the initial toucher to eliminate the mob's incentive to jump him and grab the ball. Or, it might be better to allow Major League Baseball to set the rules, because it has an interest in maximizing the value to the audience of attending a game. In other words, MLB has the right incentives to develop rules that most people will want. Regardless of the answer, focusing on these kinds of questions is much more satisfying than asking whether baseballs are more or less similar to foxes than whales.

Looking back over these cases—all staples of the first weeks of most property courses—this much should be clear: first-in-time can be a legal construction, a conclusion that relies on analogical reasoning. And what count as persuasive analogies depends on how one chooses to read the cases. They provide various options. Another case might be made similar or dissimilar if it involves hunting with beagles instead of with mastiffs, if securing the resource requires as much investment and effort as hunting it, or if the

---

28. Popov v. Hayashi, 2002 WL 31833731 (Cal. Superior 2002) [DKA & S, p. 114]; [M & S, p. 109]; [S, p. 156].

norms of the community are different for some reason. And the stakes in capture cases are not limited to wild animals and flying balls. Fugitive resources include oil and water, and resolving the competing claims of pursuers in those contexts can generate radically different incentives.

B. Creation

Another context in which first-in-time plays a dominant role is in the law surrounding original creation. First, however, the doctrine of accession and statutory protections for intellectual property need to be disentangled from the common law treatment of original creation.[29]

Accession

If someone builds a birdhouse, it should belong to her by dint of creation. Conjuring things into existence might seem to be the clearest form of original acquisition, and the easiest application of first-in-time. It is not. For where did the builder get the raw materials for the birdhouse, the wood, and the nails? Perhaps she milled the timber with her own two hands. But whose trees did she cut? For most physical resources, the act of creation generates competing claims by the creator and the original resource owner. Even when they are one-and-the-same, as when the creator also owns the trees she cuts for the wood, the same conceptual problem arises. Does she own the resulting birdhouse because she built it, because she contributed the resources, or both?

In general, ownership confers rights both over resources themselves and the products of those resources. If you own a cow, you also own the calf it bears. If you own a garden, you own the vegetables it produces, and the resulting casserole you cook with them. So if you own a tree, you should also own the birdhouse it becomes. On the other hand, it might seem awfully perverse if someone's passive ownership of an abundant resource could create property rights against someone who transformed it, through significant skill and labor, into something altogether more valuable— think, the Fallingwater of birdhouses, crafted by Frank Lloyd

---

29. See [M & S pp. 161–190] (discussing the principle of accession). Viewed broadly, accession is at work throughout the law of property. Beyond the examples below, and *rationi soli* discussed above, Merrill & Smith identify additional doctrines as also part of the broad principle of accession, including: (1) the *ad coelum* rule, that a surface owner's property rights run to the center of the earth and to the highest heavens; (2) accretion, that additions to dry land from deposits of sediment by water belong to the riparian (waterfront) owner; and (3) fixtures, that objects in buildings affixed to the buildings become part of the realty for legal purposes.

Wright himself. Should the owner of the tree really own the resulting birdhouse?

In cases like these, property law balances competing claims between the creator and resource owner. In general, if the creator transforms the resource sufficiently, or increases its value by enough, then the creator can gain title to the property (although she will likely have to pay the resource owner the value of the unimproved raw materials she took). But if the creator did not substantially transform or increase the value of the resource, then ownership will stay with the resource owner. If someone merely chops down trees, for example, the resulting logs should belong to the owner of the trees, and not the wielder of the ax.

There are open questions, though. Does it matter whether the creator expropriated the underlying resources in good faith or bad faith? Is it the extent of the transformation of the resource that should matter, the increase in its value, or some combination of both? There is doctrinal support for every option. More importantly, there are property interests at stake in these choices.

On the one hand, it is a core aspect of property that it gives to the owner a right to control what happens to the property. In general, owning a tree includes the right not to have it converted into a birdhouse. On the other, a goal of property law is to encourage putting resources to valuable use. These competing pressures, identified in Chapter 1, map neatly on to the law of accession. Protecting the resource owner vindicates the power to control property—the right to exclude. Protecting the creator encourages the transformation of raw resources from low-value to high-value ones. Accession, in short, makes even the act of creation problematic as an example of first-in-time.

There is really only one context in which the act of creation is at least potentially free from the competing claims of resource owners: invention, and the creation of intellectual property. Intellectual property, and the propertization of inventions and ideas, is therefore the cleanest setting for evaluating creation as an application of first-in-time.

Intellectual Property Statutes

Intellectual property is its own specialized field of law. It is governed, by and large, by federal statutes that fall far outside an introductory property course. The most interesting and provocative cases from a property perspective are those few that rely on common law property rights instead of federal statutes. This is not to suggest that common law property rights are where the action is. No, indeed, intellectual property in the real world is about copyright, patent, and trademark law. But the kernel of *property* can be obscured in those more technical contexts. Nevertheless, a brief introduction to the statutory regimes is useful because they manifest some of the same concerns as common law property regimes. And, if nothing else, they frame which issues *not* to discuss, because they are governed by statute rather than background principles of property law.

Federal power over intellectual property derives directly from the Constitution. Article I, Section 8 gives Congress the power "To promote the Progress of Science and useful Arts, by securing for limited Times to Authors and Inventors the exclusive Right to their respective Writings and Discoveries." This formulation expressly reflects the economic intuition that property rights are important for encouraging investment. Congress has the power to create property rights (to "secur[e] to . . . inventors the exclusive right to their . . . discoveries") in order to stimulate invention ("To promote the Progress of science"). Inventors would invent less, and artists would create less, if they could not reap the economic benefit of their creations. At the same time, invention is not valuable for its own sake. Instead, the goal is to promote the progress of science, and eventually to provide the public with access to the fruits of inventiveness. For that reason, Congress can only grant inventors exclusive rights to their inventions for a limited time. This trade-off, between allowing creators, through property, to reap where they sow, and eventually providing the public with access to the creations, is central to intellectual property rights generally.

Congress has balanced these trade-offs in different ways in each of three statutory regimes: patent, copyright, and trademark. Although these statutes deserve their own advanced courses, the basic subject matter of each is easy to articulate. Patent law protects useful, novel, and non-obvious inventions.[30] It grants inventors who file their patents with the patent office an exclusive right to the invention for a fixed term (currently 20 years). The protection is robust—patent protection is good even against an independent inventor who came up with the same invention on her own. But the term is relatively short. This contrasts with copyright, which protects creative expression against copying for the life of the artist plus 70 years. The duration is much longer than patent, but the protection is thinner in a number of important ways—it does not prevent independent creation and it includes exceptions for fair use and satire, among others. Trademark, finally, is about protecting commercial marks (think of the Nike swoosh), and its justifica-

---

30. See Trenton Industries v. A.E. Peterson Manufacturing Co., 165 F.Supp. 523 (S.D. Cal. 1958) [M & S, p. 150] (describing nature of patent protection).

tion is primarily to prevent consumer confusion. Together, these three statutory regimes leave little room for a common law of intellectual property.

Property Protection for Creation

It should now be apparent that the "creation" cases typically included in an introductory property course have two unusual characteristics: (1) they do not rely on an underlying private resource and so do not implicate accession (or do so as little as possible); and (2) they do not implicate any of the federal intellectual property statutes (or do so as little as possible). Here, then, creation claims are distilled down to their first-in-time essence.

International News Service v. Associated Press[31] is one of the best examples. The case provided the United States Supreme Court with a relatively rare opportunity to examine property rights—a topic usually within state courts' purview. This case pitted two news gathering organizations against each other: the Associated Press (AP) and the International News Service (INS). Among other allegations, AP claimed that INS was routinely copying news from AP bulletin boards and sending the stories to its own affiliates, particularly on the West Coast. Importantly, though, INS was not copying the stories verbatim. It was as if, instead of sending its reporters out into the field to cover events themselves, INS was simply sending people to cover the content of the AP bulletin boards. This was, in part, because INS had been prohibited from using British telegraph cables to send war news during World War I after it had printed some pro-German stories without approval by British censors.[32] Notice the property conundrum. AP does not own the news itself. If a truck overturns on the highway, the first reporter to the scene does not own the story. She has no legal right to exclude others from reporting the facts of the accident. Without a property interest in the news, and without a cause of action in copyright, how could AP have any sort of claim?

The Court's resolution tried to deflect the focus from property altogether, finding that INS's actions constituted unfair business practices. But the traditional tort of unfair business practices involves some kind of palming-off, someone claiming a competitor's goods as her own. That was simply not at issue here. However, the Court was willing to find unfair business practices after concluding that AP had acquired *quasi*-property rights through its labor in gathering the news. According to the Court, INS's subsequent

---

31.   248 U.S. 215 (1918) [DKA & S, p. 56]; [M & S, p. 131]; [S, p. 131].

32.   Stuart Banner, AMERICAN PROPERTY: A HISTORY OF HOW, WHY, AND WHAT WE OWN (2011).

misappropriation of this *quasi*-property substituted for the misrepresentation that was usually required for unfair business practices. It is, in other words, a property case after all, because AP had some kind of property right that INS was misappropriating.

Familiar property interests are squarely at stake in the case. The goal here? More news. This is entirely consistent with the goal in the rule of capture—more dead foxes, ducks, and whales—and the goal of statutory protection for intellectual property—more invention and creation. As in those other contexts, there is a surprisingly subtle balance to strike, and empirical questions lurk below the surface. On the one hand, gathering news for its own sake is not valuable; it is the dissemination of news that should be encouraged. By providing a rival source for news, INS was presumably making news available to more people more cheaply. On the other hand, if AP lacked the ability to exclude INS from its reporting, at least temporarily, it would have little incentive to go out and gather news in the first place. INS would have had nothing to copy because AP's bulletin boards would have been empty. Eventually, less news would have been available to the public. It is this latter intuition that the Court clearly seized upon in ruling for AP. So why extend property protection to the news?

Part of the challenge for AP is that the news is a nonrival good. Unlike tangible property, news can be consumed without reducing its value to other consumers. It is also difficult to exclude others from accessing or consuming the news. Together, these two qualities make it resemble a pure public good. And the problem with pure public goods, like national defense or flood control systems, is that people can free-ride on the benefits they provide. No one has an economic incentive to produce pure public goods because it is difficult if not impossible to reap financial rewards from them. This, in turn, means that the market, left to its own devices, is likely to under-produce the good. Enter property.

Property creates a mechanism for exclusion and therefore the ability to charge for access and make money. Indeed, property rights can be a particularly powerful solution because of the difficulty of erecting physical barriers to consumption. Even if the law did not recognize property rights in foxes, a hunter could probably still take possession and physically keep other people from coming along and "consuming" them. Not so with the news. The only non-legal way to protect the news is not to publish it in the first place, and that, of course, would defeat its purpose.

In today's digital world, the news is hardly alone in its susceptibility to copying. AP's concern about INS sending its news stories by telegraph to the West Coast seems positively quaint by comparison with the Huffington Post and modern news aggregators. The less expensive and easier it is to copy something, the more pressure there is on the legal system to provide some kind of property, or *quasi*-property, protection. Whether digital music, movies, software or designs, the ease of copying nonrival goods threatens to diminish if not eliminate the economic incentive to create such goods in the first place.

Property law is not the only solution, however, and the appeal of creating property rights should depend in part on available alternatives. Just as technology creates new opportunities for copying and disseminating digitizable works, it also creates new means of protecting them. Digital rights management (DRM) can embed anti-copying technology in the works themselves, making it exceedingly difficult, for example, to disseminate songs purchased through iTunes, or eBooks purchased through Amazon, more broadly than intended. Contract law can also step in to provide a different form of legal protection. End User License Agreements (EULAs in internet parlance) provide a kind of contractual protection for the creators of digital works. Embedded in click-through agreements on the web, or in shrink-wrap licenses attached to software packaging, EULAs can give creators significant control over a consumer's ultimate use of the work, enforceable through bilateral contracts and not property at all.

More fundamentally, too, there is an open empirical question whether any kind of protection is actually necessary to spur production of news and other nonrival non-excludable goods. The fashion industry is a case in point. Due to a strange lacuna in intellectual property regimes, fashion designs receive effectively no legal protection from copying and knock-offs. And yet, the fashion industry continues to thrive. Few people would complain that fashion's problem is too few new designs. Perhaps the value of lead-time, even if only a month or a week, is enough in fashion to reap the economic rewards of new designs. Perhaps the quality of the production is different—and higher—from the original designer than from knock-offs. Perhaps there are other characteristics of the fashion industry that account for its success despite the paucity of property protection. But maybe news is not so different after all. Consumers appear to pay a substantial premium for a lead-time of even a few minutes on the Web, in site visits if nothing else. Differences in the quality of the prose may well lead consumers to prefer one news source to another, even if the facts of the story are the same. In other words, there are tricky empirical questions behind the Court's seemingly commonsense intuition that AP's incentive to gather news depended on its ability to exclude INS. At the very least, the need for and effect of property protection is almost certainly different today than it was in 1918 when the Supreme Court found that AP had a *quasi*-property interest in the news.

Slapping the label *quasi* on AP's property interest in the news also highlights a familiar modern insight that property rights are contextual and relational—the Hohfledian move, described in Chapter 1. In 1918, the Supreme Court may well have worried that elevating the news to the full-blown status of property might have given AP the right not only to control INS's use of the news, but also consumers' use, too. By calling the news *quasi*-property, and by focusing on unfair business practices instead of the property claim, the Court implicitly recognized that some property rights—*these* property rights at least—are relational. They are good as against INS (or other competitors), but not as against the rest of the world. To a modern ear, this is true of property more generally, whether or not there is anything *quasi* about it. The idea that property rights are relational—that they are rights between people, and not rights that attach to objects—is a central insight of modern property theory and a recurring theme in this book.

As with capture, acquisition by creation undoubtedly confers some kinds of property rights based on fundamental notions of first-in-time. But it is similarly difficult to decide whose rights to protect as a creator by focusing only on formal or doctrinal categories. Can the holding in *INS v. AP* be extended to other kinds of creation cases? Even if intellectual property statutes do not protect fashion, should a similar kind of common law property claim lie against competitors in the fashion industry? That depends. Whether news is or is not like fashion cannot be answered in the abstract, or through formal definitions. One involves words, the other stitches; one requires reporters, the other designers; one is more valuable . . . I'm not saying which one. But who cares? Why is this important, and what do formal distinctions like these have to do with the content of property rights?

To decide whether an act of creation generates property rights through some kind of first-in-time claim requires a more principled inquiry. That, in turn, will depend on the goal of the property regime. Is it to recognize an entitlement on the part of creators in some abstract sense? Is it to encourage more acts of creation, or the dissemination of works to the public? Framing the inquiry this way, and exploring the underlying objectives of property law, highlights the question that opened this chapter: why do we respect first-in-time anyway? What are the normative justifications for allocating property rights first-come-first-served? Against the doctrinal back-drop of acquisition by capture and creation, it is now possible to explore some different approaches to answering this fundamental question.

C. Justifications for First-in-Time

The justifications for first-in-time closely track the underlying justifications for property rights themselves, discussed in Chapter 1. The leading candidates are philosophical and economic.

There are a number of philosophical accounts that might justify first-in-time. John Locke's is the principal one, and the same Lockean intuitions supporting the existence of property rights also justify allocating them through first-in-time. According to Locke, the world offers up a cornucopia of valuable resources, ripe for the picking. And it is in the picking itself—or tilling or capturing or otherwise taming the land—that one mixes one's labor with the resource and converts it into private property. This philosophical account comes with the same limitations discussed in Chapter 1. It applies only in the absence of scarcity—a condition that is hard to sustain in the real world. And, it does not provide any set of ready answers about what kind of labor counts, and when someone has done enough to lay claim to the underlying resource. To the committed Lockean, who should own the fox, Pierson or Post? Did Post mix his labor with the fox by starting it from its hole, or did Pierson mix his labor with it first by bashing it over the head? Moreover, the moral status of first-in-time remains contested. As one leading commentator has argued: "Mere happenstance, fortuity, or swiftness of foot can account for a person's being first, yet none carries moral weight."[33]

A more consequentialist account of first-in-time focuses on the incentives that it creates. Specifically, allocating rights by first-in-time encourages people to race to claim property. This leads to more private property, and therefore, ultimately, to more valuable resources available for use and trade. Of course, this justification does not tell us what rule, in the abstract, will lead to more property acquisition, or which will ensure that the race is a productive one. As with foxes and news, it requires balancing the incentives to encourage people to pursue in the first place with the incentives to innovate in their methods of pursuit. And, protecting first in time occasionally leads to a tragedy of the commons, which

---

33. ERIC T. FREYFOGLE, THE LAND WE SHARE: PRIVATE PROPERTY AND THE COMMON GOOD 107 (2003).

leads to over-consumption, sometimes on a massive scale. Focusing on incentives provides a framework for evaluating the effect of different rules, but does not necessarily generate uniform prescriptions.

Another economic justification for first-in-time is said to be its ease of administration. The cases above problematize that intuition. First-in-time is not always clear-cut, and can require difficult judgments (as in *Pierson* and *Ghen*). But sometimes it *is* clear-cut. The possibility of difficult cases does not mean that first-in-time is harder to administer than any other reasonable option for assigning property rights. The tough cases are important for exploring the boundary of first-in-time claims, but if the heartland of cases will attract quick consensus, perhaps that is good enough.

There can be a normative dimension to this argument, too. Property rights, unlike contract rights, are good as against the world. They are said to be *in rem* and not *in personam* rights. Property rights become difficult to respect if it is hard to discern either the content or the owner of the rights. Or, to put this positively, a benefit of clear and intuitively accessible property rights is that owners will have to invest less in enforcing them. People in the world are more likely to recognize, understand, and respect property rights that comport with their own intuitions.[34]

Ultimately, this much is clear: courts in fact often allocate property rights based on the principle of first-in-time. The doctrines of capture and creation provide ready examples of the principle at work, but also equally ready examples where the principle is problematic or hard to apply. The doctrinal and theoretical complexity is increased when subsequent owners come into the picture, acquiring the rights of previous owners. Those doctrines, including acquisition by find, gift, and adverse possession, are taken up in the next chapter.

D.   Property in the Person

Against this backdrop, it is illuminating to view property rights in the person as a special case of first-in-time. Locke, recall, reasoned that property arises when people mix their labor with resources in the world for if there is one thing we own, it is our own labor. But what about our bodies? Does it make sense to think of our bodies as our property? And what are the consequences of doing so? Here, moral concerns loom large, but there is still a place for economic and even historical analysis.

---

34. See Thomas W. Merrill & Henry E. Smith, *The Morality of Property,* 48 Wm. & Mary L. Rev. 1849 (2007).

Undoubtedly the leading case to wrestle with all of these issues is *Moore v. Regents of the University of California.*[35] It is a case one is likely to encounter multiple times in law school—in torts, health law, and bioethics. But it is the property issues that are perhaps the most difficult. In that case, the plaintiff, John Moore, had been diagnosed with leukemia. As part of his treatment, doctors removed Moore's spleen. Although they did not inform Moore, doctors used his spleen to develop and patent a new cell line that experts estimated might eventually be worth as much as $3 billion *per year*. Moore sued on a variety of theories, but the important one for our purposes is conversion, a tort asserting the wrongful expropriation of another's property (in essence, "converting" someone else's property to your own). Specifically, Moore claimed that the cells from his spleen continued to belong to him, and that the doctors expropriated them when they developed the new cell line. The conceptual problem facing Moore, however, was the nature of his claim to the cells. Moore's conversion claim required that his cells were his *property*—that he owned them and had a right of possession (or at least a right to control their disposition). Establishing a property right in body parts, including cells, turns out to be much more complicated than one might think.

There is a commonsense intuition underlying the case. Of course Moore's cells belonged to him! They were his—they *were him*—more than anything else he might possess in the world. But that does not necessarily make them "property".

California's Uniform Anatomical Gift Act (UAGA) dramatically limits people's rights to control body parts after removal. That statute prohibits the sale of body parts for transplantation, and requires their proper disposal. Following surgery, then, a patient has surprisingly few rights with regard to any severed body parts. According to the majority in *Moore,* the remaining rights were not enough to count as property. Notice the Hohfeldian move. The majority analyzed which sticks in the bundle of property rights Moore retained. Finding them lacking, the majority held that Moore had no property interest in his cells.

But this cannot be right, and indeed a dissent by Justice Mosk is entirely persuasive on this point. The right to sell is not essential to property. Indeed, there are many things in the world that cannot be sold but that are nevertheless viewed as property. Justice Mosk pointed out that hunters and fishermen can give away but are not allowed to sell what they catch. And yet, if someone untied the deer on the hood of the hunter's car and made off with it, there is no

---

35.   793 P.2d 479 (Cal 1990) [DKA & S, p. 70]; [M & S, p. 243]; [S, p. 231].

doubt that a conversion action would lie. Although the hunter did not have the right to sell the deer, it was still his property. Indeed, some things are entirely non-transferable (inalienable) and still usefully considered property: a law license, grades in a class, political office, and so on.

The majority's formalistic reasoning looks increasingly vacuous the harder one stares. If someone had stolen Moore's cells from the hospital after they had been removed from him, the hospital could have maintained a conversion action against the thief. The cells, in other words, are property for some purposes. The better question, then, is whether Moore's cells were his property *for the purpose of maintaining a conversion claim against his doctors.* This is the more sophisticated Hohfeldian move: not just recognizing that property is a collection of rights, but focusing on the nature of those rights between specific people in a particular context. And that kind of more nuanced question does not admit of any easy formalistic answer.

The more satisfying but simultaneously more difficult answer turns on the consequences of allowing the conversion claim to proceed. There are two that bear special mention.

The first is the effect on medical research of recognizing Moore's property interest. The majority appeared deeply concerned—perhaps rightly so—that allowing Moore to claim a property right in his removed cells would stifle research. There are two parts to this concern. First, and most obviously, allowing people to sell their cells would, *ipso facto*, increase the cost of obtaining cells for research. But, depending on the market for such things, and people's interest in helping science cure diseases and medical afflictions, any increase in cost might be nominal. But there is a deeper problem lurking here as well, and that is the increase in transaction costs. A conversion claim is particularly powerful because it is a strict liability tort. It does not matter whether the "wrongful converter" knew the expropriated property belonged to someone else. If the original doctors or researchers who obtained the biological material misappropriated a patient's cells or body parts, then every subsequent scientist working with the material might also be subject to conversion liability. This, in turn, might place a cloud on all biological material, because researchers would have to worry about its provenance.

It is presumably for this reason that the Office of Technology Assessment, in a report before the *Moore* court, took the view that "resolving the current uncertainty may be more important to the future of biotechnology than resolving it in any particular way."

With a rule in place, researchers could adapt and implement procedures to assure that they had rights to the biological material they were using. It would be easy enough to secure most patients' permissions to use their cells so long as doctors and researchers knew that such permission was required. But if this is right, then the future of medical research did not depend on resisting Moore's property claim, but instead on resolving the case clearly and decisively.

The stakes of the case go beyond the economics of biomedical research. There are difficult moral questions as well. Justice Arabian, in concurrence, argued that it was immoral to treat the body as property, that it would "commingle the sacred with the profane." Giving people a property right in their bodies would, he feared, convert the body into a mere commodity, as if assigning a dollar value would undermine a deeper, more intrinsic value.

The point has been most powerfully articulated by Professor Margaret Jane Radin, who argued that market alienability can interfere with human flourishing.[36] Her argument has a long philosophical pedigree, and is subtle and multi-faceted, but the basic argument is easily captured: our relationships with some things in the world are inherently undermined if they can be bought and sold. Babies are the classic example. From a purely economic perspective, there are good reasons for legalizing the sale of babies. Market transactions could result in babies ending with the families that value them the most, and thus lead to the efficient allocation of an occasionally scarce resource. But Radin argued that the existence of such a market undermines the nature of the parent-child relationship. The harm is not just to the babies. Because relationships, like parent-child relationships, are central to personhood—to people's full sense of themselves in the world—degrading those relationships by turning them into mere commodities harms everyone. The same reasoning applies to many relationships in the world, and can justify prohibitions on prostitution (the sale of sex), and on the sale of body parts. This is entirely consistent with Justice Arabian's view that permitting the sale of body parts is not just bad policy but is actually immoral.

The moral considerations are not one-sided. Whereas Arabian worried about the moral consequences of permitting the sale of bodies and body parts, Mosk—in dissent—worried about the moral consequences of failing to do so. Indeed, rejecting Moore's conversion claim allowed others to exploit parts of his body for their

---

36. Margaret Jane Radin, *Market–Inalienability*, 100 HARV. L. REV. 1849 (1987) [M & S, p. 288]; Margaret Jane Radin, *Property and Personhood*, 34 STAN. L. REV. 957 (1982) [M & S, p. 282].

personal gain. Mosk viewed the case on the same spectrum as slavery or indentured servitude, permitting "the abuse of the body by its economic exploitation for the sole benefit of another person." In a sense, the market for cells already existed; the researchers were going to profit handsomely from their work. The only question was whether Moore should be allowed to participate in that market.

The majority appeared to take comfort from Moore's ability to pursue other causes of action, like informed consent. Under the informed consent regime, a doctor must obtain the consent of a patient before using his or her cells for research. Having failed to obtain that consent in this case, Moore had a cause of action against his doctors, but a cause of action that ended with them, too. Unlike a conversion claim, it would not extend down the chain to other researchers who might end up with Moore's cell line, and the majority therefore found that this remedy more appropriately balanced the competing interests of the patient and scientific progress. But this is a strange kind of protection when coupled with the market inalienability of cells and body parts. It allows patients to refuse consent, but does not permit them to grant consent on terms that share the proceeds of the research. This seems particularly perverse, and might lead patients to refuse consent—"what's in it for me?"—when the payment of money would make important cells or other body parts available for research.

There is an interesting historical story to tell, too, although the opinions in *Moore* did not address it. It is longstanding common law precedent that bodies are not property. They are protected, if at all, by specific torts addressing the defilement of the corpse, but bodies themselves are not property. The origins of that rule, however, reveal an interesting lesson about common law evolution. While opaque and contested, the first articulation of the rule appears to come from the 1614 *Haynes Case*. But that case stood for a remarkably different proposition.[37] There, a grave robber was caught stealing the sheets off three corpses. The court ruled that the theft was from the person who had wrapped the corpses in the sheets and not from the corpses themselves, because "property of the sheets remain in the owners ... for the dead body is not capable of it." That is, a corpse is incapable of *owning* property. This is very different, however, from later interpretations of the case, which recited the language and held that a corpse cannot *be* property. In fact, *Haynes* appeared to stand for no such proposition. Nevertheless, the principle that a body is not property is by now so

---

37. This history comes from Kenyon Mason & Graeme Laurie, *Consent or Property? Dealing with the Body and its Parts in the Shadow of Bristol and Alder Hey*, 64 MOD. L. REV. 710, 713–14 (2001).

well established in the common law that the muddle of its doctrinal origins is likely no more than a historical curiosity.

The issue of property rights in body parts remains contested, and—appropriately—deeply dependent on context. In *Newman v. Sathyavaglswaran*,[38] the Ninth Circuit ruled that corneas—and specifically, the corneas of the plaintiffs' deceased children—were property for purposes of procedural due process. Specifically, the *Sathyavaglswaran* court held that the next of kin had a protectable property interest in the disposition of the body. Can this be reconciled with *Moore*? Is it possible that next of kin have property rights over body parts that people themselves do not have while alive? That seems entirely backwards. No, the more likely difference is in the nature of the claim. A body part, or perhaps cells, might not be property for purposes of a conversion claim, but might nevertheless be property for the purposes of a Due Process claim. Imagine that a California law permitted doctors to remove blood and tissue without notification or consent. California courts might well be expected to strike down such a law on constitutional grounds, while still prohibiting conversion claims.

Ultimately, then, property in the person presents an unusual kind of acquisition claim, but one that usefully highlights the benefits of property rights, on the one hand, with moral concerns on the other.

* * *

First-in-time undergirds many of our intuitions about property. As this chapter showed, it also animates a number of specific legal doctrines, from acquisition by capture and creation, to rights in the body. But it also recurs throughout the study of property. The next chapter—with its focus on subsequent possession—relies implicitly on the rights of prior possessors. It builds, in other words, from the foundation of first-in-time.

---

38.   287 F.3d 786 (9th Cir. 2002) [M & S, p. 256].

Chapter 3

CHAIN OF TITLE

While first-in-time animates original acquisition, most property was not created out of whole cloth or ripped from nature. No, most property comes from other people. Someone's claim to property typically comes from the claims she inherited from a prior possessor. This concept—referred to as chain of title—means that rights can be traced through time, as if each owner was a link in a long chain stretching back, theoretically, to some original acquisition. The topic of subsequent possession, then, is about how someone becomes the next link in the chain. This turns out to be bound up inextricably with the reasons for protecting prior possession in the first place.

Property changes hands all the time through purchase and sale, which are by far the most common forms of subsequent acquisition. The law of contracts governs these transactions, which are therefore not part of the broader study of property. Likewise, some property is inherited at death and is governed by the law of wills and trusts, also largely beyond the scope of an introductory course in property. It is the other forms of acquisition that are interesting from a property perspective, and these include finding property, receiving property as a gift, and acquiring property through adverse possession. These more specialized property doctrines each contain their own complexities, and can prove surprisingly slippery.

A. Acquisition by Find

Everyone has found property. And everyone has some innate intuition about what to do with it—pocket it, turn it over to the police, advertise it, and the like. But what legal rights are actually created by finding property? What rights do others have to property you found? There are three separate sets of rights at play in the law of finders, two easy and the other more difficult. They are, respectively, the rights of the finder against the "true" owner, the rights of the finder against subsequent possessors, and the rights of the finder against the owner of the land on which the item was found (the locus owner).

Start with the easy ones. If someone finds something on the street, and the owner returns to claim it, that prior owner is entitled to take it back. Notice that "owner" here does not necessarily mean the person who originally created or captured the property, but merely the prior possessor. The original owner is not "original" in some literal sense, but merely temporally prior to the finder.

Although the original owner has a better claim than the finder, the finder still has rights to the property. In fact, the finder has rights against anyone else who might come along, be it a Good Samaritan, bully, or thief. A finder obtains the status of "original owner" vis-à-vis the rest of the world, excepting only those who are *more* original.

Consider the small but revealing case of *Armory v. Delamirie*.[39] There, a chimney sweep "found" a jewel and brought it to a goldsmith, presumably to try to sell. The goldsmith's apprentice took the jewel and returned the empty socket, and the chimney sweep sued. The court ruled for the chimney sweep, ordering the goldsmith to pay the value of the missing jewel (or, specifically, the value of the finest jewel that would have fit in the socket, since the jewel could not be found and its actual value was therefore undeterminable).

This all seems quite basic, and it is. But it makes an important point. The chimney sweep had not bought the jewel, crafted it, inherited it, or done anything else that would have given him a claim to original acquisition. He merely found it—and it is certainly worth asking whether he might have "found" it on the bedside table in a house whose chimney he was cleaning. This is not Bert from Mary Poppins, after all! None of this changes his status vis-à-vis the goldsmith. As the prior possessor, the chimney sweep wins against everyone else except possessors prior to him. And think about this: the suit was in *trover* (for damages, as opposed to *replevin* for the return of the good). The goldsmith or his apprentice therefore retained the jewel. If one of them had subsequently lost it on the street, to be picked up by a cobbler (or some other third party), the goldsmith could sue for its recovery, even though he had obtained possession by expropriating it from the chimney sweep.

Property rights are relational. The title "owner" does not exist in some absolute sense; it represents a status in relation to other specific people. The chimney sweep is the owner of the jewel against the rest of the world, save the person (or people) who have better title. Or, as the court in *Clark v. Maloney* put it, "the finder

---

39.   1 Strange 505 (Kings Bench 1722) [DKA & S, p. 98]; [M & S, p. 220]; [S, p. 175].

of chattel, though he does not acquire an absolute property in it, yet has such a property, as will enable him to keep it against all but the rightful owner."[40]

There is a relatively straightforward consequentialist justification for the protection of prior possessors against subsequent ones. It facilitates people putting property into the stream of commerce, and discourages costly over-investment in securing physical possession. Without protection for prior possessors, finders would worry that relinquishing possession to someone else—a goldsmith, or otherwise—would make it difficult to reclaim the property. Losing possession would amount to losing all rights to the property, and so "found" property might be kept under lock and key. To put the point differently, protecting prior possession as a source of property rights means that a prior possessor often needs to prove only that she had the property first to get it back from a subsequent possessor. This makes the property more usable, and so more valuable, and eliminates the need to keep receipts for everything you own in order to establish legitimate title.

This, however, leads to the more complicated set of rights at play in the law of find: between the finder and the locus owner. If property is found on public property, or on land (or in a building) belonging to the finder, there is no question about the finder's claim to property against everyone else except prior possessors. But where the finder is on someone else's property, the nettlesome question arises whether the finder or the locus owner has better claim to the property. As between them, who should win?

Courts resolving these cases often rely on thin-seeming distinctions. Some courts examine whether the property was somehow attached to the ground or merely lying on top of it. If the former, the locus owner wins; if the latter, the finder. Other courts ask whether the property was lost or mislaid, holding that lost property can be claimed by the finder but mislaid property goes instead to the locus owner. But these distinctions prove remarkably unhelpful for resolving real cases in satisfying ways.

Consider *Hannah v. Peel*,[41] a case deservedly famous for its poor reasoning. There, plaintiff Hannah found a brooch, covered with cobwebs, that was lying on top of a window frame in a house belonging to defendant Peel. Peel, however, had never had possession of the house, since the British government had requisitioned it for quartering soldiers before he ever occupied it himself. In a suit

---

40. Clark v. Maloney, 3 Del. 68 (1840) [M & S, p. 222].

41. 1945 King's Bench 509 [DKA & S, p. 101]; [M & S, p. 233].

between Hannah (the finder), and Peel (the locus owner), who should win?

The brooch was not attached to the ground but was resting on top of it, suggesting, under one line of cases, that the finder should win. But this does not seem like a particularly useful distinction. It would suggest that the case comes out differently if Hannah had found the brooch while hanging blackout curtains in the house (the actual facts), than if he had found it buried in a box while digging a trench or foxhole out in the yard. It is hard to see why that distinction should matter.

Similarly, it would not appear to make any difference whether the brooch was lost or mislaid—whatever that might mean. Some courts have relied on the distinction between "property . . . placed by the owner and neglected to be removed, and property lost."[42] Under this rule, if an object fell inadvertently then the finder should be able to claim it as against the locus owner. But if it was placed somewhere and forgotten, then it should go to the owner. But was the brooch in this case lost or mislaid? It can be difficult if not impossible for the finder, or a court, to know whether the item was lost or mislaid, and harder still to understand why the distinction should matter. This kind of formalistic reasoning ends with the opaque holding in *Hannah,* that because "the brooch was lost in the ordinary meaning of that term," and found "in the ordinary meaning of that word," the finder wins as against the locus owner. But the court does not explain what it means for an object to be either lost or found "in the ordinary meaning." Without any sense of *unordinary* losing and finding, the case is hopelessly cryptic for future courts trying to discern a principled rule.

A better approach requires identifying the goals that the doctrines are meant to serve. For the law of finders, a likely goal is to facilitate the return of lost property to its even-earlier possessor. From this consequentialist perspective, what rule will facilitate returning property to the person who lost it? Consider some alternatives. One might be to grant the property to the locus owner on the theory that the owner is more likely to be able to retrace her steps and find it that way than if the transient finder gets to keep it. On the other hand, granting such strong rights to the locus owner might actually discourage finders from turning over the property to the locus owner in the first place. If the finder knows that the she will be able to keep the property if the true owner

---

42. *See* McAvoy v. Medina, 93 Mass. (11 Allen) 548 (1866) [DKA & S, p. 107]; [M & S, p. 241].

never returns, then she might be more willing to disclose that she found it.

Of course, it is possible to imagine separating possession from the ultimate entitlement to the property. Granting the rights to the finder so long as she leaves it with the locus owner would, for example, encourage the finder to reveal the property, which would mean that the property is left in a location where the true owner is most likely to find it. Of course, that would also create a burden for the locus owner, who receives nothing in exchange for maintaining a kind of lost-and-found. So other modifications are possible, like splitting the value of the property between the finder and the locus owner, or requiring the finder to turn the property in to the government, similar to an approach taken in Japan.[43]

But what of cases in which the return of the item to a prior owner is not a goal? In *Goodard v. Winchell*,[44] a large meteorite fell into a field. It was claimed by a scientist who "found it" lodged in the earth, but was claimed by the owner of the land as part of the soil. The case interestingly implicates two competing principles of acquisition. On the one hand, the principle of accession means that ownership of land includes ownership of everything attached to the land. "[W]hatever is affixed to the soil belongs to the soil."[45] On the other, lost or abandoned property can be claimed by a finder. "[W]hatever movables are found upon the surface of the earth ... and are unclaimed by any owner, are supposed to be abandoned by the last proprietor, and as such are returned into the common stock and mass of things; and therefore they belong, as in a state of nature, to the first occupant or finder."[46] The Iowa Supreme Court concluded, however, that the law of finders was inapplicable. The meteorite was never lost or abandoned, and so the principle of accession controlled and the landowner won.

While there is again something unhelpfully formalistic about the court's reasoning, looking as it did at doctrine of accession and the nature of meteorites, the Court is undoubtedly correct that finding a meteorite raises different issues from finding a pile of money, a brooch, or a jewel. There is no question about returning a meteorite to its rightful owner. Unhitched from the goal of facilitating the meteorite's return to someone else, the court appropriately distinguished the traditional doctrines of "found" property. That

---

43. See [DKA & S, p. 115].

44. 52 N.W. 1124 (Iowa 1892) [M & S, p. 229].

45. *Id.* (quoting district court opinion). For a discussion of accession, see *supra* note 29.

46. *Id.* (quoting district court opinion).

still does not provide an affirmative reason for favoring the locus owner over the finder, but it provides a legitimate basis for distinguishing the case.

Alternatively, then, Richard Helmholz has concluded, at least as a descriptive matter, that the real rule of find is to award title to the *good guy*.[47] That is, thieves and dishonest people, whether finders or locus owners, do not win (or at least rarely win). And this, too, can be justified normatively and consequentially. The law should, perhaps, reward people for doing the right thing: for acting honestly, for turning in lost property, and for otherwise respecting others people's property. And, consequentially, rewarding good actions might discourage bad ones, and also make it more likely that property will eventually be returned to its rightful owner.

The most important point, however, is simply this: agreeing on a substantive goal—whether returning property to the true owner, rewarding the "good guy," or something else—makes it possible to evaluate different legal rules against that goal, instead of simply drawing unprincipled distinctions between lost and mislaid property, for example.

B. Gifts

The law of gifts builds on the chain-of-title concept, but here the subsequent possessor (the recipient, or "donee") gains good title even against a prior possessor (the giver, or "donor"). It may seem surprising that there is a law of gifts at all. Giving gifts, after all, seems like the kind of entirely gratuitous act that should not require legal intervention. And for the most part, that is true. But legal disputes can arise in predictable scenarios. Most obviously, gifts are challenged when the donor gave an *inter vivos* gift (during life) and subsequently died. Beneficiaries under the donor's will may seek to unwind the gift, arguing it was ineffective, and so reclaim the property for the estate and for themselves. Similarly, if less often, the donor herself may have changed her mind, seeking to take back property that she earlier gave away. The question, then, is whether the gift was effective; that is, whether it succeeded in transferring the property to the donee. If so, the original donor (or her heirs, as the case may be) is out of luck.

Typically, an effective gift requires: (1) donative intent; (2) delivery; and (3) acceptance. Both donative intent and acceptance are conceptually straightforward. The donor must have intended to

---

47. See Richard H. Helmholz, *Wrongful Possession of Chattels: Hornbook Law and Case Law*, 80 Nw. U. L. Rev. 1221 (1986).

give away the property, and the recipient must have agreed to accept it. The former can involve complicated and messy factual findings; the latter is presumed.

Most of the action in the law of gifts therefore revolves around delivery. Delivery can take one of three forms: manual, constructive, and symbolic. Manual delivery is actual, physical delivery—handing over the property, and transferring physical possession. Constructive delivery, by contrast, involves handing over the means to take possession of the property. Classic examples include giving keys to a car, or the combination to a safe. Finally, symbolic delivery is not delivery at all, but merely giving something that symbolizes the property—typically a letter or some other kind of writing.

In general, the law requires that delivery be as perfect as possible, preferring manual delivery to constructive, and constructive to symbolic. The most difficult cases arise when the donor inappropriately relied on symbolic delivery but there is no doubt about donative intent. That is, everyone agrees that the donor intended to give her antique vase to her niece—the donor even wrote it in a letter!—but never actually handed it over. In a jurisdiction where the law requires manual delivery where possible, that gift would fail.

But why require delivery at all? If someone stands up in a crowded room and says, "I give my friend Bob $100," but does not hand over the cash, is there any reason not to hold him to the gift? Delivery may serve some evidentiary function, demonstrating intent, but it is hardly the exclusive or even the best evidence of an intended gift. After all, theft, too, results in a change in possession, but not one the law will protect (at least as against the victim of the theft). The delivery requirement is therefore often explained in psychological terms. A gift should not be effective unless and until the donor actually experiences the wrench of loss. It is easy enough to say, "Sure, I'll give you $100." But actually taking out the cash and handing it over may stimulate more serious consideration of the gift. While this makes some conceptual sense, its application in real cases turns out to be considerably more fraught.

An early case is *Irons v. Smallpiece*.[48] There, a father made a "verbal gift" of two colts to his son, but the colts remained in the father's possession until his death a year later. The Court held that delivery is required in the absence of a deed, and since there was no delivery of the colts, they continued to belong to the father at his death.

---

48.   106 Eng. Rep. 467 (Kings Bench, 1819) [M & S, p. 863].

There was, however, a wrinkle involving hay for the colts. The father agreed to provide it, but at a pre-specified price to be paid by the son. In fact, the son never paid for the hay while the colts remained his father's possession. A concurring opinion postulated, however, that the case might have come out differently if the son had, in fact, paid for the hay. But this is a peculiar claim, given the articulated need for delivery. Whether or not the son paid for the hay, the colts were never delivered. There is at least a question, then, whether delivery is better viewed as evidence of donative intent, and that other evidence could suffice. The more general point is this: courts often declare that delivery is required, but then water down the requirement in its application.

A similar case, on a more modern set of facts, is *Gruen v. Gruen.*[49] There, a father wrote a letter to his college-age son purporting to give as a birthday gift a valuable painting by Gustav Klimt.[50] The letter explained that the painting was a gift, but that the father was going to retain possession of it for his life, to keep it at his home in California. After the father's death, his wife—the son's stepmother—argued that the gift had been ineffective for lack of delivery and claimed it under her husband's will.

The case presents two complicated and inter-related questions. What was the nature of the intended gift, and was the delivery sufficient? The donor—the father—retained possession of the painting during his life. Did he, in fact, convey anything to his son at the time of the letter, or was he, in effect, making a promise to give his son the painting when he died? The court quite properly distinguished ownership from the right to possess, concluding that it is possible to separate the two. As the court saw it, the donor intended to transfer ownership of the painting to his son for his son's birthday, but to retain merely a possessory interest in the painting for his life. In property parlance, the donor was conveying some but not all of the sticks in the bundle of property rights to his son. But this can nevertheless still count as an effective transfer of property.

Of course, the painting itself was not delivered to the son. It remained on the father's wall in California. Since a painting is capable of being manually delivered, is manual delivery required, or was the father's symbolic delivery, via his letter, sufficient? The court here endorsed symbolic delivery, concluding that there would be no reason to require the father to take the painting off the wall,

---

49. 496 N.E.2d 869 (N.Y. 1986) [DKA & S, p. 174]; [M & S, p. 549]; [S, p. 151].

50. In fact, the father wrote two letters on the advice of counsel, to manage the possible tax consequences.

hand it to his son, only to take it right back since he was retaining possession for his life. Indeed, such a ritual might seem strange and unnecessarily costly. Delivery was therefore effective, and the son was able to claim title to the painting.

The outcome seems sensible and right, given the father's clearly stated intent to give the Klimt to his son. But the court's reasoning leaves open some important issues. There is no question that the painting was capable of being manually delivered. Inconvenient? Yes. But that has not typically been the standard for delivery, which requires manual delivery wherever possible. Under one interpretation, then, *Gruen* relaxes the requirements for manual delivery, and permits symbolic delivery where manual delivery is simply too inconvenient.

There is an alternative interpretation, however. After all, the gift was not of the entire painting because the father retained possession. It was, in essence, a gift of all but possession. Think of it as an immediate gift of a right to possess the painting in the future. This is subtly but importantly different from a promise to give a gift in the future, which is not generally enforceable. The former is a present gift of a future interest; the latter is a promise to give a gift in the future—a distinction considered at greater length in the material on estates and future interests.

This has potentially important consequences for delivery. While manual delivery of a painting is possible, manual delivery of a *right to possess the painting in the future* may not be. If the latter was, in fact, the content of the gift, then manual delivery may not have been possible after all. One cannot physically hand over a *right to possess in the future*. Symbolic delivery was therefore permissible and effective, not because manual delivery was too inconvenient, but because it was impossible. Under this interpretation, then, *Gruen* does not relax the requirements for manual delivery, but merely illustrates the problem of giving more abstract property interests as gifts.

The law is full of cases of ineffective gifts, often on deathbeds, and often to illicit lovers or people with dubious claims in the eyes of the court.[51] It is, in fact, easy to sense from the cases that courts use the surprising malleability in the delivery requirement to reach the outcomes they want, instead of in any particularly principled way.

---

51. See, e.g., Newman v. Bost, 29 S.E. 848 (N.C. 1898) [DKA & S, p. 167].

C. Adverse Possession

It is important, first and foremost, to recognize the tension between adverse possession and the other acquisition rules considered so far. Fundamentally, adverse possession grants good title to people, under the right conditions, against prior possessors and rightful owners. At first blush, it can look like a kind of institutionalized theft. It amounts to an interruption in the chain of title, protection for the second-in-time over the first-in-time, and true-owner status for subsequent possessors. On closer examination, however, there are sound doctrinal, normative and consequentialist justifications for adverse possession, making it an important doctrine for a well-functioning property system.

There is a straightforward doctrinal justification for adverse possession rooted in statutes of limitations. All adverse possession claims involve an interloper taking possession of someone else's property. The owner can bring an action to reclaim possession, typically trespass or ejectment for real property, or conversion or replevin for personal property. But these causes of action do not have unlimited statutes of limitations, and if the owner waits too long to sue, she may find her claim time-barred. Without a legal mechanism for re-securing possession of her property, the original owner cannot force the adverse possessor to leave. From there, it takes only one more step to recognize the adverse possessor's legal right to remain—after all, what is left of the true owner's right if she has no remedy to secure exclusive possession? But what justifies taking that additional step?

To frame the question differently, it is possible to imagine a world in which there is no statute of limitations for trespass, just as covenants and other legal obligations can run with land in perpetuity. So doctrine aside, why should the law ever reject the claims of a first-in-time owner for the claims of someone who comes later? In short, why should there be a statute of limitations at all?

Oliver Wendell Holmes articulated perhaps the most eloquent defense of adverse possession when he wrote, "A thing which you have enjoyed and used as your own for a long time, whether property or an opinion, takes root in your being and cannot be torn away without your resenting the act and trying to defend yourself, however you came by it."[52] In his elegant presentation, Holmes identified two separate but interconnected justifications for the full-blown doctrine of adverse possession. The first is an earning theory. An adverse possessor is entitled to the property after she has done enough—used the property as her own for long enough—to *earn*

---

52. Oliver Wendell Holmes, *The Path of the Law*, 10 HARV. L. REV. 457, 477 (1897).

title to it. This is Holmes' concern for protecting as property those claims that have taken root in the soul. But the flip side of the same coin is a sleeping theory, suggesting that the true owner loses a claim to her property if she sleeps on her rights for too long. As Holmes put it, "If [the owner] knows that another is doing acts which on their face show that he is on the way toward establishing such an association [with the property], I should argue that in justice to that other he was bound at his peril to find out whether the other was acting under his permission, to see that he was warned, and, if necessary, stopped."[53] Imagine that the strength of owners' and adverse possessors' respective claims slope in opposite directions over time: the owners' diminish while the adverse possessors' grow. At a certain point, those lines will cross and adverse possessors' claims will be stronger then (prior) owners.

Typically, some measure of both earning and sleeping is required to perfect an adverse possession claim. The adverse possessor must have done enough through her use of the property to earn a right to it, and simultaneously the true owner must have so slept on her rights that she deserves to lose the property. Combined, the earning and sleeping theories encourage people to put property to productive use, and discourage owners from ignoring their property for too long. This is part of the general story of property: rewarding effort and industry and discouraging unproductive claims.

Another and less grand justification for adverse possession is rooted in administrative efficiency and the desire to minimize transaction costs. Adverse possession can vindicate people's expectations about ownership when records are either ambiguous or wrong, or where the true owner is simply too difficult to identify or find. If someone lives on land for long enough, wrongly believing it to be his, the law will eventually protect those settled expectations. After all, if the entire world is under the same misapprehension, the *actual* owner may be very difficult to identify. Adverse possession in this view can serve to clear title that might otherwise be hopelessly cloudy.

The black-letter doctrine of adverse possession reflects these theoretical justifications. In order to gain title to property, an adverse possessor must demonstrate that her possession was: actual, open and notorious, exclusive, adverse under a claim of right, and continuous and uninterrupted for the statutory period.[54] Each is a different element—although some are occasionally subdivided or named differently—and each contains its own complexity.

---

53. *Id.*

54. 2 C.J.S. Adverse Possession § 29 (2011).

Actual Entry. Actual entry seems easy enough. An adverse possessor must actually enter and possess the property for her claim to run. The contested issue in this element tends to involve how much property is being adversely possessed. That is, how much of the property did the adverse possessor actually enter?

Imagine that someone, call him Owen (for "owner"), owns forty acres of property. Alice (for adverse possessor) tills and tends thirty of those forty acres. If all of the other elements below are met, how much of Owen's property does Alice own? All of it? Only the thirty acres that she actually cultivated? The rule, typically, is that an adverse possessor can claim actual entry of the amount of property that she was using as a true owner would use the property. If a true owner would, for example, typically leave ten acres fallow (for runoff, crop rotation, or otherwise), then Alice can claim all forty after the adverse possession period has run. But if not, then Alice can claim only the property that she actually used.

There are two important exceptions to this rule, however. First, if the adverse possessor enclosed the property, then she can assert constructive possession of the whole. Erecting a fence around the entirety of the property, but only cultivating a part, is usually enough to establish an adverse possession claim for the whole.

Second, if the adverse possessor has a "color of title" claim to the property, then she can also adversely possess the whole. "Color of title" is a term of art, meaning a claim based on a written instrument. This typically occurs when someone attempts to buy property and is given title, but the title is defective for some reason. If the ineffective buyer subsequently takes possession for the statutory period and in the requisite manner, she may then take good title by adverse possession—and may also take title to the entire property, regardless of the amount that she actually occupied or cultivated.

This exception has everything to do with clearing title to property. If the intended buyer takes possession and treats the property as her own for long enough, the law will eventually approve the ownership claim, giving effect to people's settled expectations and allowing subsequent buyers to take good title in turn.

Open and Notorious. The notoriety requirement, as it is often called, requires that the adverse possession be sufficiently obvious to put the true owner on at least constructive notice that someone else is using her property.

This is most obviously related to the sleeping theory of adverse possession. The true owner is not sleeping on her rights unless she has reason to know that someone is infringing them. While there is no bright-line rule establishing what counts as open and notorious use, it must generally be the kind of use to which a true owner would put the property, and it must, above all, be visible. The true owner, on periodically walking (or investigating) her property, should be put on notice that someone else is actually in possession.

In *Marengo Cave Co. v. Ross*,[55] someone discovered the entrance to a cave that extended, underground, under his neighbor's property. He then "occupied" the entire cave for nearly 50 years, charging admission to the public. After a dispute eventually arose with his neighbor, he claimed title to the cave by adverse possession. The court rejected the claim, finding that the use—although advertised to the public—was not sufficiently visible since it was underground. While use of the cave itself was open and notorious, the fact that the cave extended under his neighbor's land was not. Adverse possession, then, is not about treading lightly or leaving a soft footprint on the land. It requires something altogether more visible: building a house, erecting a fence, tilling the fields, and the like.

Mannillo v. Gorski[56] increased the notoriety requirement in cases of minor border encroachments. There, defendants' 14–year-old son built concrete steps that—unbeknownst to anyone—encroached on their neighbors' property by 15 inches. More than 20 years later, the neighbors recognized the encroachment and sued for trespass, essentially asking to have the stairs removed and the property line reestablished. The defendants countered that they had acquired title to those 15 inches by adverse possession. After clarifying the required mental state, discussed below, the court rejected the defendants' adverse possession claim on grounds that the plaintiffs had not known the steps were on their land. In other words, they did not have notice of the adverse possession. But that seems odd! Concrete steps are entirely open and notorious. Their existence and their precise location were obvious to anyone who bothered to look. The court, however, found that plaintiffs were not on notice of the adverse possession because they did not know the exact location of their own property line. In essence, the court held that plaintiffs had not slept on their rights for failing to have a survey conducted that would have identified the exact location of their property line.

Stepping back, this case illustrates one common context in which adverse possession claims arise: shifting boundaries in suburban communities. Neighbors frequently colonize each other's prop-

---

55. 10 N.E.2d 917 (Ind. 1937) [M & S, p. 190].

56. 255 A.2d 258 (N.J. 1969) [DKA & S, p. 136].

erty, inadvertently or not, by extending gardens, mowing lawns, building fences, or erecting concrete stairs. Requiring actual notice of an encroachment bails out those owners who do not police their boundary lines to the inch. But perhaps that is in the best interests of neighborly peace and harmony. If the suspicion of a shifting line caused people to run to the local surveyor or risk losing precious inches from their property, then legal conflicts are likely to be not too far behind. On the other hand, a fence that exists in the wrong place for long enough may well create reliance interests in the adverse possessor that the law should recognize, whether or not the owner had actual knowledge of the invasion. Doctrinally, though, this much is clear: the open and notorious requirement is typically satisfied by a use that puts the true owner on constructive notice of the occupation, except when it comes to minor border encroachments in which case, as in *Mannillo,* actual knowledge may be required depending on the jurisdiction.

Exclusive. The exclusivity requirement works just as it sounds. Two or more people cannot simultaneously adversely possess property if they are also adverse to each other. Nor can an adverse possessor share possession with the true owner (or her agents or tenants). On the other hand, two or more people can adversely possess property together so long as they are not adverse to each other. A husband and wife, say, or even friends or business partners may together be able to adversely possess property, resulting in a co-tenancy of one kind or another.[57]

If this distinction seems obscure, consider what it is intended to capture. Multiple squatters, all simultaneously occupying a building or some land, are unlikely to satisfy the exclusivity requirement for adverse possession. This is obviously not based on any kind of sleeping theory; the true owner sleeps on her rights no less if two or more people are on her property rather than just one. Instead, it appears to reflect social judgments about the kinds of uses, and the kinds of people, that should be able to obtain title to property through adverse possession. This may have less to do with coherent doctrine than judicial attitudes towards disfavored activities, like squatting.

Adverse and Under a Claim of Right. The adversity requirement (sometimes referred to as hostility) means simply that the adverse possessor's possession cannot be with the owner's permission. For this reason, a valid lease can never ripen into adverse possession, no matter its duration. Sorry, renters: consent will always defeat an adverse possession claim.

---

57. For discussion of co-tenancies, see Chapter 5.

Claim of right, however, is one of the most contested elements in adverse possession cases, and it takes on different meanings in different jurisdictions. Notice, though, that this element refers to something completely different than the *color of title* described above. Color of title exists when adverse possession is founded on an ineffective instrument; claim of right, on the other hand, refers to the mental state of the adverse possessor.

A traditional but now disfavored approach, called the Maine rule,[58] required the adverse possessor to be acting in bad faith. That is, the adverse possessor had to know that she did not own the property she was occupying, and was attempting to assert title to it. This rule is often criticized for rewarding the bad actor, the person who deliberately seeks to appropriate the property of another. An alternative approach, then, is to require the opposite: good faith. That is, the adverse possessor must mistakenly believe, in good faith, that the property she possesses actually belongs to her.

The more typical approach, and the one favored by most commentators, is to abandon the mental state requirement altogether. That is, the mental state of the adverse possessor does not matter, so long as all the other elements are met. Importantly, this does not eliminate the hostility requirement; the possession must still be *non-consensual*, but there is no subjective mental state requirement for the claim to run.

The mental state requirement varies by jurisdiction. Adding to the difficulty, courts are not always consistent in their application of the claim of right. *Van Valkenburgh v. Lutz*[59] is a perfect example. There, the Lutzes occupied land adjacent to a lot that they owned. They built a shack for a family member on the neighboring property, built a garage partly on it, cultivated some gardens, raised chickens, partially cleared, and otherwise used the land. After a confrontation with some neighbors' children, the neighbors—the Van Valkenburghs—bought the contested property in a tax sale and sought to have the Lutzes removed. The Lutzes initially responded that they had an easement over the property, and later amended their argument to assert an adverse possession claim.

Rejecting the Lutzes' argument, the New York Court of Appeals relied, in part, on two internally contradictory holdings. The Court first held that the shack did not establish an adverse possession claim because the Lutzes knew that it was not on their own property. That is, they built the shack on land they knew was not

---

58. Preble v. Maine Cent. R. Co., 27 A. 149 (Me. 1893) [DKA & S, p. 133]; [M & S, p. 199].

59. 106 N.E.2d 28 (N.Y. 1952) [DKA & S, p. 122].

theirs. However, the Court also rejected the adverse possession claim resulting from the garage encroachment because the Lutzes mistakenly thought they were building it on their own property. What mental state does the New York Court of appeals then require for adverse possession? It appears to reject both good faith and bad faith as bases for adverse possession.

No one thinks that the case actually did away with adverse possession in New York, however. Instead, the case illustrates the confusion that can surround the mental state requirement. Or, perhaps the case illustrates something even more troubling: how adverse possession doctrines can disfavor certain people and certain uses. The Court appears to have disapproved of the Lutz's relatively low valued use of the property, favoring instead the well-heeled Van Valkenburghs, newcomers to the community.

Continuous and Uninterrupted. The final requirement is that the possession be continuous and uninterrupted for the statutory period. The duration varies by jurisdiction, but is typically between 5 and 21 years. Of course, the requirement does not literally require continuous occupancy; the adverse possessor can leave for groceries! Instead, as with the notoriety requirement, the adverse possessor is only required to occupy the property the way a true owner would. Still, this element hides two important complexities: tacking, and disabilities.

Tacking permits an adverse possessor to transfer her adverse possession claim to someone else. Paradigmatically, one person can adversely possess property for the first half of the statute of limitations and then transfer her interest to someone new who can adversely possess for the second half. Notice that this is at least superficially in tension with the exclusivity requirement. In effect, it allows several people to divide their adverse possession claims over time. It also appears hard to square with an earning theory, because each individual adverse possessor has not satisfied the statute of limitations.

The tension is somewhat illusory, however. The earning theory is broad enough to include the possibility that a partially earned adverse possession claim can be transferred or sold. In fact, such alienability increases the value of adversely possessing property, encouraging industry and investment in a manner entirely consistent with the earning theory. But this raises an important question about the relationship required between successive adverse possessors that is required for their claims to tack together.

Consider, for example, *Howard v. Kunto.*[60] In that case, owners of three adjacent waterfront parcels each owned summer houses on the lots. However, a new survey revealed—much to everyone's surprise and dismay—that each person was one lot off. That is to say, each person was actually the record owner of the property one lot to the west of the house he actually occupied. Although people had bought and sold property, and had been living on the property in reliance on the misinformation, everyone in fact was living on someone else's land. Making matters worse, the defendants, the Kuntos, had taken property from a previous owner less than a year before. Therefore, they could not have adversely possessed the property in that time, unless they inherited a claim from the previous owners.

This case is a perfect example of how adverse possession can be used to clear title to property, and to give effect to people's expectations even when they are inconsistent with land records. It is easy enough to see what the solution should be; the parties should be given title to the property that they reasonably believed they owned, and on which they—or their predecessors in interest— had relied for years. Actually reaching that result required some difficult doctrinal work, however.

Under traditional rules, for claims to tack, successive adverse possessors had to be in privity with each other. Privity—an elusive concept that returns periodically and in more detail throughout this book—is typically supplied by a deed between parties. That is, when one party conveys a deed to another for the sale of property, it supplies privity between them as to that property. That privity exists even where the seller has expanded her property through adverse possession. If a deed purports to convey ten acres of land, but the seller has been occupying and cultivating an additional acre for the statutory period, while meeting the other requirements for adverse possession, then the sale of the ten-acre lot is enough to establish privity for the additional acre. Instead of buying just the ten acres recited in the deed, the buyer is able to acquire all eleven acres. This is how tacking and privity typically work.

The problem in *Howard v. Kunto*, however, was that the deed between the Kuntos and the prior owners *entirely* misdescribed the property. It is as if the prior owners had conveyed to the Kuntos a deed for the Brooklyn Bridge. They actually had no connection to the property described in the deed. This would not have created privity under traditional tests, and so the Kuntos would not have been able to inherit their predecessor's claim.

---

60.   477 P.2d 210 (Wash. Ct. App. 1970) [DKA & S, p. 142]; [M & S, p. 208].

The Court, however, sensibly loosened this doctrinal straight-jacket, finding that "[t]he technical requirement of 'privity' should not, we think, be used to upset the long periods of occupancy of those who in good faith received an erroneous deed description." That, after all, is the crux of much adverse possession doctrine: vindicating reasonable and settled expectations about the ownership of property. The *Kunto* court therefore held that privity requires only some "reasonable connection between successive occupants," and not necessarily a deed describing some or all of the property.

So who does not have privity in Washington after this case? Successive trespassers, squatters, and people with no clear connection to each other would not be allowed to tack their periods of adverse possession. Here, again, deep social judgments are on display in the doctrine of adverse possession. True owners are sleeping on their rights no less when their property is occupied by successive trespassers instead of others. And a vacant property may take equal root in the soul of a squatter as in other people. Shantytowns worldwide—often erected on others' land—make that point plainly as they become permanent homes for many families.

The other pressing issue regarding the statute of limitations is the tolling of the statute of limitations when the true owner is suffering from a disability, which is narrowly defined. Where the true owner was either a minor, mentally incompetent, or imprisoned when the adverse possessor first entered the property, the statute of limitations is tolled for the duration of the disability. Typically, the true owner can maintain an action for trespass or ejectment against an adverse possessor for the regular statutory period, or ten years (or some other specified amount of time) after the disability ends, *whichever is longer*. The disability defense is rooted squarely in the sleeping theory of adverse possession. The true owner is due no demerits for sleeping on her rights if she was not in a position to defend them.

Perhaps the most interesting aspect of the disability doctrine is not that it exists, but that it has such limited application. The list of disabilities is exclusive, not illustrative. And the only disabilities that will toll the statute of limitations are those that existed at the time the adverse possession began. So, if the owner of property was 12 years old when an adverse possessor first entered her property, but then subsequently became imprisoned and eventually mentally ill, the adverse possessor will still end up with the property 10 years after the *original* disability ends, because that was the only one in place at the time the adverse possessor entered. On facts like these, the true owner may never have had a meaningful opportunity to protect her rights; each disability overlapped with the next. Nevertheless, that is not enough to prevent the statute from running and the adverse possessor ending up with title to the property. The disability doctrine thus reflects a compromise; it provides some protection to the true owner, rooted in a sleeping theory, but at some point will still allow the adverse possessor's claim to run. Successive disabilities will not prevent the adverse possessor from earning title to the property eventually.

The government suffers from the ultimate disability. Although not typically construed in terms of disability, the rule is ironclad: adverse possession does not run against the government. The underlying justification for this rule is familiar from disabilities, however. The law will not charge the government with the demerits of failing to monitor its property. The public, or its agents, should not have to walk all the federal and state lands to make sure people are not encroaching or adversely possessing. It may also be inappropriate and a source of mischief if people could impoverish the public by capturing government-owned lands. The relationship between public land and private actors is quite complex, and this is by no means the last word. The subject is taken up again in the context of the public trust doctrine, and also the Takings Clause.

* * *

To summarize, this chapter has surveyed different ways of acquiring property from others: find, gift, and adverse possession. That list is not exclusive—conquest, for example, is often treated in a property class[61]—but the core insights are apparent. The various legal doctrines can only be applied in any principled way by identifying some underlying principles or goals animating each area of law. The project here is not to insist on any particular goal, but rather to explore how different goals translate into different doctrinal choices. Against this backdrop, then, the next topic is how property can be divided and rebundled.

---

61. See Johnson v. M'Intosh, 21 U.S., 8 (Wheat.) 543 (1823) [DKA & S, p. 3]; [M & S, p. 113]; [S, p. 98].

Part II

DIVIDING PROPERTY

Having explored how people acquire property and property rights, the next topic is how people can divide them. This is not merely mechanical—although the technical aspects loom large in this Part—but also reveals something important about the nature of property.

A considerable amount of the private law is devoted to dividing up property rights in new and creative ways. Bundling and unbundling property can create tremendous value, and can allow people to structure their holdings to meet their specific needs. By allowing people to buy individual songs instead of entire albums, iTunes created value for consumers—value that Apple partially captures with every sale. This is a result of selling property in smaller and increasingly thin slices. Additional examples are everywhere. The same building might sell for more money divided into smaller apartments than sold as a whole. Converting a condominium into a time-share allows people to buy a week or a month at a time, perhaps increasing the value for the entire unit. Many bankers on Wall Street make most of their money inventing new kinds of increasingly esoteric ways of disaggregating financial interests.

There is a countervailing pressure, however. The more finely divided property interests become, the more difficult and expensive it can be to put them back together again. Sometimes property rights are divided too finely. Individually, these thin rights cannot be put to productive use, but the act of rebundling them may prove prohibitively expensive. This worry, about minimizing transaction costs and keeping property in efficiently sized chunks, presses back against unrestrained alienability and the fractionated rights that can result.

Throughout the material that follows, then, it is important to see both pressures: one toward flexibility, and increased divisibility of property rights; the other toward the opposite, constrained flexibility and restraints on how property rights may be divided.

The first Chapter examines how to divide property intertemporally (across time). The second looks at how to divide property concurrently (among individuals at the same time). In both, a central issue is how the law deals with potential and actual conflicts among the various parties who have property interests in the same underlying resource.

Chapter 4

ESTATES AND FUTURE INTERESTS

The system of estates and future interests, governing conveyances of real property, is as arcane, baffling, and technical as any subject in the common law. The goal of presenting the material here is not to detail or even summarize the specific rules and intricacies governing this area of law. That work is better left to the many reference texts specifically devoted to the subject. The project in this Chapter is simultaneously more grand and more modest: to understand why the system exists, and to explore the tensions it reflects. Although the discussion below necessarily begins with a broad outline of the system, that description operates only at the most general level.

Fundamentally, "estates and future interests" refers to the system of land ownership inherited from English feudalism, although today it applies more often to trusts than to land itself. It describes rights in land and trusts, and ways of dividing those rights among present and future interest holders. At the end of this sometimes baffling material, the principle takeaway is that several people simultaneously can share interests in the same property, even though only one person actually possesses it at a time. In short, estates and future interests is a system for dividing interests in property among people inter-temporally.

A. History

The system of estates in land descends directly from feudalism in the Middle Ages. Although the details fill volumes, the general outline of the history is important to understand.[62]

The King was at the center of the original feudal land system. Land was owned by the King, who distributed it to his subjects through a hierarchical system of "tenure." The King would grant land to tenants in exchange for their promises to provide knights for service to the crown. Those tenants could then "subinfeudate" the land, making themselves lords (literally, "land lords") and creating new tenants whose fealty was owed to them. The lords would then demand knight service from their new tenants, and

---

62. For those interested in more detail, the leading volume is A.W.B. Simpson, A History of the Land Law (2d ed. 1986).

those knights could then be used to satisfy the lords' obligation to the King. The arrangement was iterative, too, so that the tenants could further subinfeudate their land, passing along their obligations to new tenants, and so on.

Notice, then, that the person at the bottom of this hierarchy—the person in possession—was not the "owner" of the land. The King was the owner, and everyone else was his (or his intermediaries') tenant. This bottom-most person in possession was said to hold a "fief" (as in fiefdom), eventually called a "fee." The fee-holder possessed the land subject to his obligations to his lord, and those obligations were quite personal—providing knights and, eventually, other kinds of services as well. As a result, the fee interest could be subinfeudated, but could not be transferred and did not survive death. When the fee-holder died, the fee interest would return to the lord to be redistributed as he pleased. It became customary, however, for the lord to return the land to the fee-holder's heir upon some kind of payment.

Eventually, the law began to recognize a conveyance to a tenant that would, in fact, allow the property to be transferred to the tenant's heir at death without first reverting back to the lord. A lord wishing to create such a fee interest in a tenant, call him "A,"[63] would convey the land "to A and his heirs." Then, when the tenant died, the land would transfer automatically to the tenant's heirs, and so on.

It is important to see, however, that even this fee interest was not alienable. Although it would descend to the fee holder's heirs at death, it could not be transferred *inter vivos*, during the fee holder's life. A conveyance of land "to A and his heirs" meant that A's heirs—typically his eldest son—would automatically take the property when A died. A could not transfer his interest, nor cut short his heirs' interest, during his lifetime.

That eventually changed. Inalienability can create grossly inefficient distributions of land. An individual fee holder may well value the land less than someone else, but without alienability of fee interests, the land is kept out of the hands of the higher value user. The legal system finally caught up with the pressures for increased transferability, reinterpreting the language of a conveyance "to A and his heirs." Instead of giving A's heirs an actual legal entitlement to take at A's death, this conveyance was reinterpreted to create an alienable interest held by A . That is, the addition of "and his heirs" in a conveyance meant that the property would not

---

63. By convention, the grantor in land conveyances is usually denoted "O" (for owner), and the recipient or recipients are denoted A, B, C, etc., as necessary.

return to the grantor (the lord) at A's death, but instead that A could control what happened to the property. This included alienating it during his life. Therefore, a conveyance "to A and his heirs" was simply a conveyance to A, with a grant of control over the disposition of the property.

Alienability created new forms of ownership, however, and this is where the feudal history remains so relevant today. Already this brief history has identified three different interests that a fee holder might have. In the original version, the fee would simply end at the fee holder's death and return to the lord. In the second, the fee could not be transferred *inter vivos* but would automatically transfer to the fee holder's heir. And in the last, the fee would be freely alienable by the fee holder during life, and at death by will. These describe three very different kinds of legal relationships, and grantors needed ways to describe which they wanted to create.

Enter the formal conveyancing system! Very specific, formal language creates each of these different kinds of interests in land, language that persists to this day even as its feudal origins recede into the mists of time. For example, in order to create a freely alienable interest, a grantor typically conveys property "to A and his heirs." This is not a grant to A's heirs, who have no stake at all in what A does with the property. Instead, this is technical language, describing the nature of A's interest in the land. To create an interest that lasts only for the grantee's life, a grantor conveys property "to A for life." And to create an interest that descends to the grantee's heir at death, the grantor can convey the property "to A and the heirs of his body." (This last interest, however, called a "fee tail," has been revoked in every state, for reasons considered in detail below.)

Although hardly a model of clarity, the modern conveyancing system at least makes more sense against this historical backdrop.

B. The System

Any conveyance of property necessarily involves at least two people: the grantor (the previous owner) and the grantee (the recipient of the property). The conceptually rich material here involves conveyances to more than one grantee at a time.

The fee simple absolute is the unitary heart of the system. It is what people typically think of as ownership. It is undivided temporally, extending forward in time indefinitely. It is, perhaps, useful to think of the fee simple absolute as an atom (or a pie, for the scientifically disinclined). When a grantor conveys that atom to a grantee or grantees, it can be divided temporally, but it cannot be destroyed. That is to say, all the parts of the atom (or the pie) must continue to exist. If a grantor does not convey everything, then whatever is left over she automatically retains. Think of this as the "conservation of mass" principle of estates and future interests.[64]

At the most general level, land ownership is divided among people holding present possessory interests—people with a legal right to possess the land now—and future interest holders—people with a right to possess the property sometime in the future. A grantor can therefore divide her property among different grantees, one of whom takes a present possessory interest, and others of whom will take, if at all, only in the future. While this quickly becomes complex, it is useful to think about the formal conveyancing system as a set of tools for accomplishing goals that real people are likely to have in specific situations.

Imagine, then, that Othello (for "Owner") owns Blackacre in fee simple absolute. (By convention, most land in a property course is named Blackacre—think here of some aristocratic estate with a grand house and lands, all together named "Blackacre." Of course, the name is generic and can denote the smallest and most modest lands, too.) There is no temporal limit on Othello's ownership, and there are no future interest holders lurking in the shadows waiting to take possession of Blackacre sometime later. When Othello dies, he has full control over the disposition of Blackacre, and can do with it as he pleases. Othello, however, wishes to convey Blackacre to his sister, Amanda. He has several choices. He can convey everything that he has to her, essentially transferring the atom (or the pie) whole. A conveyance by Othello, "to Amanda and her heirs," accomplishes this. It creates a fee simple absolute in Amanda, which is alienable and has no future interests associated with it. In this case, Othello has given up everything he has, and transferred it to Amanda.

But Othello has some additional options. Perhaps Blackacre is the family homestead that he inherited from his parents. He wants to allow his sister to live on Blackacre for her life, but he wants it back for his family after she dies. This can be accomplished by creating a life estate. Othello can create one by conveying Blackacre, "to Amanda for life." But notice, here, that Othello has now split the atom (or divided the pie). The subatomic particles are the life estate that Amanda now holds, and what happens to Blackacre after Amanda dies. In other words, the conveyance specifies what happens to Blackacre during Amanda's life; she is in possession of

---

64. See [M & S, p. 518] (labeling this principle "conservation of estates").

it. But the conveyance says nothing about what happens afterwards. Therefore, Othello has not given everything away. He has only given away possession of Blackacre for Amanda's life. After she dies, Blackacre will revert back to him (or to his heirs, if he is already dead). Othello thus has a future interest in Blackacre—an interest that comes after Amanda's present possessory interest for life. And, for the sake of precision, what Amanda has is called a life estate in Blackacre, and what Othello has is called a reversion.

Othello might have other conveyances in mind, too. Instead of granting a life estate to Amanda, and retaining a reversion, he might want to specify a third party to take after Amanda dies, perhaps Othello's son, Xavier. In this case, Othello simply needs to convey Blackacre "to Amanda for life, then to Xavier." Now, after splitting the atom, Othello has given both parts away and left nothing for himself. Amanda will take a present possessory interest for her life, and Xavier will take a future interest—now called a remainder—in the rest. And when Xavier takes, sometime in the future after Amanda dies, he will take in fee simple absolute. What he technically has, then, is a vested remainder in fee simple absolute.

The rest of the system of estates and future interests includes variations on this basic theme. The grantor may, in the conveyance, specify conditions that have to occur before someone else takes. This creates the generic form of a defeasible fee and, depending on the grammar of the conveyance and the holder of the future interest, might be a fee simple determinable, a fee simple subject to a condition subsequent, or a fee simple subject to an executory limitation, each of which is followed by its own specific future interest—a possibility of reverter, a right of entry, and an executory limitation, respectively.

Importantly, some forms of future interests are not certain to become possessory. These are contingent interests, contingent on something occurring or not occurring in the world. An example is a conveyance "to A for life, then to B if she outlives A, otherwise to C." In this case, B and C both have contingent interests. Neither one is certain to take—it depends whether or not B outlives A. But imagine that B dies sometime later, while A is still alive. B has not outlived A, so it is now certain that C will take the property after A dies. At that point, C's interest is no longer contingent but is now vested, meaning it is certain to become possessory sometime in the future. This is true even if C dies before A. C herself may never take possession of the property, but her *interest* will become possessory; her heirs, or beneficiaries under her will, can inherit her interest even if she predeceases A. A vested interest is a certain one, and this has important consequences for the rule against perpetuities taken up below.

There are many additional complexities, requiring lawyers to distinguish between contingent remainders and vested remainders subject to divestment. Nuances pile on. The terminology and the details are often important, with property rights hanging in the balance. But all of it takes this general form. Aside from a fee simple absolute, every present possessory interest in property is followed by one or more future interests that may or may not become possessory sometime in the future. Each has its own name, and is created by different language, but the basic idea remains the same throughout.

Property students can also take some comfort from the fact that the American Law Institute has recently adopted the Restatement Third of Property, proposing an altogether different and more streamlined approach to the entire law of estates and future interests. Although not yet the law anywhere, the new system radically compresses the number of present possessory and future interests, dividing them simply into the fee simple absolute, the fee simple defeasible, the life estate, and the term of years, the latter three of which are followed either by a reversion if held by the grantor, or a remainder if held by a third party. Vesting rules are also simplified. Property students in the future may have a much simpler system to learn, but the change in the law has not happened yet.

C.   Managing Relationships Between the Parties

Dividing property interests over time raises the possibility if not the probability of conflicts between the various interest-holders. One of the law's central goals in this area, and central challenges, is to manage these conflicts when they arise. The conflicts can be between the holders of present possessory interests and future interests, or between grantors and grantees.

Life Tenants Versus Remaindermen: the Problem of Waste

One likely source of conflict is between present possessors and future interest holders. The problem, quite simply, is that the holder of a present possessory interest like a life estate has every incentive to consume as much of the property as possible, leaving as little as possible to the future interest holders.

Consumption in this context can have various meanings. Most obviously, if land contains a consumable resource—timber, minerals, oil—then the present interest holder has an incentive to capture as much of that value as possible. The future interest holders might be left taking a clear-cut, strip-mined, resource-depleted lot. But the problem can take more subtle forms as well. The owner of a life estate who fails to maintain a house on the property is saving herself money—effectively, consuming the house—and imposing the costs on future interest holders who will take over a house in disrepair.

Notice, too, that dividing ownership in this way presents two distinct but related problems. The first is one of equity between interest holders. The owner of the present possessory interest may be able to capture more than her fair share of the total value of the property. But the second, and perhaps more profound, is that the incentives of the present possessory interest holder may reduce the overall value of the property. Deferring maintenance, for example, may save $100 today, but impose $10,000 in loss tomorrow if the roof starts to leak, or the house just falls apart. Likewise, a life estate holder might want to cut down trees before they are mature, or otherwise over-consume available resources in a way that re- duces the total value of the property.[65] In theory, remaindermen should be able to bargain with the life estate holder to avoid actions that actually reduce the total net value of the property. Both parties can be made better off by negotiating to maximize the total value of the property over time, and dividing the surplus between them. However, the remaindermen may be children, or even un- born or unascertained people, and so there may be no one available to negotiate with the life estate owner.

Both problems are addressed through the doctrine of waste.[66] It prevents present possessors from acting in a way that unreasonably interferes with the expectations of future interest holders, and protects the total value of the property over time. The common law recognizes three different kinds of waste: affirmative, permissive, and ameliorative.

Affirmative waste occurs when a person in possession of the property takes affirmative actions that decrease the value of the property to future interest holders. An action for waste will lie, for example, when a life estate holder strips all the timber or minerals from the land during her period of possession. However, the law generally recognizes the right of the life estate holder to capture some of the value of the property, so if mining operations were already underway they can continue at the scale and pace that

---

65. See RICHARD A. POSNER, ECONOMIC ANALYSIS OF LAW 73–74 (7th ed. 2007).

66. Waste is also relevant for concurrent interests, where possessory interests are divided among people at the same time instead of inter-temporally. For more discussion of concurrent interests, see Chapter 5.

already existed. Timber can be removed consistently with sound forestry practices, and presumably in ways that an owner of a temporally undivided interest would log the land.

Permissive waste, on the other hand, refers to a failure to act, as when a present possessor simply allows property to fall into disrepair, fails to pay property taxes resulting in a tax foreclosure, or does not eject adverse possessors. It also includes acts of negligence that result in harm to the property—for example failing to take reasonable fire-prevention measures, which leads to a damaging fire.

Ameliorative waste is more difficult conceptually. It occurs when the actions of the present possessor alter but *increase* the value of the property for the remaindermen. A good example is *Woodrick v. Wood.*[67] There, George Wood left property in his will to his wife, Catherine, with a remainder to his two children. The facts are ambiguous about whether Catherine was the remaindermen's mother or stepmother. Regardless, Catherine sought to tear down a partially rotted horse barn on the property. One of the two remaindermen, Patricia Woodrick, objected and filed suit, seeking an injunction against destruction of the barn. Woodrick argued that the barn had a positive value of $3,200 and that its destruction would amount to waste. Catherine countered that the barn actually decreased the value of the property as a whole, and that paying to have it demolished was increasing the value of the property to the remainder beneficiaries. The trial court refused to grant an injunction, but ordered Catherine to pay Patricia $3,200 (the value of the barn) if she decided to tear it down.

The lower court's holding might seem uncontroversial, but as the *Woodrick* court explained, "At common law, anything which in any way altered the identity of leased premises was waste, regardless of whether the act happened to be beneficial or detrimental to the remainder interest."[68] The notion in the common law was that remainder beneficiaries were entitled to take the property in the form the property existed when their interest was created. Under this doctrine, tearing down the barn would change the character of the property and be impermissible whether or not it increased the value of the remainder beneficiaries' expectations.

The *Woodrick* court refused to follow the common law doctrine and affirmed the trial court. It held that Catherine would not be

---

67.   1994 WL 236287 (Ohio Ct. App. 1994) [DKA & S, p. 218].

68.   *Id.* Although the language refers to leased property, instead of property divided inter-temporally between present and future interest holders, the principle is the same.

committing waste if she tore down the barn, because "the value of the property will not be diminished by the barn's destruction." The case nevertheless remains somewhat peculiar for two mutually inconsistent reasons.

First, if destroying the barn really would not constitute waste, why should Catherine pay Patricia the value of the barn if she decided to tear it down? It would seem that destroying the barn would make both Catherine and Patricia better off, and the resulting increase in value to Patricia's remainder interest should be sufficient compensation for the loss of the barn. It is as if Catherine would be paying Patricia twice. The *Woodrick* court did not wrestle with this problem, finding only that the trial court appropriately sought to "protect the interests of both parties and to reach a fair resolution of their dispute according to the law." Courts apparently enjoy considerable freedom to craft different remedial options.

Second, it is perhaps not so obvious that a court should approve changes to property, even with compensation to the remaindermen. A parent leaving the family homestead to his sister for life, remainder to his children, would presumably not want his sister to be able to change the form of the homestead—replace it with a bowling alley or a gas station—even if it increased the value of the future interest. A significant purpose of the original grant was to convey the homestead itself to the grantor's children, and not merely its equivalent or better in money. It will not do to replace childhood bedrooms with a mattress store, at least unless the remainder beneficiaries consent. To put it in economic terms, the remainder beneficiaries may well have subjective personal values tied up with the property that the common law doctrine of ameliorative waste seeks to protect.

The common law rule is overbroad, however, working like a kind of prophylaxis, protecting remainder beneficiaries from nonconsensual changes whether or not they actually had any connection to the property at all. It is unclear on the facts of *Woodrick* why Patricia Woodrick objected to the barn being torn down. Perhaps she had a terrible relationship with the defendant and was merely being obstructionist, in which case the court was presumably correct to allow the ameliorative waste. But it is also possible that Patricia had a deep connection to the barn; maybe she was the only person in the family who rode, that it was the source of her emotional connection to her father, or that it had strong sentimental value for some other reason. If any of these were true, then the mere fact of an increase in *market value* may not justify tearing down the barn if it was harming Patricia more than it was benefitting Catherine (the life estate holder).

In *Baker v. Weedon,* the Mississippi Supreme Court confronted a situation where there was no likely claim to subjective value on the part of the remaindermen.[69] There, a 73 year-old man died, leaving his farm to his 30 year-old widow, Anna Plaxico. The conveyance, however, provided that if Anna died without children, then the farm would go to the grantor's grandchildren at Anna's death. Anna therefore had a life estate, and the grantor's grandchildren had contingent remainders (contingent on Anna not having any children of her own; if she did, the grantor's grandchildren would not take). As it turns out, Anna had no children and remained on the property for decades, living primarily off of her farming operations and later a meager rental income from the farm.

The grantor's grandchildren were not even aware that they had a remainder interest in the farm until Mississippi sought to condemn some small part of it for a new road and contacted them about their interest in the property. With continuing stress on Anna's finances, however, she sought permission to sell the farm, with the proceeds placed into trust for her for her life, with any money remaining at the end to go to the grandchildren. In other words, she sought to have the farm converted into cash.

The trial court granted Anna's request for a judicial sale. It found, in essence, that changed conditions in the area made the property much more valuable if it were put to some other non-agricultural use. That is, continuing to use the property as a farm was a kind of waste, and selling it to a higher valued user would be a more productive use of the property. This is, however, a strange kind of waste, because selling the farm would not actually increase its value. The value of the farmland would be the same whether in Anna's hands or a developer's. The only question is who gets to realize that value: Anna or the remainder beneficiaries. In other words, Anna was not asking for permission to act in a way that would increase the value of the property; she was only asking to realize the increased value of the property arising from changed circumstances.

Nevertheless, both the lower court and the Mississippi Supreme Court viewed the problem through the lens of waste. The Supreme Court found that selling the property did not adequately protect the remainder beneficiaries who were entitled to receive the property itself and not merely cash. The court acknowledged that sale might sometimes be appropriate, but only after meeting a higher threshold of necessity than the lower court found.

---

69.   262 So.2d 641 (Miss. 1972) [DKA & S, p. 210]; [S, p. 653].

The court's opinion is unsatisfyingly formalistic, and also misapprehends the economic stakes of its decision. The court is not protecting the remainder beneficiaries' subjective value in the farm, because they did not even know they had an interest in the farm until more than 30 years after their grandfather died. Nor can the court claim to be enforcing the grantor's wishes, because it takes no real stretch to imagine that his principle interest was providing for Anna's comfort during her life. The court instead appears beguiled by the grandchildren's evidence that the property was going to increase in value dramatically sometime in the near future, so that selling it now would actually be under-valuing the property.

Evidence at trial purported to demonstrate that the property was worth $168,500 today, but would be worth $336,000 within the next four years. But that is nearly impossible. If the property really would be worth $336,000 in four years, then its value is higher than $168,500 today. Think of it this way: how much should someone pay today for property that was going to be worth $336,000 in four years? More than $168,500! In fact, someone would pay $336,000, discounted to present value (which will depend on interest rates, carrying costs, and the like). Even at 15% interest, the value today would be approximately $200,000. If the property was really worth only $168,500 today, then evidence of substantially higher value in the future must have included significant speculation about coming economic changes in the area. Really, then, by refusing to authorize the sale, the court was protecting the remainder beneficiaries' desire to gamble that the property was going to increase in value in the future.

Perhaps, though, there are good reasons for the common law rule of waste to be over-broad. Subjective value is notoriously difficult to identify, let alone to measure. By protecting remainder beneficiaries' rights to the property as-is, courts are freed from the potentially difficult factual inquiry into the existence and extent of subjective value. That is at least the effect of the court's rule in *Baker*, even if the reasoning is less than pellucid.

Today, most common law actions for waste have been replaced by statute, the content of which varies by jurisdiction. They specify whether and when ameliorative waste is cognizable. And, most importantly, they specify the available remedies.

There are, in fact, three possible remedies for a successful waste claim. The first is damages. The life estate holder can be forced to compensate the remaindermen for harm done to their future interests. This might include compensation for the valuable assets impermissibly extracted from the land, or for harm resulting from negligence, for example. The second is injunctive relief. The life estate holder can be made to stop affirmative or ameliorative waste, or can be made to act to prevent permissive waste. Finally, the most rare but perhaps most valuable remedy is termination of the present possessory interest. The life estate holder can lose the life estate, at which point the property will transfer to the future interest holders prematurely. In general, these are escalating remedies, and each becomes available only as the degree and kind of waste increases. Permissive waste resulting from negligence may be remedied through damages alone; reckless or intentional permissive waste may result in injunctive relief, as may affirmative waste. Loss of possession is reserved for the most egregious forms of waste, and courts narrowly construe the statutes authorizing this remedy.

Grantors Versus Grantees: The Rule Against Perpetuities

The second and less obvious conflict that the law must sometimes mediate is between grantors and grantees. Through the sophisticated use of conveyances, a grantor can control the disposition of property far into the future. If a grantor wants to ensure that property remains in his family forever, he might try to leave it "to my son, A, for life, then to his first child, then to that child's first child, then to that child's first child, and so on forever." Or if a grantor wanted to ensure that property was used only for a specific purpose, like the maintenance of a hat store, she might leave property "to A for so long as the property is used as a millinery, otherwise to B."

The problem with such grants, as the law has long recognized, is that the grantor can substantially constrain the alienability of property far into the future. The grantee may want to replace the millinery with a sporting goods store, since few people wear hats anymore. But under the terms of the grant, she will forfeit her interest in the store if she closes the millinery. This can lead to all kinds of suboptimal and inefficient uses of property. As a result, theorists in the Nineteenth Century railed against this so-called dead hand control, arguing that it reduced the alienability of property.[70]

But all is not so simple. Freeing beneficiaries from limits in property conveyances does increase alienability *as to them*, but it reduces alienability *as to the grantor*. The grantor's freedom to control the disposition of her property is reduced if the law prevents her from conveying the property on whatever terms she

---

70. *See* Gregory S. Alexander, *The Dead Hand and the Law of Trusts in the Nineteenth Century*, 37 Stan. L. Rev. 1189 (1985).

wants. Alienability, then, is something of a zero-sum game. Expanding the reach and forms of dead hand control increases the alienability of property for grantors, but reduces it for grantees, and vice-versa.

The notoriously difficult rule against perpetuities is the law's attempt to mediate this conflict. It allows grantors to tie up property but not indefinitely, putting a kind of temporal restriction on property conveyances. The rule against perpetuities does not impose a strict time limit, however. It requires instead that contingent interests must necessarily become not contingent (either vest or fail), and that executory interests must become possessory or fail, within 21 years of the death of a life in being at the time of the conveyance. The mechanics of the rule can be quite baffling, and are sidestepped here. The important point, for this discussion, is to understand the purpose of the rule and the choices that it reflects.

Fundamentally, the rule against perpetuities represents a compromise between the interests of grantors in controlling their property, and the interests of grantees in being free from inherited restrictions on property. Implicit in this trade-off is the insight that the value to the grantor of encumbering property is likely to decrease over time. A grantor may care deeply about what happens to her property for the next generation, less so for the following, and be relatively indifferent to anything after that, except in the most abstract sense. Simultaneously, the interests of beneficiaries in freeing themselves from dead-hand control increase as the world and people's preferences increasingly diverge from the grantor's original expectations.

That understanding provides some purchase for the rule's byzantine structure. It allows future interests to remain uncertain until the next generation reaches adulthood—for 21 years after the death of people alive at the time of the original conveyance. A grantor can know, and care about, people currently living. And she might even be able to anticipate their children growing into adulthood. But the future grows foggy beyond that, and conveyances that contain uncertainties extending further in time are simply void.

It is important to understand, too, that the rule against perpetuities is a rule about certainty, not a rule about possession. It does not require that all remaindermen in fact take possession of the property within the perpetuities period, but only that the contingent interests become certain one way or another—either vest, or actually fail.

A number of states in recent years have adopted perpetuities reform. Some have taken a relatively modest approach, enacting what is called "wait and see." Traditionally, the rule against perpetuities is a rule of logical proof; a conveyance that might violate the rule against perpetuities under some set of facts is void from the outset. Under a wait-and-see approach, the conveyance will be judged by what actually happens in the world, not what might have happened.

The newly adopted Restatement Third of Property takes just such a wait-and-see approach, but also combines it with some more novel reforms. Instead of measuring the perpetuities period by a "life in being," the new Restatement uses generations, treating all members of the generation the same, whether or not they were lives in being at the time of the conveyance. Moreover, it replaces the focus on vesting with a focus on the time that future interests will terminate, either by failing or becoming possessory. This eliminates the need to distinguish between contingent and vested future interests—a distinction that can become quite slippery. While the Restatement is not the law of any jurisdiction, it may at least be an indication of what the future holds, and if so, it looks a bit brighter indeed.

Some states, however, have gone so far as to repeal the rule against perpetuities altogether. In those states, grantors can in fact create interests in land (and, importantly, in trusts) that will last for generations, in perpetuity. It remains to be seen what will happen 50, 100, or even 200 years from now when the trusts remain—perhaps with entirely anachronistic restrictions—but the original grantor is long gone. One suspects that courts or legislatures will eventually find ways to ease those restrictions, to make the trusts something less than perpetual after all, because some limits on dead hand control may be essential to protecting interests in the future from entirely outdated restrictions by long-dead grantors.

D. Limits on the Forms of Ownership

At the most general level, the rule against perpetuities is a restraint on alienability (at least for the present generation), preventing grantors from conveying property in ways they might want. Through this lens, the rule against perpetuities is part of a broader story about property. The law imposes substantive limits on interests a grantor can create, and these limits reveal important lessons about the nature of property rights generally. A telling example is the abolition of the fee tail.

Abolition of the Fee Tail

Recall that in its feudal origins, one early version of the fee would pass automatically to the fee holder's heir at death. While the language creating this fee, "to A and his heirs," later came to create a fee simple absolute, the original form remained through a conveyance "to A and the heirs of his body." This language created a fee that automatically descended to A's lineal descendants. When A died, the property transferred to A's heirs, typically his eldest living son; when A's heir died, the property transferred to his heir, and so forth. In its strongest form, the fee tail would end only when A's lineal descendants died; that is, when A's bloodline ran out.

There are two important aspects to the fee tail. First, while the *possessory* interest could be alienated, the fee would automatically transfer back to the grantee's next lineal descendants on the death of the grantee. Second, the fee tail could last for a long time. Bloodlines may persist for centuries, if not longer. While Masterpiece Theater dramas are full of bloodlines ending in myriad tragic ways, many families persist through innumerable generations.

The two points are related. One effect of inalienability is to protect landowners from creditors. If land is entailed (placed in a fee tail), creditors may not be able to get at it. An owner of a fee tail who goes broke or even bankrupt does not have the power to convey fee simple title to a creditor, and so the property will remain in the family through good times and bad. And the fee tail potentially has this effect for a long time, generation after generation. This begins to look very much like an aristocracy.

Exacerbating this condition is the effect of the fee tail on property supply. As more property is held in fee tail, less becomes available to everyone else. At least partly as a result, in England in the 18th Century, few farmers lived on land that they owned, while in Colonial America almost everyone did.[71]

America, in the founding era, largely rejected the fee tail. Legislation spread throughout the states proclaiming that a conveyance "to A and the heirs of his body" created a fee simple absolute, and not a fee tail after all. This rejection of the fee tail is not just some minor and mechanical change in the law of estate and future interests. It was, at its core, a stand against aristocracy, and a move toward more democratic land ownership. Although it may seem like a small change in the law, Thomas Jefferson himself viewed the abolition of the fee tail in Virginia as one of the most important moments in the creation of the Republic.[72]

---

71. ERIC FONER, TOM PAINE AND REVOLUTIONARY AMERICA 3, 90 (1976).

72. John F. Hart, *"A Less Proportion of Idle Proprietors": Madison, Property Rights, and the Abolition of the Fee Tail,* 58 WASH. & LEE L. REV. 167, 168 (2001).

If nothing else, this history demonstrates that the forms of property conveyances are not mere technicalities. Allowing grantors to bind land to a particular family forever creates a perfectly coherent form of ownership, but one with consequences that the American legal system could not abide. The system of estates and future interests hides within it important tensions in the law of property more generally.

Numerus Clausus

Notice how the above struggles between grantor and grantee, possessor and remainderman, and among classes of holders generally, involve a limited set of property interests. While the ultimate arrangements at stake are quite diverse, they are built on recurring categories, such as the life estate, the fee simple, and the fee simple subject to executory limitation. Professors Thomas Merrill and Henry Smith have offered a more general economic account of these limited forms of property ownership. They identified what they refer to as the *"numerus clausus"* principle of property law: "that property rights must conform to certain standardized forms."[73] This is notably distinct from the law of contracts.

It is a core feature—indeed, a core virtue—of contract law that it can be endlessly manipulated. Parties can agree to almost any terms they want and are not constrained by standard forms. Not so with property. Conveyances that do not fit within the standard forms will either be struck down or forced into a recognized box.

Johnson v. Whiton is illustrative.[74] In that case, Sarah Whiton attempted to convey to a buyer property that she (and some relatives) had inherited through her grandfather's will. The buyer refused delivery on grounds that Sarah did not have the power to sell it. The relevant conveyance in the will read:

> After the decease of all my children, I give, devise, and bequeath to my granddaughter Sarah A. Whiton *and her heirs on her father's side* one-third part of all my estate. . . . (emphasis added)

What estate does this conveyance create? It is easy enough to infer what general rights the grantor intended to create. It seems as though the grantor intended to leave the property to Sarah for her life, and then to her heirs on her father's side, intentionally omitting any heirs she might have on her mother's side. The problem is that this particular language—"heirs on her father's side"—does not fall within any of the recognized property forms; it

---

73. Thomas W. Merrill & Henry E. Smith, *Optimal Standardization in the Law of Property: The* Numerus Clausus *Principle*, 110 YALE L. J. 1, 4 (2000).

74. 34 N.E. 542 (Mass. 1893) [M & S, p. 543].

seems like a kind of fee tail, but with the property only descending on one side of the family. Since property forms are limited, and grantors cannot create new ones in their conveyances, the *Whiton* court held that the limitation in the conveyance was void. Sarah Whiton therefore received the property in fee simple absolute, and had the power to alienate the property, conveying good title to the plaintiff.

It is important to understand the nature of the court's concern here. There is nothing inherently wrong with the grantor trying to leave the property to Sarah for her life, and then to her heirs on her father's side. In fact, that could easily have been effectuated by conveying the property "to Sarah A. Whiton *for life, and then* to her heirs on her father's side." That conveyance would have been entirely valid, even though it closely resembles the invalid conveyance in the case. The differences are subtle but important.

In the language of the actual grant, as the court interpreted it, the language "to the heirs on her father's side" is a limitation that constitutes Sarah's interest in the property. The grantor appeared to be attempting to create a new kind of property interest, one in which the heirs on one side of the grantee's family automatically take at death. This, says the court, the grantor may not do.

And there is a real difference between the language in the conveyance and the alternative conveyance suggested above. In the alternative language, Sarah does not have a fee interest at all, but only a life estate. In that case, she would have had the property for her life, and her heirs on her father's side would have had a future interest in the property, specifically a remainder in fee simple. Under this interpretation, however, Sarah Whiton would not have been able to sell the property in fee simple to the plaintiff, because she did not have a fee simple interest to sell.

So why not allow a grantor to create whatever interest he or she wants? This added flexibility would allow for greater tailoring of interests, and would increase the value of the property to the grantor. After all, owners would presumably prefer more flexibility than less in conveying their property. Professors Merrill and Smith offer a powerful explanation. They argue that property interests are different from contractual interests because they are *in rem*. They run with the property, and are therefore good against the rest of the world. The more complicated the property system, then, the greater the information costs for third parties. With relatively few forms of ownership, it is easier for attorneys performing due diligence to understand what rights people have. Language conveying property "to A and her heirs"? That is a fee simple. A conveyance, "to A for life, then to A's daughter," creates a life estate in A, and a remainder in fee simple in her daughter. There is little ambiguity, and well-drafted conveyances require little legal effort to interpret.

Professors Merrill and Smith argue that the more complex the system of rights is, the more expensive it will be for people to understand those rights when seeking to honor or acquire them. To put it differently, complexity in property arrangements imposes a kind of externality on third parties. It is possible that the grantor will internalize some of the costs, at least to the extent that they are capitalized into property values. People will pay less for property with uncertain title, for example, so people are wise not to convey or acquire property in complex or ambiguous forms. But at least some of the costs are borne by society as a whole, because information costs generally increase as complexity in the forms of property increases.

Not everyone agrees. First, and most obviously, simplicity and transparency do not appear to be among the virtues of the existing system of estates and future interests. Moreover, the system is already malleable, allowing for nearly limitless arrangements if lawyers are sufficiently sophisticated and creative. The *numerus clausus* principle can therefore look more like a trap for the unwary than a substantive limit on the arrangement of property rights.

Professors Hansmann and Kraakman offer a different response.[75] They argue that standardized rights are less important than verifiable rights. As they succinctly put it: "So long as there are clear definitions and labels for the forms most needed, the ability of parties to transact in those forms will not be compromised by the availability of additional forms."[76]

Nevertheless, the *numerus clausus* principle provides an important description of, and justification for, the existence of limited forms of property rights. This, too, demonstrates that the archaic-seeming system of estates and future interests implicates important tensions at the heart of property law.

* * *

Ultimately, the system of estates and future interests continues to impose substantial burdens on lawyers and law students seeking to master its byzantine rules. But hidden among that technical complexity are important concepts. The system mediates conflicts between different interest holders and also constrains the forms that conveyances can take because of their costs to society.

---

75. Henry Hansmann & Reinier Kraakman, *Property, Contract and Verification: The* Numerus Clausus *Problem and the Divisibility of Rights,* 31 J. LEGAL STUD. 373 (2002).

76. *Id.* at 381.

Chapter 5

CONCURRENT INTERESTS

The system of estates and future interests provides mechanisms for dividing interests in property over time. It is also possible to divide interests in property concurrently so that multiple parties share ownership of property at the same time. This is immediately familiar to anyone who has had a spouse, a roommate, or a joint bank account, but the legal forms and consequences of holding concurrent interests are less than obvious.

A. The Forms of Co-ownership

In keeping with the *numerus clausus* principle introduced in the last chapter, concurrent interests take one of only three basic forms: tenancy in common, joint tenancy, and tenancy by the entirety. The term "tenancy" here does not refer to renters, but instead to the form of possession of property. Co-tenants are, in other words, owners of the property at the same time.

At the core of all three of these forms is the claim of each co-tenant to an undivided interest in the entire property. Each concurrent interest holder—each co-tenant—has an undivided interest in the whole. That might seem odd, like people together owning more than 100% of the property. But this is not The Producers of property law. In fact, the intuition should be familiar to anyone who has ordered a pizza with friends. If two people order a pizza together, they each "own" the whole pizza together. Neither person is entitled to any particular slice; each may take whatever slice he or she wants. And, even if they split the cost and therefore have an equal interest in the pizza, they each have a one-half undivided interest in the whole and so one person may still eat more than the other. Translated into real property, co-tenants in a house each have the right to possess or use the entirety of the house. Each may use and occupy all the rooms, subject to the rights of her co-tenant (or co-tenants) to do the same.

While all three forms of concurrent interest share the basic feature of undivided ownership, they contain important differences.

1. Tenancy in Common. A tenancy in common is the most basic form of concurrent interest in property. Each co-tenant has an undivided interest in the whole property, owns that share outright, and is free to do whatever he or she wants with the interest. If A and B are tenants in common in a piece of land, and A wants to sell her interest to C, she may do so without changing the nature of the tenancy. B and C would then become tenants in common, and B's interests would be unaffected.

Tenants in common can also own unequal shares in the property. One person might own two thirds of the property, and someone else the remaining third. Each, again, has a right to use the entirety of the property. But if the property is sold, or generates income, that money will be divided proportionately to each person's ownership stake.

2. *Joint Tenancy*. A joint tenancy functions just like a tenancy in common except that it comes with a right of survivorship. When a joint tenant dies, her share is automatically transferred to the other joint tenants. This can have powerful consequences. To see why, consider the differences between a tenancy in common and a joint tenancy in the following situation:

> Allison and her brother Bob own a house together. Allison has a daughter, Clara. In her will, Allison leaves all of her property to Clara. If Allison dies before Bob, who will own the house?

If Allison and Bob owned the house as tenants in common, then Clara will inherit Allison's share of the house when Allison dies. As a result, Bob and Clara own the house together as tenants in common. But if Allison and Bob owned the house as joint tenants, then at Allison's death, her interest in the house will automatically transfer to Bob. She will not have any interest remaining in the house to pass through her will. In fact, it will not pass through probate at all. As a result, Bob will own the house outright, and Clara will have no interest in it whatsoever.

A joint tenancy reflects a legal fiction that all joint tenants are, together, a single entity, so that the death of one joint tenant does not affect the interests of the entity as a whole. But in order to create this powerful right of survivorship, the common law traditionally required a joint tenancy to be created in a very particular way. According to traditional doctrine, a joint tenancy required four unities: time, title, interest, and possession. All joint tenants had to share identical interests in these four dimensions.

First, then, the interests of the joint tenants must have been created at the same time, meaning they had to be created by the same conveyance and vest or become possessory at the same time. For this reason, under traditional common law rules, a property owner could not unilaterally create a joint tenancy in his own property. Imagine that Adam owned Blackacre in fee simple, and wanted to create a joint tenancy with his daughter, Bertha, so that she would take Blackacre automatically when he died. He could not simply convey Blackacre to her, nor convey one-half of Blackacre to her as a joint tenant. Their interests would not have been created at the same time. To circumvent this requirement, Adam would have had to convey Blackacre to a third party—a so-called straw-man—who could then convey it back to Adam and Bertha together as joint tenants.

Second, a joint tenancy had to be based on the same instrument, providing a unity of title. When property is transferred by act of law, as when someone dies without a will, it could not create a joint tenancy.

Third, the interests had to be identical. As a result, it was impossible to have uneven fractional ownership, and each of the joint tenants' interests had to be of the same duration.

Finally, each joint tenant was required to share the unity of possession, meaning that each had a right to possession of the whole.

In modern times, a number of states have dispensed with these strict requirements and allow the creation of a joint tenancy simply by expressly declaring it. In other jurisdictions, however, the common law requirements persist.

If creating a joint tenancy can be difficult, terminating one is very easy. Under traditional rules, breaking any one of the four unities would sever the joint tenancy. Thus, if a joint tenant conveyed her interest to a third party, this would break the unities of time and title and automatically convert the joint tenancy into a tenancy in common. Importantly, a conveyance would have that effect even if the other joint tenants did not know about it. The conversion could happen in secret, and the right of survivorship could be eliminated without any warning whatsoever.

That power was pushed to its limits in *Riddle v. Harmon*.[77] There, a husband and wife owned some real estate as joint tenants. The wife, however, decided that she did not want her husband to take her share of the property at her death, and instead wanted to leave it to someone else by will. To sever the joint tenancy, she therefore transferred her interest in the property to herself— imagine handing a deed from one's left hand to one's right—for the purpose of converting the joint tenancy into a tenancy in common. She died 20 days later.

---

77. 162 Cal.Rptr. 530 (Ct. App. 1980) [DKA & S, p. 324]; [M & S, p. 616]; [S, p. 666].

The California legislature had previously amended the common law to allow for the creation of a joint tenancy by direct transfer; that is, without the use of a strawman. But California had not yet wrestled with the question whether termination of a joint tenancy still required an actual transfer to a third party or whether one joint tenant could sever the joint tenancy by conveying her interest to herself. The *Riddle* court reviewed the history of joint tenancies and concluded that the "actual transfer" requirement was an anachronistic vestige of feudal rules. Since the requirement of a strawman had been eliminated for the creation of a joint tenancy, the court reasoned that it could be abandoned for terminating a joint tenancy as well. Any other rule would require needlessly complicated transactions that served no purpose except enriching lawyers and catching up the unwary.

The *Riddle* court clearly represents the modern trend, but it is at least worth asking whether the justifications for requiring actual transfer are different for terminating a joint tenancy than for creating one. Doctrinally, they seem equivalent. But the opportunity for one joint tenant to disadvantage another, and even commit fraud, seem higher in the former than the latter. Mr. Harmon received no notice that his joint tenancy had been converted to a tenancy in common. If he had an estate plan, he did not know that he might have additional property to be disposed of by will; his wife would not necessarily take automatically at his death, the way he would have expected.

There is also a particular opportunity for fraud. Imagine two joint tenants, Alison and Bob. Alison has decided that she does not want Bob to take the property if she dies first, but she does want to take the property if Bob dies first. Alison therefore transfers her joint tenancy to herself—as in *Riddle v. Harmon*—and then places that conveyance in a sealed envelop with her will. Once the conveyance has been executed, the joint tenancy has been converted into a tenancy in common, but no one else on the planet aside from Alison knows it. If Alison in fact dies first, someone will find the conveyance with her papers, and will know that the joint tenancy had been severed during her life, and her interest in the property could then pass through her will. But if Bob dies first, Alison can simply tear up the conveyance with no one the wiser. While this is not literally effective to restore the joint tenancy—it was severed the moment she executed the conveyance—if no one knows about it, then no one can object to her taking automatically at Bob's death.

This is a non-trivial problem, but it is important to ask whether and to what extent the "actual transfer" requirement protects against this kind of fraud, and at what expense. True, if

Alison had to use a strawman to sever the joint tenancy, then at least someone else in the world would know that the joint tenancy had been terminated. But this is no guarantee that the information will ever come out when Bob dies. If Alison hired a random attorney to effectuate the transaction, or simply used a close friend of hers, the termination of the joint tenancy might still be kept secret if Bob dies first. And even if the actual transfer requirement provides some modest protection, it does so at substantial cost by requiring expensive and unintuitive formalities for all those people who are not acting in bad faith. On balance, the modern trend makes good sense.

Joint tenancies present an altogether different problem when it comes to interactions with third parties, and specifically mortgagees. Despite their ease of termination, joint tenancies are not so fragile that the conveyance of any interest will result in a tenancy in common. In *Harms v. Sprague,*[78] one joint tenant mortgaged his interest in the property and then died. The question was whether that mortgage severed the joint tenancy and, if not, whether it survived the joint tenant's death. Although a mortgage is an interest in real property, and in some states even includes a conveyance of the underlying property to the lender, Illinois followed the so-called lien theory of mortgages, finding that a mortgage is no more (and no less!) than a security interest in the underlying property.[79] And, according to the court, a joint tenant may unilaterally create a lien on the property without severing the joint tenancy. That lien, however, will not survive the death of the borrower, so when he dies, his joint tenants will take the property free and clear. If the lender had foreclosed on the lien during the borrower's life, that would presumably have severed the joint tenancy. But without such an action, the lien was extinguished at the joint tenant's death.

As a practical matter, this means that banks generally will not make loans secured by property held as joint tenancies unless all the joint tenants consent. In cases like *Harms,* though, where the mortgagee is not a bank but an individual, the mortgagee may find himself holding an unenforceable note if the borrower dies before his other joint tenants. It is, in short, a trap for the unwary, and a cause for caution and due diligence.

By far the more effective form of asset protection, though, comes from the tenancy by the entirety.

---

78. 73 N.E.2d 930 (Ill. 1984) [DKA & S, p. 330]; [M & S, p. 611].

79. For a discussion of mortgages, see Chapter 8.

3. *Tenancy by the Entirety.* Fewer than half the states today recognize a tenancy by the entirety.[80] But where it exists, it is identical to a joint tenancy except that it is only available to married people, and—in general—it cannot be unilaterally severed.[81] Had Mrs. Riddle and her husband owned their property by the entirety, she could not have converted the property to a tenancy in common without her husband's consent, even with the use of a strawman.

The principal benefit of a tenancy by the entirety is not to prevent the Mrs. Riddles of the world from secretly conveying away their interests, however. The real benefit is protection from creditors. When property is held by the entirety, a creditor of one spouse cannot attach his or her share of the property. This can be a powerful form of asset protection.

The only way to sever a tenancy by the entirety is through consent by both parties or divorce, which is said to sever the unity of marriage. Therefore, a creditor of only one spouse cannot reach assets held by the entirety.

B. Managing Relationships Between the Parties

As with inter-temporal divisions of property, the law plays a central role in mediating conflicts among concurrent interest holders. The worry is that each co-tenant has an incentive to consume as much of the co-owned property as possible, externalizing the consumption on the other co-tenants. In addition to removing valuable resources from the property, this can include occupying as much of the property as possible—grabbing the bigger bedroom, claiming the better building site, or simply taking up more space.

Concurrent interest holders are often sufficiently small in number, and sufficiently connected by social bonds—siblings, spouses, parents and children—that conflicts are dealt with outside the law. If friends order a pizza together, they do not need recourse to property law concepts to divide up the slices. Everyone takes her share, respectful of the others. But if people know ahead of time that someone in their group often eats too much, they may suggest converting the co-owned pizza into private property, asking everyone to buy her own, or dividing the pizza into individually-owned slices before starting to eat. Or, if the situation is really problematic, friends may ask the over-consumer to pay more for the extra

---

80.   [DKA & S, p. 321].

81.   A minority of state permit unilateral conveyances by one spouse. See HANOCH DAGAN, PROPERTY 9 (2011).

pizza she ate. As it turns out, precisely this same set of remedies is available for concurrent interests generally, through actions for Partition, Ouster, Accounting and Contribution.

Partition

A key protection for co-tenants is the ability to end their common ownership and revert to individual ownership. Concurrent interest holders can of course effect this transformation voluntarily at any time; if all the interest holders agree, they can divide up or sell the property as they wish. But if the parties are not able to agree, then any tenant in common or joint tenant can file an action for partition, which will terminate the concurrent interests.[82]

Partition, however, can take one of two forms. It can either be in kind, or by sale. Partition in kind literally divides the physical property among the owners, giving them each their share outright. This is like dividing pizza slices among the various friends. Partition by sale, on the other hand, involves a judicial sale of the property with the proceeds divided among the owners in proportion to their respective interests in the property. While the party seeking partition can express a preference for one or the other, it is ultimately up to the court to decide which form of partition to award. To be clear: a concurrent interest holder is always entitled to partition; the difficult legal question is simply whether the partition is in kind or by sale.

There are strong competing concerns. Partition by sale is the easier of the two administratively. It does not require the court to draw physical lines. The court can simply order the property sold and the proceeds divided. The market determines the value of the property, and each receives the value of her respective share.

Partition by sale, though, does involve the non-consensual dispossession of the non-petitioning concurrent interest holders. Imagine three siblings who inherit their childhood home from their parents as tenants in common. The two brothers love the house, but their sister wants out and files an action for partition. If the court awards partition by sale, all three of them may lose the house. Not only does this seem like an extreme remedy, it also threatens to wipe out whatever subjective value the two brothers have in the property, destroying real value.

Of course, the brothers are perfectly capable of bidding for the property in the judicial sale. If the property is in fact most valuable to them because of their sentimental attachments, then they should

---

82. Notice that an action for partition is not available in a tenancy by the entirety, which cannot be unilaterally terminated.

be the winning bidders. Their subjective value will be preserved. But this is no perfect answer. First, the brothers may have liquidity constraints that make it difficult for them to bid on the property to the extent of their actual preferences. They may also suffer from some kind of free-rider problem, making coordination with each other expensive, at least where there is more than one co-tenant interested in bidding on the property. Moreover, even if the brothers are able to submit the winning bid, the judicial sale will transfer some of their subjective value in the property to their sister. Say the market value for the property was $300, but the brothers bid $330 because of their attachments (adding as many zeros as you like to make the example realistic). By submitting the winning bid, the brothers would, in effect, transfer an additional $10 to their sister, who would receive $110 instead of the $100 market value. This may seem unfair.

Partition by kind avoids the problems of forced dispossession, allowing the non-petitioning co-tenants to remain on their share of the property. But it creates its own problems, most notably drawing lines that divide the property fairly among the various parties. *Delfino v. Vealencis* is representative of the challenges.[83] There, the Delfinos owned 20.5 acres of land as tenants in common with Vealencis. The Delfinos wanted to develop the property into a residential subdivision, and so sought partition by sale, presumably seeking to buy out Vealencis' interest at a judicial sale. Vealencis, however, was using a portion of the property as a rubbish and garbage removal business and sought partition by kind instead, seeking to keep her business intact.

The *Delfino* court held that partition by sale is only appropriate where two conditions are met: (1) the physical conditions of the property are such that it cannot be practically or equitably divided; and (2) the owners' interests would be better protected by sale. These are conjunctive, not disjunctive, and courts must find both. In this case, the Delfinos argued that Vealencis' rubbish business was inconsistent with their use of the property as a residential subdivision, making partition by kind inappropriate. The court rejected the argument, finding that the "economic gain of one tenant" did not necessarily outweigh the fact that the other tenant "derives her livelihood from the operation of a business on [a] portion of the property, as her family before her has for many years." The court therefore remanded for partition of the property by kind.

---

83.   436 A.2d 27 (Conn. 1980) [DKA & S, p. 338]; [M & S, p. 599].

This case, then, explicitly recognizes the potential unfairness of partition by sale. Vealencis and her family had been on the property for years, and her co-tenants' action for partition should perhaps not force her off the land. But the unsentimental economic position favors the opposite result. If Vealencis valued the property more than the Delfinos, she would have been free to bid on it herself. If she lost, then by definition the property was worth less to her than it was to them, and partition by sale results in the higher valued use. Sale, in other words, helps to identify the highest-valued use and user. And it is almost unimaginable that a single rubbish collector would outbid a residential developer for the property. Denying partition by sale, then, responds to a more abstract fairness concern, and an implication that Vealencis' longtime use of the property is somehow incommensurable with the residential development; it simply does not translate into "willingness to pay" as the economic account would have it.

There is obviously no one correct way to resolve this problem, but *Delfino* nicely reveals the stakes. Doctrinally, this much is clear: most courts hold that partition by sale is more extreme than partition by kind, and should therefore be awarded only in unusual circumstances. In fact, however, these pronouncements are mostly lip service and courts frequently award partition by sale. Perhaps courts prefer sale because it avoids the difficult problem of line-drawing, and perhaps because they care more about the property ending up in the hands of the highest value user as tested by the market.

Ouster

While partition provides a mechanism for terminating a co-tenancy, ouster is about allocating the beneficial value of the property among the co-tenants. Specifically, it is a claim by one co-tenant for the reasonable value of the other co-tenant's use of the property.

Ouster poses a conceptual hurdle because of its tension with the core principle of co-tenancies: that each co-tenant has a possessory right to the whole property. Although one person may extract more value from the property, this cannot be at the expense of the other co-tenants' right to do the same. Ouster arises, then, precisely when one co-tenant's use of the property does, in fact, interfere with her co-tenants' possessory rights. At that point, an action for ouster can force the tenant in possession to pay the fair value of her use of the property.

To see the nature of the problem, imagine that a husband and wife die, leaving their house to their three children, Adam, Ben, and Clara, as tenants in common (although precisely the same analysis would apply to a joint tenancy). Adam has been renting an apartment in his hometown, and immediately moves into the house. Ben and Clara, however, both have families and live across the country. They have no interest in actually possessing the house, although they do not want to see it sold. The question is whether Adam, the only co-tenant actually using the house, is obligated to pay the fair rental value of his use to his co-tenants.

Intuitions about the equitable result might diverge, and a lot may depend on family circumstances. But the doctrinal point is relatively straightforward. Adam has a right to possess the house; he is simply living on property he owns. He is doing nothing more than his co-tenants could do, if they wanted. The fact that his siblings have no interest in possessing the house themselves does not somehow obligate Adam to pay for his use.

That would change, however, if either Ben or Clara were to arrive on the doorstep seeking to move in too, and be prevented by Adam's possession. If Adam does not let them in, or if his possession actually dispossess his co-tenants, then they have an action for ouster. At that point, Adam has interfered with his co-tenants possessory rights and is liable to them for the value of his own use.

The interesting legal issue is deciding what actions by a co-tenant constitute ouster. In *Spiller v. Mackereth,*[84] one of the co-tenants, Spiller, was exclusively using a co-owned warehouse. His co-tenant, Mackereth, wrote a letter demanding either that Spiller vacate half of the building or start paying rent. Spiller did neither. Mackereth also alleged that Spiller had placed locks on the doors, preventing Mackereth's entry. As a result, Mackereth claimed ouster, seeking the rental value for the property. But the *Spiller* court held that Mackereth had not demonstrated ouster—that writing a letter was not enough, and that the locks on the doors were merely to secure the premises and were not necessarily intended to exclude Mackereth. Had Mackereth asked for keys to the locks and been denied, that might have been a different matter. But on these facts, the court found no ouster.

Does this make sense? It seems inefficient to require a co-tenant to actually arrive at the doorstop to try and gain entry, and also likely to lead to conflict. A letter should perhaps be enough. On the other hand, Mackareth had no right to demand that Spiller move out of half of the warehouse. Spiller was entitled to use as much of it as he wanted, subject to Mackareth's use, and if Mackareth was not in fact using it, then he had no real objection.

---

84.   334 So.2d 859 (Ala. 1976) [DKA & S, p. 348].

Under this analysis, it would be difficult for a co-tenant to "use" part of the property by keeping it empty or vacant, but this is consistent with the law's preference for productive use of property, described in Chapter 2.

It is worth noticing that the ouster remedy is relatively crude. It does not seek to mediate conflicts between co-tenants. It does not, for example, provide a mechanism for deciding which half of the warehouse Spiller can use. A tenancy in common does not come with a pre-packaged governance structure or specified set of rights, as would a corporation or formal partnership. That is its strength and its weakness; it is therefore useful mostly for people in close relationships with each other, people who have the capacity to work through most of their disagreements informally. And, of course, if that fails, they retain partition as a powerful fallback.

It is also important to see the relationship between ouster and adverse possession. A co-tenant's use, even of the entirety of the property, does not necessarily rise to the level of adverse possession because the use is not inherently adverse. Instead, a co-tenant must claim absolute ownership of the entirety of the property to start the adverse possession statute running, and this might require, for example, an attempt to sell the property, or to rent it out in its entirety without paying anything to the co-tenants. In short, the ouster threshold, while high, is still lower than for adverse possession.

Accounting and Contribution

A different set of rules applies to rents and other payments received from third parties. The problem of third-party leases is the most interesting.

A tenant in common is typically permitted to lease her property interest to a third party. Of course, she can convey away no more rights than she herself possesses, which is to say that any lessee rents the property subject to the use and possession rights of the other tenants in common. When it comes to leases of co-owned property, however, rents from the third-party lessee must be divided among the owners in proportion to their ownership share. If the rental payments are not divided, co-tenants may bring an action for an accounting, seeking to recover their share, net of expenses.

The question, then, is why this remedy is available for third-party leases and not against a co-tenant in possession herself. The action for accounting applies whether or not there was ouster. The co-tenant lessor does not have to pay rent if she occupies the property herself without ousting her co-tenants, but she does have to pay a share of actual rent collected from a third party for the identical possession.

Perhaps the best explanation is administrability. When it comes to a tenant in possession, courts would have to assess the fair rental value for the property, and this might be difficult to measure. In an action for accounting, the lessor is obligated only to pay her co-tenants a share of the rents actually received. There is no problem of valuation. Moreover, courts may worry that the obligation of a tenant in possession to pay rent to her co-tenants might discourage use of the property at all. If the tenant in possession has a cash flow problem, or wants to put the property to a suboptimal use, she might end up paying more to her co-tenants than the property was actually worth to her. That is, the fair rental value standard will not take into account the idiosyncratic uses that owners routinely make of their property, and so may cause some co-owners to prefer not using the property at all over using it and having to pay the fair rental value to her co-tenants. But if the property is leased to a third party there is no such worry, since the co-tenant will never be obligated to pay more than a proportional share of the rents actually received, whether or not they are below the fair rental value of the property.

Finally, contribution is like the flip side of accounting, allowing a co-tenant who is incurring carrying costs on the property to seek money from the other co-tenants. In general, though, actions for contribution are limited to taxes, mortgage payments, common charges, and the like. They are sometimes but rarely available for repairs, with some jurisdictions allowing contribution for necessary repairs, following notice to the other co-tenants, but many not.

* * *

The three forms of concurrent interests allow property to be divided among multiple owners at the same time. Conflicts often emerge when several parties own undivided interests in the same property, and property law provides various ways of mediating those conflicts. Partition transforms the concurrent interest into individual ownership, while ouster, accounting, and contribution create mechanisms for sharing the benefits and burdens within a co-tenancy.

Chapter 6

MARITAL PROPERTY

Marital property is, fundamentally, a kind of concurrent interest. It implicates sufficiently important social judgments and economic concerns that it deserves special treatment. The question is whether and to what extent someone has an interest in property acquired by his or her spouse, simply by dint of the marriage.

This is necessarily a gendered discussion. The law has developed in the shadow of a particular conception of marriage involving one spouse—typically the husband—who is the dominant wage earner, and the other—typically the wife—who has domestic responsibilities but who earns little money herself. The issues of marital property therefore principally involve the rights of the non-wage-earning spouse to property earned or acquired by the wage-earning spouse during the course of the marriage. Legal conflicts can arise when the marriage ends, either through divorce or the death of one spouse. At divorce, to what extent can the non-wage-earning spouse claim a share of the money and property earned by the other during the marriage? Or, if a wage-earning spouse dies and attempts to leave all of his money and property to someone else—charity, a child from a prior marriage, a mistress—to what extent can the non-wage-earning spouse claim part of that property as her own? This Chapter addresses these questions.

A. Community and Separate Property Systems

The United States has inherited two very different approaches to marital property: community and separate property systems. Although similarities between the two have increased over the past decades, they have very different histories and reflect very different judgments about the nature of marriage.

Community property is a relative rarity in the United States. It descends primarily from civil law traditions and has been adopted in only a few, mostly western states. It is important conceptually, however, because it reflects a particular view of marriage. In a community property jurisdiction, a married couple is treated like a single economic unit in which both spouses share equally. Wages paid to one spouse are therefore literally earned by both spouses. The law implicitly recognizes that both spouses contribute to the marriage, even if only one earns wages, so that both are entitled to share in the economic benefits.

In separate property jurisdictions, by contrast, each spouse retains separate ownership over the assets earned or acquired during the marriage. The evolution of separate property systems reveals an important story about the power dynamics embedded in property law.

The separate property system is feudal in its origins, and in reality amounted to a husband-owns-all system. Originally, and into the nineteenth century, property that a woman brought into a marriage became the property of her husband. Although there were some exceptions, the legal landscape did not change fundamentally until states in the mid-nineteenth century began to enact married women's property statutes, effectively allowing women to retain ownership of their property in the marriage, and to dispose of it by will if they outlived their husbands.[85] Today, then, a separate property system is just that: a system in which spouses retain their own property during the marriage. Wages one spouse earns during the marriage belong to him or her; property acquired by a spouse can be held individually.

Despite the married women's property acts, the separate property system can still foster economic dependency. After all, if one person earned all of the money during the marriage, he or she—and typically, "he"—would then own all the property when the marriage ends.

To respond to concerns about the inequitable division of marital property, separate property jurisdictions enacted various statutory protections for the non-wage earner. The law of wills, for example, creates a forced spousal share that the surviving spouse can claim, as of right, against the estate of the pre-deceasing spouse. Although the amount of the share varies tremendously by jurisdiction, it prevents someone at death from disinheriting his or her spouse entirely (in the absence of a valid prenuptial agreement). Similarly, at divorce, property is now subject to equitable division, meaning that a court will divide marital property between the spouses without being constrained by who holds title, or who actually earned the money.

There remains tremendous diversity in the application of these protections, however. In part, this is because two very different kinds of justifications animate protections for the non-wage-earning spouse: the partnership theory, and the support theory.

The partnership theory is entirely consistent with community property jurisdictions. It views the marriage as a true partnership.

---

85. Reva Siegel, *Home as Work: The First Woman's Rights Claims Concerning Wives' Household Labor*, 1850–1880, 103 YALE L. J. 1073, 1081–85 (1994).

Even if one spouse earned most of the money in the marriage, the partnership theory assumes that the other spouse contributed to the partnership in other ways, giving the non-wage-earning spouse an entitlement to a share of the earned wages. A support theory, by contrast, seeks to ensure that one spouse cannot impoverish the other at death or divorce. It would be unjust, and an inappropriate burden on society, to allow someone with means to force his or her spouse onto the public dole.

These underlying rationales generate very different doctrinal prescriptions for spousal protections. Should equitable division, and the spousal forced share, apply to property acquired by a spouse prior to marriage? Under a partnership theory, the answer is "no." The marriage partnership did nothing to acquire the property, and so it does not need to be shared with the other partner. But under a support theory, the answer is, "yes." If the justification for spousal protection is to ensure the support of a spouse who otherwise does not have means of support, the source of the funds should not matter. If money is available to one spouse, a share must be made available to the other if it is needed for his or her support. The same analysis applies to property received by gift or bequest during the marriage. Gratuitous transfers to one spouse should not be included under a partnership theory, but should under a support theory. And, finally, what if the surviving spouse, or non-wage-earning spouse, is independently wealthy? Under a partnership theory, the financial wherewithal of the surviving spouse should be ignored; if property was acquired by the marriage partnership, a share should be available regardless of need. The opposite is true under a support theory, where independent wealth should bar any claim for support.

Even where these spousal protections apply broadly, they do not actually mimic a community property jurisdiction. Consider what happens if the non-wage-earning spouse dies first. In a separate property jurisdiction, even one following a partnership theory, no spousal protections are even triggered. In a community property jurisdiction, on the other hand, the non-wage-earning spouse literally owns half of the marital property. He or she can therefore control the disposition of half of the marital assets at death. In a separate property jurisdiction, that pre-deceasing spouse who earned no wages during the marriage has no property to control.

For a time, this created real tax differences between separate and community property systems. The IRS imposes an estate tax at death. While that tax today applies only to high-valued estates, it traditionally taxed people with relatively modest estates at death.

100

Any wage earner subject to the estate tax received a substantial advantage in a community property jurisdiction because half of the wages already belonged to the non-wage-earning spouse during life. To take a simplified example, imagine that the estate tax is simply a flat tax of 25% of the entire value of an estate, and that a husband saved $1 million over the course of a marriage to a non-wage-earning wife who survived him. In a separate property jurisdiction, his $1 million savings would be subject to the 25% estate tax, requiring him to pay $250,000 to the IRS at his death. But in a community property jurisdiction, he only owns $500,000 at his death; his wife already owns the other $500,000. Therefore, he will be taxed on this lower number, and owe only $125,000. Assuming in both examples that he leaves everything to his wife, she will end up with $125,000 more in a community property jurisdiction than in a separate property jurisdiction.

These tax advantages were so substantial, in fact, that a number of states in the mid-twentieth century considered switching from a separate to a community property system. Instead of encouraging this change, the IRS changed its estate tax rules, creating what amounts to an estate tax credit for bequests to a spouse, thus eliminating the tax advantage of the community property system.

If nothing else, this story illustrates the interconnectedness of property issues and political power. The dynamic here is easy to see. Moneyed interests, mostly men, wanted the tax advantages of the community property system, but did not want to relinquish that much control to their wives. They were willing to do so for the tax benefits, but managed to secure instead favorable tax treatment without a loss of control. Now, the principle wage earner in a separate property jurisdiction can leave everything to his or her spouse without having to pay taxes, but is not automatically sharing wages during the marriage.

The doctrinal niceties of these various approaches are typically taken up in the advanced study of family law and the law of wills. These are areas of law governed almost entirely by state statute and not the common law of property. Core property concepts emerge starkly, however, when it comes to the equitable division of property at divorce in separate property jurisdictions.

B. Rights to Marital Property at Divorce

In separate property jurisdictions, as discussed above, spouses continue to own their own property during the marriage. A husband owns what he brings into the marriage, and a wife the same.

But upon divorce, modern courts must divide marital property equitably between the spouses. Although the standard for equitable division varies state by state, it often requires courts to decide whether, and to what extent, the non-wage-earning spouse has some kind of entitlement to the separate property of the wage earner, often with a presumption of equal division.

It is important here to distinguish the division of marital assets—a property issue—from alimony, which is based on future obligations of support.[86] As one article usefully puts it, "property division is backward-looking (looking at the marital relationship while it existed), while alimony reflects the law's concern with the post-divorce financial situation of the parties, their future needs, and their prospective abilities."[87] Alimony is an issue better left to the study of family law. The concern here is how property rights arise during and because of marriage.

A gendered lens reveals the problem and the typical legal treatment. Imagine a husband who is a partner in a law firm making substantial amounts of money, and a wife who has never pursued a career, instead staying home, raising their children, and running the couple's domestic life. If, during the marriage, the husband buys their house but puts it in his own name, can his wife claim a share of the house at divorce? The husband may argue that the money for the house came from his work, that he bought it, and that he should be entitled to keep it. But the wife may argue that it was her work maintaining the house and raising the children that allowed her husband to have a successful law practice. She can argue that her work and support on the home front were equally responsible for their ability to acquire and maintain the house, and that she should therefore be entitled to a share of it. The law has developed generally to recognize the wife's claim in this situation, to presume that her non-economic contributions to the marriage made her husband's economic contributions possible. This is not to suggest that courts will necessarily divide the property 50–50, but they often will, and this broad conception of contribution at least provides a starting point for the equitable division analysis.

Intuitions around equitable division become complicated, however, when the property to be divided is less tangible and more personal to one spouse. Then, core questions again emerge about the nature of property, and the source of property rights. Professional licenses are a perfect example.

---

86. Alimony can, in fact, take a number of forms: permanent alimony, rehabilitative alimony, limited duration alimony, and reimbursement alimony.

87. Carolyn J. Frantz & Hanoch Dagan, *Properties of Marriage*, 104 COLUM. L. REV. 75, 99 (2004).

What happens if, during a marriage, one spouse goes to law school with the other's emotional and economic support? If they divorce after graduation, who owns the value of that law degree? Is it even property that is subject to equitable division? In *In re Marriage of Graham*,[88] the Colorado Supreme Court addressed precisely this question. There, Anne and Dennis Graham were married. She worked as an airline flight attendant, providing 70% of the family's income while her husband went to business school. Shortly after he graduated and secured a job, he filed for divorce. Anne claimed equitable division of the value of his MBA. The Court rejected her claim, finding that a degree is simply not "property" subject to equitable division within the meaning of the Uniform Dissolution of Marriage Act. A degree lacks exchange value, is not transferable, and terminates at death. If the marriage had lasted longer, and Dennis' increased earning capacity had translated into an actual house, or a bump in the family bank account, those tangible and more transferable assets would have been subject to equitable division. But the business degree by itself was simply not property, according to the court.

The court's reasoning is unconvincingly formalistic. Asking whether a business degree is "property" is suspiciously analogous to asking whether bodies or a spleen are property.[89] And, as discussed in Chapter 2, something can still be considered "property" even if it is inalienable and cannot be transferred at death. Those are important sticks in the typical bundle of property rights, but property can nevertheless exist without them. Moreover, imagine if the government tried to strip someone of her law degree or other professional license. It could not do so without triggering Due Process protections, rooted in the constitutional protection for life, liberty, and *property*. An educational degree is undoubtedly property for some purposes, and the *Graham* court is unconvincing when it baldly concludes the opposite.

There is, however, something to the court's intuition that an educational degree is not like a house or more typical marital assets. The salient characteristic may not be alienability, though, but instead the extent to which the degree is personal to the graduate. Anne Graham did not sit through Dennis' classes, take his exams, or otherwise distinguish herself as a business student. But on this score, is a degree really so different from a house? While Dennis' school performance was his own, it was Anne's financial support that made it possible for him to go to school at all,

---

88.   574 P.2d 75 (Co. 1978) [DKA & S, p. 371].

89.   See Chapter 2(D).

and it may well have been her emotional support that allowed him to succeed.

This intuition can be pushed even further when the property is unmoored even from a degree and amounts simply to an increase in earning capacity. If Michael Jordan had married at the beginning of his NBA career, and divorced halfway through, should his wife have been entitled to a share of his earning potential as a basketball player? Here, it may be even harder to attribute any of his basketball abilities to the efforts of his wife, because they seem so innate and ineffable. On the other hand, a basketball career is more than just physical ability. And it may again be the emotional and other support of a spouse that makes the difference between a third-stringer in the European League, and a star in the NBA.

If that intuition remains elusive, Frederica von Stade's divorce provides another useful example, in the case of *Elkus v. Elkus*.[90] Von Stade is, to this day, a famous opera singer. Over the course of her marriage, from 1973 to 1989, her annual income rose from $2,250 to $621,878. During a divorce in 1989, her husband claimed a share of her career and celebrity status. His contributions evidently included, his "active involvement in [von Stade's] career, in teaching, coaching, and critiquing her, as well as in caring for their children".

New York already recognized professional licenses as marital property, and the question for the state's appellate division was whether the same reasoning should apply to unlicensed professions. The court held that it should—that it is the enhanced earning capacity represented by a professional license that counts as marital property, and not simply the license itself. According to the court, the purpose of equitable division is to recognize that marriage is an economic partnership, and to prevent inequities in distribution. Distinguishing between licensed and unlicensed professions would needlessly discriminate against people whose spouses were engaged in profitable but unlicensed professions.

It is interesting to ask about both *Graham* and *Elkus* whether the outcome would have been the same if the genders had been reversed. There is nothing in either court's reasoning that makes gender obviously relevant, but the contrasting outcomes are provocative. In the first, the court found that the wife gets no economic credit for her husband's degree—he earned it himself. In the latter, the court found that part of Frederica von Stade's career is, in fact, attributable to her husband's labor. Or, to put it bluntly, the man's

---

90. 572 N.Y.S.2d 901 (App. Div. 1991) [DKA & S, p. 378]; [M & S, p. 626]; [S, p. 705].

work was his own, but the woman's was partly attributable to her husband. Of course, the cases arose in different jurisdictions and so may simply reflect different attitudes to marital property, but the issue of gender is at least important to consider.

There is no consensus about including degrees or professional licenses in marital property subject to equitable division. New York widely includes them.[91] Other states do not. The property question, though, should turn on the nature of marriage, and not on formalistic distinctions between the resources in question—a house versus a professional degree versus an opera career.

Even if this is right, the equitable division of property raises difficult remedy questions that also implicate core property concepts. When a state or state court does include increased earning potential or an educational degree in the property subject to equitable division, how should the court actually divide it? First, a court must value the increased earning potential; second it must structure an award.

The valuation problem is factually difficult but conceptually straightforward. Consider the value of a law degree. An expert can compute the expected wages of an average person with and without a law degree. That difference constitutes the impact of the law degree on earning potential. If the difference is, for example, $50,000 per year, then the value of the law degree today is the present value of that increased income stream (i.e., what someone would pay, today, for the right to receive $50,000 per year into the future). At 6% interest, and 20 years to retirement, the present value would be approximately $575,000. That expected value can then be equitably divided between the spouses. Of course, inputting different numbers will generate very different results.

While valuing an educational degree—or any form of increased earning potential—is conceptually easy enough, actually effectuating the equitable division is more complicated. In reality, family law governs these outcomes and the actual remedy in any particular jurisdiction may be well established. Nevertheless, property law can illuminate the range of theoretically possible options, which are therefore worth viewing through the twin lenses of fairness and efficiency.

One remedy is simply to perform the net present value calculation, make the equitable division, and divide the increased earning potential at the termination of the marriage. If, on the assumptions above, the equitable division is equal shares, the holder of the law

---

91.   See O'Brien v. O'Brien, 489 N.E.2d 712 (NY 1985) [DKA & S, p. 377]; [M & S, p. 626]; [S, p. 697].

degree would owe his or her spouse $287,500. That has the benefit of being simple and definitive. But it creates a potential cash flow problem. The degree-holder has not yet earned this future income, and may not have the money to make the equitable division. The court could award a lump sum, but payable in installments to avoid the cash flow problem. Alternatively, if there are other marital assets, this money can be offset against them, but there may not be—and in the case of *Graham*, there were not.

The more profound problem is the lack of assurance that this particular law degree, in this particular person's hands, will in fact generate the projected increase in earning. He or she may have planned to go into public service, pursue less remunerative career paths, or have more trouble than usual obtaining a high-paying job. Using either the average or median in increased earning potential still means that some significant number of people with law degrees will in fact earn less, and the division will be unfair to them.

This concern is highlighted in the value of celebrity, like Frederica von Stade's. In fact, in applying equitable division to her increased earning potential, the New York Appellate Division cited, approvingly, a case permitting the equitable division to Joe Piscopo's career at his divorce. The citation is illuminating. Joe Piscopo was a big television star in the early 1980s. He was famous for his roles on Saturday Night Live, in particular. He appeared to have significant future earning potential, and his career at the time was worth a lot of money.[92] Shortly after his divorce, however, his career took something of a nosedive, and he appeared only infrequently in television and movies after that, remaining a household name only for people of a certain generation. Earning potential naturally includes some discount rate to reflect the risks of the money not coming in, but it still presents an opportunity for unfairly inflating the value of the property subject to equitable division. Of course, it is also possible that a degree, or celebrity, or other source of earning capacity may turn out to be much more valuable than expected—Joe Piscopo's career could have taken off.

A different approach, then, would be to award a percentage of the actual money earned in the future, on an ongoing basis. This has the benefit of not penalizing the degree-holder for money he or she does not actually earn. But it comes with its own problems. Chief among them is administrability. An ongoing obligation to pay faces enforcement problems, and also creates a long-running con-

---

92. Not reproduced in *Elkus v. Elkus,* the *Piscopo* court based its valuation of his celebrity goodwill on a percentage of his average past earnings over a 5–year period. Those earnings were over $600,000 per year—a substantial amount in the late 1980s. See Piscopo v. Piscopo, 232 N.J.Super. 559, 557 A.2d 1040 (App.Div.1989).

nection between the ex-spouses when both might strongly prefer a clean break. But the problem is deeper than that, too. Forcing someone to pay a pre-set percentage of future wages to a former spouse functions like a tax; it decreases the marginal utility of earning money. Someone choosing whether to work an extra hour, or take a higher paying job, will discount the remuneration by the payment to the spouse. Whereas a lump-sum payment up front may force a spouse to work at a different, higher paying job than he or she otherwise would have chosen, an ongoing obligation to pay may have the opposite effect, discouraging extra work.

An entirely different alternative, then, is to award reimbursement alimony, at least where the equitable division is based on a professional degree. This is not alimony in the sense of ongoing support, but is instead an equitable remedy that provides compensation for a spouse's contributions to the other spouse's benefit—often paying for a degree, or making other financial contributions. Since Anne Graham put her husband through business school, even paying for his tuition, she should get her money back.

This approach does not require any complicated speculation about future value. It has the benefits of certainty and relative simplicity. Nevertheless, it embodies a very different conception of the nature of the marital partnership. Reimbursement alimony is a bit like returning the purchase price for a house, instead of awarding a share of its increased value. A cold-blooded view sees marriage as a kind of investment; each makes contributions in anticipation of future rewards. Anne Graham had several investment options for her money. She could have bought a house, put it into the stock market, or—as she actually did—help to put her husband through graduate school. Returning her money to her does not seem to recognize the extent of her financial expectations. Of course, any investment has risk. Her husband could have turned out to be bad at business, the job market could have soured for people with MBAs, her husband could have died prematurely, or, as happened, he could have left her.

One way of framing the question, then, is to ask whether a spouse should bear the risk of divorce as well as these other risks. When "investing" in a spouse's education, is divorce one of the risks a spouse should consider? That, of course, depends on one's conception of marriage. As common as divorce has become, it may not be a risk that the law, for normative and expressive reasons, wants people to assume when "investing" in a marriage.

But this may be too dispassionate by half. The fundamental question may really just be about the nature of ownership in marriage, and whether and to what extent a spouse's support creates an entitlement to the economic benefits of that support at divorce. Reimbursement alimony will restore the supportive spouse to the position he or she would have occupied without the marriage; equitable division of increased earning potential comes closer to a measure of expectation damages.

C. Same-sex Marriage

Any modern discussion of marital property must consider the issue of same-sex marriage. In states that permit same-sex marriage, there is no question that all of the principles of equitable division apply equally to same-sex marriages. The question is whether, and to what extent, some of these same ideas and principles can extend to relationships in states that do not permit same-sex marriage.

From the perspective of property, marriage is important because it can be the source of concurrent interests. There is something about a marriage that can give someone a claim to his or her spouse's property. The property question, then, is whether other kinds of relationships besides marriage can generate similar claims to each other's property.

Consider a variety of hypotheticals. Can college roommates, who share domestic responsibilities while in college and provide each other with emotional support, claim title to a share of each other's property at graduation? Can friends who cohabitate for years eventually claim a share of each other's property? How about lovers? And, finally, can a same-sex couple, in a jurisdiction where marriage is not available to them, claim equitable division of property when the relationship ends?

Consider the case of *Marvin v. Marvin*.[93] There, an unmarried man and woman lived together for 7 years, and accumulated significant assets all held in the man's name. At dissolution of their relationship, the woman sued for an equitable division of the property. The California Supreme Court ruled that the woman could recover on the theory that the couple had entered into an explicit contract ahead of time, entitling the plaintiff to half the property acquired during the relationship. But the court went further than this and also articulated a broad theory of implied contract that could entitle a non-married partner to a share of the property, not under the relevant California statute but instead as a matter of equity. The court reasoned that a non-married partner's

---

93.   557 P.2d 106 (Cal. 1976) [DKA & S, p. 395]; [M & S, p. 635].

contributions, including services, could be the basis for an equitable division of property at dissolution, as well as a claim for unjust enrichment. Importantly, the *Marvin* court acknowledged that traditional rules prevented this kind of recovery, largely because the law disfavored non-marital relationships, but that changing social mores made the old rule anachronistic. The same kind of reasoning can apply to same-sex partners as well, providing a mechanism for equitable division even in jurisdictions that do not permit marriage.

* * *

Marital property is a particular form of concurrent interest. The doctrine of equitable division recognizes that property rights can develop from the nature of marriage itself. Marital property, then, implicates both the acquisition and division of property, revealing how the non-wage-earning spouse can acquire rights to marital property, and how that property is divided between spouses.

Chapter 7

LEASEHOLDS

The final form of concurrent interest to consider is a leasehold. A lease divides interests in the property between the owner-landlord (who is not in possession of the property), and the tenant (who is). But why are leaseholds the subject of property at all? The landlord-tenant relationship is governed by the lease, which appears to be nothing more than a contract between two parties. It is, however, a contract for a particular kind of interest in property, and it is precisely the property relationship at the heart of the lease that requires special scrutiny. In fact, the most important part of the discussion that follows is how and why the law of property constrains the kinds of transactions that landlords and tenants are allowed to enter.

The law of leases presents three separate property issues. First is identifying different kinds of leases. As with property conveyances, leases take one of a limited number of pre-specified forms. The differences revolve primarily around how the lease can be terminated. Second, leases—especially residential leases—can impose some important implied obligations, especially on landlords. The strongest of these are even non-waivable, which distinguishes them from most contractual provisions. Finally, landlords and tenants have some ability to alienate their respective property interests. The law here specifies the forms that such conveyances can take, and also defines the content of the parties' ongoing obligations to each other.

It is important to understand, however, that statutes govern most of the modern law of leases. State and local laws define landlords' obligations to their tenants, tenants' duties, and their remedies against each other. In fact, most of the common law of leases has been replaced by statute. Nevertheless, since the goal here is to understand the nature and content of property broadly, the focus is on the common law of property, and not on the more specific legal tools that landlords and tenants today tend to wield against each other in actual disputes.

A. Types of Leases

The common law recognizes four kinds of leases: (1) Term of years; (2) Periodic tenancy; (3) Tenancy at will; and (4) Tenancy at sufferance. They are distinguishable primarily by how and when they can be terminated.

The term of years does not actually refer to "years" but to any lease for a pre-specified amount of time. Leases "for one month," or for "ten years," are both called a "term of years." The lease ends automatically when the term of years ends. Therefore, there is no notice requirement for either the landlord or the tenant to terminate the lease at the end of the term.

A periodic tenancy, by contrast, is a tenancy for a fixed period of time, but that then renews automatically in the absence of adequate notice to the contrary. A typical example would be a month-to-month periodic tenancy. Although the lease term is only one month, by default the lease will continue to renew itself at the end of every month. The parties do not need to enter into a new lease to continue to be bound by its terms. Typically, notice to terminate must be given one "period" in advance, with an outer limit of 6 months. Therefore, to terminate a month-to-month periodic tenancy by the end of December, the landlord or tenant would have to provide notice to the other by the end of November. But, for a year-to-year periodic tenancy, only six months notice is required. These timing requirements have been modified by statute in many jurisdictions, but the basic principle remains the same: notice is required to prevent the periodic tenancy from being automatically renewed.

A tenancy at will is, in some sense, the opposite of a periodic tenancy. It is a leasehold without any fixed term at all. It lasts only so long as both the landlord and tenant want, and either may terminate at any time. Today, by statute, even a tenancy at will requires some reasonable notice for termination. Typically, 30 days is required, or the period between lease rental payments. This statutory change makes the tenancy at will hard to distinguish from a periodic tenancy. However, unlike a periodic tenancy, a typical tenancy at will is automatically terminated at the death of the landlord or the tenant, or upon transfer of either's interest to a third party.

The final form of leasehold is a tenancy at sufferance and it is technically not a leasehold at all. A tenancy at sufferance arises by operation of law when a tenant remains in possession of the property after expiration of a lease. It amounts to a kind of remedial status and provides the landlord with two options: evicting the tenant, or holding the tenant over to a new lease term. In essence, the landlord has a choice: get rid of the tenant and seek to recover damages, or create a new periodic tenancy with an ongoing obligation by the tenant to pay rent.

As with estates and future interests, leases are limited to these four forms, and courts will usually force efforts to create new leaseholds into one of these boxes. A classic example is an attempt to lease property "for the duration of the war." Because the war has no pre-specified ending date—unfortunately, the nature of war!—this cannot be a term of years. And because it has no built-in period, it cannot be a periodic tenancy. Instead, a court will typically view this as a tenancy at will, and allow either the landlord or the tenant to terminate the lease, with adequate notice, at any time, even before the end of the war.

This example highlights the central legal problem raised by these four forms of leaseholds: deciding how to characterize any particular lease. True, it is often easy enough. Leases with pre-set termination dates or month-to-month or year-to-year tenancies are easy to identify as terms of year or periodic tenancies, respectively. But at the edges, where parties enter into more creative leases, or where documents are not professionally drafted, the characterization problem can become much more complex. And, with periodic tenancies, identifying the period can also prove difficult. For example, what should courts make of a lease "with an annual rent of $12,000, payable monthly"? Most courts will interpret this is a periodic tenancy, but are likely to differ whether the period is a year or a month. The complexities increase from there. At stake, always, is whether and how the lease can be terminated.

Garner v. Gerrish reveals the problem.[94] There, two people entered into a residential lease using a fill-in-the-blank lease form. The lease provided that it was "for and during the term of quiet enjoyment from the first day of May, 1977 which term will end— Lou Gerrish has the privilege of termination [sic] this agreement at a date of his own choice." Four years later, the landlord died, and the executor of his estate, Garner, sought to terminate the lease. Gerrish resisted, arguing that the lease actually granted him a tenancy for life, subject to his own unilateral right to terminate.

Looking at the face of the document, the parties' expressed intent appears relatively straightforward. The lease contemplates that Gerrish has the right to remain on the property for as long as he wants; it provides no mechanism for termination by the landlord.

---

94. 473 N.E.2d 223 (NY 1984) [DKA & S, p. 423]; [M & S, p. 545].

As a matter of property law, though, this lease did not fit obviously within any of the recognized lease forms. The traditional common law rule restricted parties' freedom to create unilateral termination rights, requiring that a lessee's right to terminate must be accompanied by a reciprocal right for the lessor. A lease granting the tenant the right to terminate should therefore imply a reciprocal right for the landlord, making this a tenancy at will. Under such a rule, Gerrish's lease would have terminated automatically upon the landlord's death, and Garner would be entitled to reclaim the property.

Interestingly, the *Garner* court abrogated the traditional common law rule, finding, in essence, that it was based on anachronistically formal reasoning. The court recognized that Gerrish's leasehold was functionally equivalent to a determinable life estate; it would last until he wanted it no more, or at the latest until his death. While a lease is most decidedly not a legal life estate, the court nevertheless held, in essence, that there was no reason to prohibit a landlord from creating in a lease what a grantor could create in a conveyance of real property. The result was that Gerrish could continue leasing the property for as long as he wished, and that Garner had no right to terminate the lease and make him leave.

This is a very modern-sounding holding. It is at odds with the *numerus clausus* principle articulated by Professors Merrill and Smith, and reflects something of a contractualization of the property law of leases. It marks a shift away from rigidly formal property categories, and to an over-arching concern with parties' intent. This trend is by no means ubiquitous, but is on display in other areas of landlord tenant law as well.

B. Obligations Running With Leases

Delivery of Possession

Under the traditional American view, a lease was a conveyance of an estate in land to a tenant. The landlord's only meaningful obligation, then, was to convey the estate. This did not necessarily include a conveyance of possession, but merely the *right* to possession of the property. Therefore, if a prior tenant held over and remained on the property past the expiration of the previous lease, a new tenant's action would be against that holdover, and not against the landlord. This can be put in very personal terms. Imagine renting a new apartment, showing up on the first day of the lease, and finding that the prior tenant has not yet moved out.

What remedies should be available? Under the traditional American rule, the exclusive remedy would have been an action against the holdover tenant, not against the landlord, and you would still have been bound to pay rent by the terms of the lease.

Of course, you could have bargained for a different rule if you had wanted. A landlord could include an express covenant to deliver possession, instead of merely the right to possession. But the American rule, anyway, puts the burden to include such a covenant on the contracting parties. Courts will not infer one. *Hannan v. Dusch*[95] is typical in this regard.

All of this is in contrast to the English rule in which courts imply a covenant in a lease to deliver possession to a tenant. That rule has been followed in a number of American jurisdictions as well. When such a covenant is implied, the tenant has additional remedies against a landlord who fails to deliver possession. If a prior tenant has held over, or the property is otherwise not ready to be occupied, the tenant can sue the landlord for damages. In some jurisdictions, the tenant is also likely to be able to seek termination of the lease, and can be freed from any ongoing obligation to pay rent.

Does the American rule or the English rule make more sense? It depends, in large part, on one's intuitions about the relative capacities of landlords and tenants. The American rule implicitly assumes that tenants have adequate opportunities to bargain for the legal protections that they want. The parties can allocate the risk of holdover tenants between them, and the law should not imply terms into a lease that the parties did not expressly include. This view may well make good sense in commercial leases where both landlords and tenants are sophisticated actors with considerable experience in renting property.

The assumption is less plausible in the context of many residential leases, where the landlord is more likely than the tenant to be a repeat player in the rental market. The landlord is therefore the party more likely to know the relevant law and to understand what risks the lease is and is not allocating to the tenant. Moreover, the landlord may be in a substantially better position than the tenant to assess the risk of a holdover tenant, or the property otherwise being unsuitable for possession at the start of a new lease. After all, it is the landlord who has dealt with the prior tenant, has had some opportunity to foresee and prevent the possibility of that prior tenant holding over, and who has more information regarding the condition of the property. The new

---

95. 153 S.E. 824 (Va. 1930) [DKA & S, p. 438]; [M & S, p. 659].

tenant is unlikely to have more than an abstract sense of the risk of a holdover. The best justification for the English rule is the information cost advantages landlords typically enjoy, especially in the context of residential leases.

Implied Covenant of Quiet Enjoyment

Possession is not the only covenant that courts will sometimes imply in leases. Often, courts will also imply an ongoing covenant of quiet enjoyment—that is, a covenant not to disturb the tenant's possession. But what happens if the landlord breaches this covenant?

There is a conventional understanding of the covenant of quiet enjoyment that provides a useful starting point for the analysis. It turns, fundamentally, on the independence of covenants in a lease.

In the terminology of contracts, a covenant is a commitment to engage in, or to refrain from engaging in, some specified conduct. At the least, a lease involves a covenant on the part of the tenant to pay rent, and a covenant on the part of the landlord to deliver a right to possess the property (if not possession itself, discussed above). There may well be other explicit covenants, too, depending on the terms of the specific lease. But in an important doctrinal move, courts have long held that most of the covenants in a lease are independent from one another, which means that breach of one does not excuse performance under the others. Therefore, under a traditional rule, if the landlord breached a covenant in the lease, the tenant remained obligated to pay rent, and the exclusive remedy was to sue for damages.

The only meaningful exception to this independence of covenants was for actual eviction. If a landlord evicted a tenant, the tenant would not have to continue paying rent (mercifully!), because the landlord had breached the covenant to not interfere with the tenant's possession—a covenant on which the tenant's covenant to pay rent was dependent. This, then, is the origin of the implied covenant of quiet enjoyment. If a landlord interferes enough with the tenant's use and enjoyment of the property, it can amount to constructive eviction. Having been "evicted" (constructively), the tenant could invoke the doctrine of dependent covenants and stop paying rent.

In a nutshell, this is the traditional use and power of the implied covenant of quiet enjoyment: provide tenants with a way out of a lease if conditions on the property render it sufficiently unusable. In fact, as discussed below, the implied covenant of quiet enjoyment is now somewhat broader than this, and a breach can give rise to a broader range of remedies, but the origins of the doctrine provide a useful frame for understanding its potential significance.

Even this traditional and relatively straightforward account of the covenant of quiet enjoyment hides considerable complexity, like deciding what constitutes constructive eviction. According to the court in *Reste Realty Corp. v. Cooper*,[96] constructive eviction includes "any act or omission of the landlord . . . which renders the premises substantially unsuitable for the purposes for which they are leased, or which seriously interferes with the beneficial enjoyment of the premises." Moreover, the condition must be "permanent." The *Reste* court found constructive eviction from property when the leased premises—the basement of a building—flooded whenever it rained. This, according to the court, rendered the premises unsuitable for the tenant's use and enjoyment, and therefore allowed him to vacate and stop paying rent.

Another complexity is the extent to which the implied covenant of quiet enjoyment extends to a landlord's inaction. The doctrine's original application was to prevent landlords from physically ousting tenants from possession of the property.[97] This has extended relatively easily to affirmative actions by landlords that make conditions somehow intolerable, or at least unsuitable for the leasehold interest—think, here, of landlords turning off the heat in the winter. If the implied covenant did not extend to these situations, landlords could effectively evict someone by simply making the conditions on the property bad enough. But what of inaction by the landlord—specifically, what of actions by other tenants that the landlord fails to stop?

In *Blackett v. Olanoff*,[98] residential tenants sought to terminate their leases because of a loud cocktail lounge operating on the ground floor of their building. The tenants found it intolerable and wanted to move out. They invoked the implied covenant of quiet enjoyment, but the landlords argued that the noise from the lounge should not be attributable to them. The court agreed with the tenants, holding that tenants were relieved of their obligation to pay rent because "the disturbing condition was the natural and probable consequence of the landlord's permitting the lounge to operate where it did, and because the landlords could control the actions at the lounge." The court distinguished the situation from the "usual annoyance of one residential tenant by other," which is

---

96.   251 A.2d 268 (N.J. 1969) [DK & S, p. 483]; [M & S, p. 669; 688; 705].

97.   For an account of this history, see Jean C. Love, *Landlord's Liability for Defective Premises: Caveat Lessee, Negligence, or Strict Liability*, 1975 Wis. L. Rev. 19 (1975).

98.   358 N.E.2d 817 (Mass. 1977) [M & S, p. 666]; [S, p. 785].

not typically chargeable to the landlord. In other words, the inherent incompatibility of the uses in this case, and the fact that it was within the landlord's power to require the lounge to produce less noise, rose to the level of constructive eviction.

Together, these two cases provide a sense of the potential breadth of constructive eviction and implied covenant of quiet enjoyment claims. Some important issues of mechanics remain, however. First, to the extent the implied covenant of quiet enjoyment is breached only when the landlord constructively evicts a tenant, it would appear that the tenant would have to vacate the property before bringing a claim. Indeed, in the typical case, the implied covenant of quiet enjoyment is asserted as a defense against a claim by the landlord for nonpayment of rent after the tenant leaves. That was the situation in *Olanoff.*

But is constructive eviction necessary for a breach of the implied covenant of quiet enjoyment, and must the tenant actually vacate the premises? As noted above, original quiet enjoyment claims were based on an analogy to actual eviction from the property. If the interference must be significant enough to amount to physical dispossession, then the tenant must vacate in order to assert a claim. The scope of the covenant of quiet enjoyment has expanded from those origins, however. A landlord's breach the covenant need not rise to the level of constructive eviction. In such a case, the tenant should be able to remain in possession and sue for damages. Courts, however, can be somewhat muddled in their reasoning about constructive eviction, and this sensible result is by no means a foregone conclusion.

Consider, in this regard, the problem of complete eviction from only part of the property. According to Justice Holmes in *Smith v. McEnany*,[99] the duty to pay rent cannot be apportioned, meaning that eviction from some of the property amounts to eviction form the whole. This comes from the common law notion that a lease springs directly from the land as a whole. As a matter of contract law, though, it is an odd result. It is easy to imagine an eviction from a part of the property that does not rise to the level of material breach of the lease. After all, constructive eviction is based on the idea that, at a certain point, violating the implied covenant of quiet enjoyment amounts to a material breach and failure of consideration. But it would seem that complete eviction from a part of the property could constitute partial breach for which the remedy is damages and not termination of the lease. The *McEnany* court did acknowledge a *de minimis* exception for small enough "evic-

---

99.   48 N.E. 781 (Mass. 1897) [M & S, p. 656].

tions," but the facts in that case involved only a nine-inch encroachment into the tenant's property, and so it is hard to know what would fall within the exception. In *McEnany*, at least, constructive eviction from part of the property was material breach as to the whole.

Constructive eviction and vacating the property is required where the tenant seeks termination of the lease instead of damages. The tenant must then vacate the property within a reasonable time of the actions (or inactions) constituting constructive eviction. The tenant waives a constructive eviction claim by remaining in possession of the property—conditions must not have been as terrible as the tenant claimed. But what counts as a reasonable time is often in the eye of the beholder. In *Reste*, for example, the basement flooded every time it rained, and it had for years before the tenant finally vacated. The court, however, agreed that the tenant had not waived his claim because he left within a reasonable amount of time after the "crowning blow" of a rainstorm. But there will always be a crowning blow; viewing waiver in terms of the *final* act instead of the *first* one goes a long way to blunting the force of the waiver doctrine.

This reasoning—while potentially broad—is mindful of the risk to tenants of vacating. As the *Reste* court emphasized, "Vacation of the premises is a drastic course and must be taken at [the tenant's] peril." In most cases, after vacating, the tenant will have to secure a substitute lease. Residential tenants need a place to live, and commercial tenants presumably want to stay open. They will then be obligated to pay rent under their new leases. That is all well and good, and may come out roughly evenly, so long as they were, in fact, constructively evicted. But if the original landlord sues to collect rent under the old lease, and a court rules that the tenant had not, in fact, been constructively evicted, then the tenant may find herself paying double rent: rent on the new lease, and rent on the old. The only sure way that a tenant can avoid this risk is to seek a declaratory judgment, prior to vacating, that the conditions on the property really did constitute constructive eviction. Even a summary proceeding can be lengthy and costly, however, and is not practicable in every case.

A final important observation about the implied covenant is that parties are free to contract around it. This can happen explicitly in the lease or, more interestingly, implicitly if the tenant knew of an offending condition when entering into the lease. If a tenant knows there is a loud nightclub downstairs, or that the basement floods in every rainstorm, her decision to lease the property anyway will typically preclude a subsequent constructive eviction claim.

However, courts have sometimes been flexible in applying the rule. *Reste* is again illustrative. There, the tenant entered into an original five-year lease without knowledge of the repetitive flooding on the property. However, the landlord and tenant subsequently entered into a second lease, on slightly different terms, at which point the tenant was clearly aware of the flooding. The *Reste* court nevertheless found constructive eviction, because the landlord—or his agent—had made representations before entering into the second lease that the flooding problem would be fixed. The tenant was allowed to rely on that representation instead of on the actual condition of the property. In short, the implied covenant of quiet enjoyment is waivable by the tenant, but it is not always obvious what will count as waiver.

Implied Warranty of Habitability

During the past half century, courts in many jurisdictions have increased the protection that leases afford to residential tenants, implying not only a covenant of quiet enjoyment, but now also a warranty of habitability. This doctrine is both narrower in scope but more protective than the implied covenant of quiet enjoyment. It is important to understand the differences between these similar-seeming implied terms in a lease.

The implied warranty of habitability is just that: a warranty that the property will, in fact, meet minimum levels of habitability. Courts adopting this doctrine have reasoned that the traditional rule of *caveat lessee* does not make sense in the context of modern residential leases, where tenants are not primarily leasing estates in land, but rather places to live, with functioning amenities and conditions suitable for human habitation. A low bar, perhaps, but an important one! As a consequence, the warranty of habitability will only be implied in certain kinds of leases. In many jurisdictions, it simply does not apply to commercial leases, or even to long-term leases, or to leases of single-family residences as opposed to apartments. It also only applies to conditions that implicate basic habitability; a defective hot tub will not trigger the warranty, even if it was the primary reason the tenant rented the apartment. The implied covenant of quiet enjoyment therefore applies to a broader category of leases, and potentially covers a broader range of defects.

When a court implies a warranty of habitability, however, it provides the stronger protection, as *Hilder v. St. Peter*[100] demonstrates. There, plaintiff rented a truly horrific apartment from the defendants. It had a broken window, broken toilets, no lock on the front door, sewage in the basement, a collapsed ceiling, and other

---

100. 478 A.2d 202 (Vt. 1984) [DKA & S, p. 493]; [S, p. 805; 832].

defects. Plaintiff sued for repayment of rent, and the Vermont Supreme Court held that plaintiff's residential lease came with an implied warranty of habitability and ruled in her favor. Plaintiff could not have brought a constructive eviction claim in this case because she remained in possession. She was not seeking termination of the lease; instead she was seeking an abatement of rent to reflect the deplorable condition of the premises. Furthermore, it may have been difficult for the plaintiff to make an implied covenant of quiet enjoyment claim because she knew about most of the defects in the apartment when she rented it.

The warranty of habitability is therefore particularly powerful for two reasons: (1) it is non-waivable; and (2) the tenant can remain in possession and either withhold rent or sue for damages (including punitive damages if the landlord's conduct is egregious enough).

Non-waivability is perhaps the most important aspect of the implied warranty of habitability, but is conceptually problematic. Even if the tenant was aware of the uninhabitable quality of a rental property when she leased it, she can still withhold rent until the landlord brings it up to snuff, or can pay to repair it herself and deduct those costs from her rent payments. In this way, the implied warranty of habitability helps to ensure that residential tenants will be entitled to rental property that at least meets some minimal level of quality.

While this may sound like an altogether sensible outcome, the equities are not quite so clear. Imagine that the landlord in *Hilder* knew that he would be subject to an implied warranty of habitability. He would then face a choice: either improve the property to meet the habitability requirement, or not rent the property at all. Depending on the rental market and the landlord's financial situation, he may well prefer to keep the apartment empty than investing in making it habitable. But what if a tenant nevertheless wants to rent the apartment even on those terms—or perhaps especially on those terms? It may well be that the market value of a refurbished apartment is more than the tenant could afford. Given the choice between renting a truly deplorable apartment and sleeping on the street, she may prefer the former (especially in Vermont where winters can get cold). But the implied warranty of habitability is non-waivable; the landlord in this situation therefore cannot rent the property to the tenant even on terms they would both prefer, because the landlord may just be exposing himself to liability.

Perhaps a useful way to conceptualize this conflict is to ask which side someone interested in the rights of the poor should take. On the one hand, it might seem eminently sensible to litigate against inadequate housing conditions. Slumlords who do not provide adequate heat or other necessities can unjustly burden tenants, and the implied warranty of habitability provides a powerful remedy. On the other hand, working to ensure that all housing is above a minimum condition might reduce the availability of housing to the very poor. A strong warranty of habitability may well eliminate some leases that both landlords and tenants would have preferred.

There are, however, justifications for what amounts to prohibiting leases of certain kinds of property. Most importantly, there is an empirical question lurking here that is not easy to answer. The implied warranty of habitability can be seen as a kind of tax on landlords; it increases the costs of maintaining rental property—especially property in poor condition—which, in turn, can be expected to reduce the available supply. But if landlords were forced to improve terrible apartments, would this actually result in reduced supply or increased costs? The answer presumably depends on the elasticity in the local market for residential leases. Landlords may respond in one of two ways. They might—as tenant advocates hope—renovate apartments without upping rents, effectively reducing their own profits. Alternatively, they might improve their rental units but pass those costs on to tenants. Or, if that is impossible, they might just not lease the property. It is not entirely clear how landlords will react to the implied warranty of habitability, and the answer will vary significantly depending on local housing conditions.

Beyond these empirical questions, the warranty of habitability may have as much to do with tenants' dignitary interests—and with society's concern for those interests—as with anything economic. There is something unabashedly paternalistic about the warranty of habitability. Its non-waivability means, in essence, that it prevents some people from renting property on terms that they would voluntarily choose. But just as society will not let people sell themselves into indentured servitude, it may not let people rent "uninhabitable" apartments. Or, more precisely, it will not allow landlords to lease uninhabitable apartments, even if there are tenants who are willing to rent them. It may be that society is not willing to allow people to rent apartments like the one in *Hilder*.

A final complexity is the remedy for a breach of the warranty. The mechanisms for obtaining relief are easy enough. The tenant must first inform the landlord of necessary repairs. If the landlord fails to make them, the tenant has several choices, including: (1) withholding rent; (2) suing for damages (which can include seeking repayment of rent already paid, and a rent abatement going forward); or (3) undertaking the repairs herself and setting off the expense against rent due. Under the first two options, however, how should the rent abatement—or damages—be valued?

It might seem as though the measure of damages should be the difference between the rent charged and the actual value of the property, as some courts have held. The problem is that this measure of damages can provide a way around the non-waivability of the warranty. If a landlord charges the actual rental value of the property in its uninhabitable condition, there would seem to be no damages to assess. Imagine, for example, that the fair rental value of an apartment in reasonable shape is $700 per month. In fact, however, the apartment has various hazards and problems—look no further than *Hilder* for an example—so that its actual value is far less, say $300 per month. If the landlord rented the property for $700 per month, the tenant would of course be able to recover the difference between rent paid and the value of the property in its current condition. The landlord could, however, set the rent at $700, but recite in the lease that the rent is being reduced to $300 to account for the condition of the property. Now what are the damages? It would seem there are none. The landlord is charging only the value of the property as it actually exists, and therefore there is no difference between the rent being charged and the fair rental value of the property.

Perhaps for this reason, some courts have adopted other measures of damages. In *Hilder,* the court held that damages are measured by "the difference between the value of the dwelling as warranted and the value of the dwelling as it exists in its defective condition." Other courts use a percentage diminution approach. Both, of course, raise complicated valuation problems. It is no easy task to determine by what percentage a defect decreases the value of property. And, divorcing the measure of damages from the actual rent paid by the tenant could lead to remedies with no basis in the economic reality of the lease.

Consider a lease for property with a fair rental value in habitable condition of $700 per month, a fair value in its current condition of $300, and an actual rent of $300 per month. Under the *Hilder* approach, damages may be assessed at $400 per month—the difference between the value of the dwelling as warranted, and the value of the dwelling as it exists—meaning, in theory, that the landlord owes the tenant $100 per month (or at least that the tenant owes nothing), despite an apartment that is worth $300 per month. Presumably, this concern is at the heart of the *Hilder* court's pronouncement that "In determining the fair rental value of the dwelling as warranted, the court may look to the agreed upon rent as evidence on this issue...." In other words, the agreed-upon rent is presumptively the fair rental value of the property *in habitable condition*, since the non-waivability of the warranty means that the lease was, in fact, for the property in habitable condition. This requires a willing suspension of disbelief about the sophistication of the lease negotiations.

There is no simple answer to the problem of remedy, and courts continue to disagree about how damages should be characterized and measured. The important point here is just to see the complexity of the issue. Nevertheless, the implied warranty of habitability remains a powerful legal tool for residential tenants, and in the typical case, allows the tenant to remain in possession and withhold rent.

C. Restrictions on Landlords

If leases were purely private arrangements, indistinguishable from other private contracts, then parties would have tremendous freedom to structure their transactions however they might choose. Landlords could freely select the parties with whom they want to deal, and bargain for the remedies they might want in the event of breach. In leases, however, the law imposes important substantive restrictions on landlords. First are Fair Housing Act limits on a landlord's ability to discriminate based on race or other protected characteristics in the selection of tenants. The second are limits on self-help and landlord remedies in the event of breach. The third are limits on the ability of landlords to prevent subleases and assignments, and to reach those third parties when they breach.

Fair Housing Act

If property owners truly had an unfettered right to exclude, they could choose their tenants based on any criteria, no matter how offensive or discriminatory. In fact, however, federal law provides an important limitation on landlords' free alienability in the Fair Housing Act, enacted in 1968 as part of the Civil Rights movement. That statute broadly prevents landlords from discriminating in the selection of tenants on the basis of race, color, religion, sex, family status, handicap, or national origin.[101]

At one level, this Act pits private property rights against broad concerns about discrimination. The Fair Housing Act is, after all, a restriction on owners' property rights, prohibiting them from en-

---

101. 42 U.S.C. § 3604 (2011) [DKA & S, p.431]; [M & S, p. 435]; [S, p. 926].

gaging in certain kinds of conduct on their property, namely: discriminating in proscribed ways. One obvious justification is simply that prohibiting discrimination is more important than individual property rights. But that is not obviously true in all settings. After all, federal law does not presume to restrict whom someone invites for dinner, no matter how offensive someone's reasons for not extending an invitation. The landlord's interests in exclusion must therefore be lower, or concerns about discrimination higher in this context. In fact, both are true.

The right to exclude is obviously central to private property. But it is not necessarily a trump, especially where—as here—the owner is voluntarily choosing to lease property to *someone*. Nothing in the Fair Housing Act requires people to become landlords; it requires only that if people voluntarily choose to rent property, they cannot discriminate in the selection of tenants.[102] The importance of preserving the owner's right to exclude is diminished in this context where the owner is affirmatively seeking to allow someone else to take possession of the property.

Moreover, housing is a context in which discrimination is particularly pernicious (as with employment, covered by Title VII of the Civil Rights Act). The history of racial segregation in the housing market continues to bedevil efforts at meaningful integration. This issue obviously implicates important constitutional and policy questions going far beyond property law, and they are largely put aside here. It is enough simply to point out that America has a troubled history of residential segregation in particular, and so concerns about housing discrimination remain high.

The Fair Housing Act, then, embodies a compromise between the interests of owners in controlling their own property, and the interests of tenants in avoiding discrimination. In *Attorney General v. Desilets*,[103] the Massachusetts Supreme Court applied both federal and state law to two landlords' decision not to rent to unmarried couples because of their own religious convictions. This case pitted the landlords' free exercise of religion against the tenants' rights to be free from discrimination in housing. And the Court remanded the case for trial, permitting the State to demonstrate its interest in eliminating housing discrimination based on marital status, and particularly in the community at issue. Fundamentally, though, the Court recognized the need "to balance the State's interests against

---

102. The Act also applies to the sale of property, a point considered in more detail below.

103. 636 N.E.2d 233 (Mass. 1994) [M & S, p. 439]; [S, p. 967–68].

the nature of the burden on the defendants ... [which concerned] the business of leasing apartments, not ... the participation in a formal religious activity.''

The Fair Housing Act also recognizes that the nature of the landlord may change the equation. Notably, most of the anti-discrimination rules do not apply to the owner of a single-family residence seeking to lease it out (so long as she does not own more than three single-family residences), nor to a landlord in a building with no more than four separate units, so long as the landlord actually lives in one of them. In other words, the central provisions of the Act do not apply to very small-scale landlords, or to landlords who will be living in close proximity to their tenants.

Even then, however, some of the Act's provisions do apply, most notably the prohibition on advertising that discriminates based on any of the protected categories. This may seem strange. The Act permits actual discrimination based on race, just not advertising the discrimination. This has everything to do with the expressive content of discrimination. There is something particularly offensive about allowing people to advertise "No blacks," regardless of the substance of their decision. The harm of such an advertisement may also be spread more broadly than the substantive selection of a tenant. A discriminatory advertisement has some effect on anyone who reads it. Those being discriminated against may feel stigmatized. And for others, such an advertisement may send a tacit signal that discrimination is permissible and even mainstream. The actual discrimination in the selection of tenants is far worse for the excluded tenants, of course, but is much narrower in its reach.

Ultimately, the Fair Housing Act embodies a number of trade-offs, sometimes awkwardly, between the interests of property owners and the interests of tenants and society. This is a conflict not restricted to landlord-tenant law, however, and will return in later chapters.

Limits on Self–Help

Another limit on the landlord's right to exclude comes from limits on the landlord's right to use self-help to evict a tenant. Self-help, in this context, typically means removing the tenant's possessions and changing locks on doors. Under a traditional common law rule, a landlord was entitled to use self-help to remove a tenant so long as two conditions were met: (1) the landlord was legally entitled to possession; and (2) the landlord used peaceable means of reentry. And, as a matter of property law, the use of self-help in this situation may make good sense. After all, if the landlord was legally entitled to possession, then the tenant is effectively a trespasser. A tenant who stays past the expiration of her lease, for example, has no right to the property anymore. Self-help might look like nothing more or less than allowing owners to protect their own property interests.

In fact, however, most jurisdictions forbid the use of self-help. If landlords want to remove tenants who are illegally in possession, they must avail themselves of judicial remedies, typically summary eviction procedures that, while quick, may still take weeks or months to navigate. Courts have expressed concern that self-help poses too much of a risk of a breach of the peace. That policy justification was at the heart of the court's holding in *Berg v. Wiley*[104] prohibiting self-help in Minnesota. The court reached its conclusion even though the landlord went to the property accompanied by a sheriff while the tenant was away to change the locks on the doors. The chance of physical conflict was therefore almost zero.

The prohibition on self-help reflects, to some extent, the nature of the relationship between the landlord and the tenant. A tenant who holds over is simply not in the same position as a random trespasser who illegally enters property. The tenant has a relationship with the landlord—a relationship that the landlord voluntarily undertook—and that may justify limits on the landlord's ability to exercise self-help if the tenant holds over or otherwise illegally remains in possession.

It is important to understand, however, that this is not an entirely pro-tenant rule. While it undoubtedly provides legal protection to current tenants, it does so at some cost to future tenants. After all, if a landlord has re-rented property beginning at the end of a prior lease, a tenant who remains in possession harms both the landlord and the incoming new tenant who cannot take possession of the property. Even more importantly, increasing the costs of evicting a tenant also increases the stakes for landlords to rent to tenants who will not need to be evicted. This, in turn, can result in more scrutiny on the front end to avoid the higher costs at the back end. Landlords may engage in more due diligence, require more financial resources, references, credit checks, and greater security deposits, all to offset the relatively high costs of judicial eviction as opposed to self-help. In other words, landlords may pass some or all of the costs of increased judicial process on to tenants on the front end, making leases more expensive and harder to get. States that have eliminated self-help are implicitly asserting that those up-

---

104. 264 N.W.2d 145 (Minn. 1978) [DKA & S, p. 460]; [M & S, p. 388]; [S, p. 771].

front costs are lower than costs associated with self-help remedies. That may well be true, but it is important to understand the nature of the trade-off.

Subleases and Assignments

The alienability of leasehold interests presents another challenge to landlord remedies. At least at their inception, leases are bilateral. The landlord (lessor) rents property to the tenant (lessee) on terms specified by the lease. But those interests are theoretically transferable. It is important first to understand the consequences of such transfers, and then to look to limits.

As a bilateral contract, a lease creates privity of contract between a landlord and a tenant. If either breaches the terms of the lease, the other may sue. But what happens if one of the parties has transferred her interest to a third party? Specifically, what happens if the tenant has transferred her interest in the lease to someone else?

The complexity of such transfers is that the new tenant was not a party to the original lease. She is not in privity of contract with the landlord. Therefore, if she breaches the terms of the original lease, the landlord would appear to have no claim against her, at least as a matter of contract law. Property law can provide an additional basis for privity, however. If a tenant assigns all of her interest in a lease to a third party, that third party is now in *privity of estate* with the landlord, despite the absence of privity of contract. They are connected through the property. Privity of estate can serve as a basis for a claim directly between the landlord and the assignee, without having to go through the original lessee. This does not apply, however, to subleases where the original tenant conveys less than her entire leasehold to a third party. Subleases do not create privity of estate between the landlord and sublessee.

If this all seems somewhat convoluted, focus on the connections between the parties. At the time of the original lease, the landlord (L) and tenant (T1) are in both privity of contract and privity of estate. That is, they entered into a contract—the lease—with each other, and so can sue each other for breaches of that agreement. But they are also in privity of estate, meaning, in essence, that they are connected to each other through the land. The tenant, after all, is living on or at least is in possession of the landlord's property. This is an alternative form of privity—privity of estate—and provides a different basis for suit.

Now what happens when the original tenant transfers her interest to a new tenant (T2)? T1 and T2 have a new agreement between them—the sublease or assignment—that undoubtedly creates privity of contract *between them.* If anything goes wrong with the sublease or assignment, T1 and T2 can sue each other. Furthermore, it is possible that this sublease or assignment will give the landlord a basis for suing T2 directly. Some courts have been willing to find that a sublease or assignment is a third-party beneficiary contract for the benefit of the original landlord. Typically, this exists only when the new tenant agrees expressly to be bound by the covenants in the original lease. Where this occurs, the landlord is, in fact, in privity of contract with T2, and can sue as a third-party beneficiary. But where this does not occur—either because the agreement between T1 and T2 does not include the covenants in the original lease, or because a court refuses to recognize such agreements as third-party beneficiary contracts— the range of options is more limited. If the agreement between T1 and T2 is an assignment, then the landlord and T2 are now in privity of estate, and can again sue each other directly.

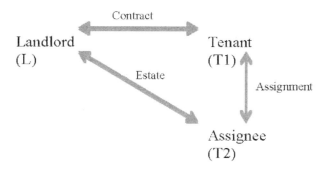

But where that agreement is a sublease, any suit between the landlord and T2 must go through the original tenant, T1.

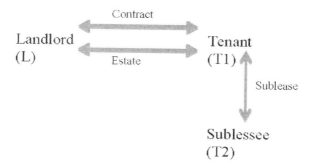

To be clear, the landlord retains a claim against the original tenant in any case. They remain in privity of contract no matter what. Even in an assignment, if T2 breaches covenants in the original lease—say, stops paying rent—the landlord can still sue T1 for that breach. In practice, this may not be an adequate remedy because the landlord may have trouble finding the original tenant who is no longer in possession of the property, or because the original tenant has no money to pay damages.

The landlord's remedy against T2 may therefore depend on the characterization of the transaction between T1 and T2 as a sublease or assignment, but it is not always easy to distinguish between them. In *Ernst v. Conditt*,[105] for example, landlords (the Ernsts) leased property to Rogers for a Go–Cart track. Shortly after taking possession, Rogers conveyed his interest to Conditt. Both Rogers and Conditt approached the Ernsts, seeking explicit permission to "sublet" the property. Rogers agreed to remain personally liable on the lease, and the Ernsts explicitly consented. Less than one year later, Conditt stopped paying rent and the Ernsts sued, seeking the remaining rent due. Conditt, however, argued that he was not liable to the Ernsts; that his agreement with Rogers was a sublease, and so lacked privity with the landlords. Specifically, he argued that Rogers' agreement to remain personally liable retained for Rogers a kind of reversionary interest in the lease, so that Rogers did not, in fact, convey away the entirety of his interests.

Traditionally, the difference between a sublease and an assignment depends on whether the original tenant has any possessory interest remaining in the property. If a tenant transfers less than her entire interest to a third party, by retaining a reversionary interest for example, it is a sublease. An assignment only occurs

---

105.   390 S.W.2d 703 (Tenn. Ct. App. 1964) [DKA & S, p. 442].

when a tenant transfers her whole interest to someone else. In a term of years lease ending on August 31st, if the tenant transfers her interest to a third party until August 30th, it is a sublease. If the tenant transfers the lease through the 31st, it is an assignment.

The *Conditt* court acknowledged, however, a modern trend in the law towards focusing on the parties' intent instead of strictly on the formal elements of the agreement—an example, perhaps, of the gradual contractualization of property law. An assignment exists when the parties intended it. The court held that the agreement between Rogers and Conditt was an assignment under either the traditional or the more modern approach. Although the parties called their agreement a sublease, it did not change the substance of the underlying transaction, which was to give Conditt the right of possession for the entirety of the remaining lease. Therefore, the Ernsts could sue Conditt directly for non-payment of rent, and did not have to sue Rogers. Had it been a sublease, however, the Ernsts' only remedy would have been to sue Rogers.

It may seem as though landlords have nothing to lose from subleases and assignments. After all, the original tenant remains liable. And, in many situations, the new tenant is also liable, expanding the people from whom the landlord can recover. In reality, though, legal remedies are landlords' last resort. Far better, from their perspective, is to select responsible tenants who will pay rent, maintain the property, and meet the requirements of the lease. For that reason, subleases and assignments can be threatening to landlords who, in effect, lose the right to control who is actually occupying their property. Landlords often include clauses in leases either prohibiting subleases and assignments, or at least requiring the landlord's approval. Such clauses, however, may not be enforceable.

Restrictions on lessees' ability to alienate their leaseholds have come under attack from both property and contract principles. Property law, recall, strongly favors alienability. Just as old feudal restraints on alienability resulted in the inefficient allocation of property rights—property owners being unable to transfer their interests to higher-valued users—restraints on the ability to alienate leaseholds can lock people into inefficient arrangements. Although the example is somewhat trivial, *Ernst v. Conditt* is again revealing. There, the original lessee turned out to have had less interest in running a Go–Cart track than Conditt. True, Conditt himself was not particularly successful in the enterprise, but he might have been. For almost every unsuccessful restaurant or business, there is a lessee seeking to get out of her obligations under the lease, and—at least in good times—another new business interested in taking over the property. In the residential context, too, people might get a job in a new city, have an unexpected addition to the family (twins!), or face some other change making their rented homes inadequate or unnecessary. Restricting the alienability of leasehold interests can keep commercial spaces empty, residential property in the hands of people who do not want it, and can keep both out of the hands of people who actually value it more.

On the contract side, too, restrictions on the alienability of leaseholds have come under attack by the duty to mitigate damages. Under the traditional rule of leases, even if a tenant vacated the premises prematurely, the landlord was still bound by its independent covenant to provide quiet enjoyment and so could not retake possession of the property. The landlord's remedy was to sue for damages, and often at the end of the lease. But that rule, too, has started to change, sometimes requiring the landlord to mitigate damages in such circumstances by making reasonable efforts to re-lease the property to someone else.[106] Under this rule, a landlord might be obligated to accept a replacement tenant if the tenant breaches, which begins to look like a requirement to accept reasonable subleases and assignments.

That is precisely what the court held in *Kendall v. Ernest Pestana, Inc.*[107] On a complicated set of facts, the California Supreme Court held that in a commercial lease requiring the consent of a landlord before the tenant could sublease or assign the property the landlord could not arbitrarily withhold consent. This remains a minority rule. Nevertheless, where applicable, the rule in essence creates a right to sublease or assign property, at least to a reasonable sub-lessee or assignee.

It is important to recognize the effect of this rule on a landlord, however. It gives the tenant the ability to capture an increase in value in the leasehold. Imagine the realistic hypothetical of a landlord entering into a commercial lease for 5 years at a monthly rate of $3,000. Two years into the lease, the rental value of the property has increased dramatically, perhaps to $5,000 per month. If the tenant has a right to sublet the property (or the landlord has no right to withhold consent absent good cause), she can charge the market rate—$5,000—and keep the difference for herself. But if the landlord can withhold consent, then the landlord is likely to bargain for a substantial share of that increased value. That is, the

---

106. See Sommer v. Kridel, 378 A.2d 767 (N.J. 1977) [DKA & S, p. 469]; [M & S, p. 702]; [S, p. 774].

107. 709 P.2d 837 (Cal. 1985) [DKA & S, p. 450]; [S, p. 758].

landlord can refuse permission to sublet the property absent some payment to reflect the increase in rental value. At stake, then, is who gets to capture increases in the value of the property during the term of the lease.

Allocating that right to the tenant may, in fact, be entirely appropriate. After all, if the property decreases in value during the lease, the landlord is under no obligation to charge less rent. And, if the original tenant did not attempt to sublet the property, the landlord has no opportunity to try to capture the increased value. If the tenant simply stays in possession, she gets that increased value herself. At least as an economic matter, there is no obvious reason why an effort to sublease or assign the property should trigger an opportunity for the landlord to extract additional rental value from the property.

Pressing questions remain, though. How broad is the prohibition against unreasonably withholding consent? The *Kendell* case arose in the context of a commercial lease, and courts (and state legislatures) have typically been less hostile to landlords withholding consent in the context of residential leases. This appears to be based partly on an intuition that alienability is less important to tenants in residential leases than commercial ones. But it may also be that residential leases tend to be of shorter duration, and so limits on alienability are less burdensome. And there may also be a better reason to allow residential landlords more discretion in the selection of tenants. A residential subtenant may well have the financial qualifications of the original tenant, but be less desirable as a tenant for some other reason: she is a student, a smoker, has a dog, etc. This, then, leads to the other open question: what counts as a reasonable basis for withholding consent to a sublease or assignment?

There is no clear consensus about the reasonable bases for a landlord to withhold consent. A sublessee or assignee must, presumably, demonstrate the ability to meet the financial obligations under the lease. But there are other considerations that a court may well feel are reasonable for a landlord to consider. For example, a landlord may not be required to consent to a sublease or assignment to a competitor of the landlord. Likewise, a landlord may not be required to consent where the new tenant reduces the overall value of the landlord's other rental property; the owner of a shopping mall may not need to consent to a sublease by Macy's to a dollar store, no matter how secure the dollar store's finances are.

The question becomes more complicated, however, when more subjective concerns are the basis for refusal. A landlord, for example, may have religious or moral objections to certain kinds of businesses, and courts appear to diverge over whether such subjective concerns constitute a reasonable basis for refusal. On the one hand, forcing the landlord to accept a subtenant is in tension with the landlord's right to exclude. It amounts to forcing the landlord to do business with someone not of her choosing. On the other hand, the landlord has voluntarily agreed to become a landlord, and that already subjects her to a number of legal limitations on her right to exclude—the Fair Housing Act being the most important. In this view, an owner voluntarily chooses to become a landlord— which is primarily a commercial status—and so can be limited to commercial considerations in withholding consent to subleases and assignments. There is no real consensus in this area, and intuitions may change depending on the characteristics of the landlord. A professional commercial landlord may have less discretion than a small residential landlord, for example.

* * *

Dividing property between landlords and tenants again reflects broader property themes. Leases take limited forms, and the law of leases mediates the conflicts between the parties' competing property interests. Most importantly, the property aspect of leases imposes substantive restrictions on the rights and duties of both landlords and tenants in ways that go beyond what contract law would typically require.

Chapter 8

LAND TRANSFERS

It is perhaps unconventional to include land transfers in the broader discussion about dividing property rights. Real estate transactions seem more about acquiring or relinquishing property, and not about dividing it. There are, indeed, a host of quite technical doctrines in this area of law that provide little conceptual payoff about the division of property rights. A closer look, however, reveals an unexpected but quite profound connection to the broader theoretical themes in this Part. Land transfers become contested primarily when multiple parties assert competing claims to the same underlying real estate, for example when someone sells the same piece of property to more than one person. This does not actually divide property rights between the two buyers; only one of them will end up with the property. But the law of recordation is, fundamentally, about mediating the competing property claims of two purchasers of the same property. Similarly, when a mortgage gives a lender a security interest in property, it is an interest in the property itself that may even ripen into outright ownership through foreclosure. The mortgagee and mortgagor therefore both have an interest in the property. While the doctrinal discussion that follows can sometimes seem quite divorced from the rest of the study of property, the underlying issues are more similar than they might at first appear.

A. The Land Sale Transaction: An Overview

Buying and selling land (real property) is often different from buying and selling personal property. The transactions typically involve more steps and more parties and the integrity of the system is an abiding concern. A land sale transaction typically includes four separate steps: (1) entering a contract; (2) securing financing (a mortgage); (3) closing on the property; and (4) recording the deed. Each is important and creates different rights and responsibilities.

A land sale transaction begins in earnest when a buyer makes an offer for property that the seller accepts. Basic contract law governs this agreement. Because it is a contract for the sale of land, however, it is subject to the statute of frauds and so must be in writing (with some limited exceptions). The contract does not legally transfer property from the seller to the buyer however. It is instead an executory contract promising to transfer the property if certain contingencies are met. When executing the contract, the buyer will also typically provide a substantial down payment on the property that may be retained by the seller if the buyer does not perform.

Once the land sale contract is executed, the seller still owns and retains possession of the property. However, an equitable interest in the property passes to the buyer at this point; she has a right to the property, so long as she fulfills her obligations under the land sale contract. This division of ownership typically imposes on the seller a duty to maintain the property until closing. However, the risk of fire or other damage to the property now lies with the buyer, who is generally obligated to carry insurance on the property during this period, unless the parties agree otherwise.

The usual land sale contract is contingent on the following: the buyer securing financing; a satisfactory inspection of the property; and the seller conveying marketable title. Each of these contingencies may be waived, and buyers will sometimes do so to obtain an advantage over competing bidders. Once the contract is executed, however, both parties are under a duty of good faith to try to satisfy the requirements in the contract.

The first two requirements are clear enough. If the buyer does not have cash on hand to buy the property outright, she must make reasonable efforts to secure financing (and the contract may sometimes be contingent on the buyer's ability to secure financing on specific terms). This will usually involve a bank, from which the buyer will secure a loan to buy the property subject to a mortgage, discussed below. The buyer will also arrange to have the property inspected for physical defects. If there are substantial ones, the contract will typically give the buyer a predetermined number of days to inform the seller, and to either arrange to have the defects remedied, renegotiate the purchase price, or back out of the deal with a return of the down payment.

The covenant of marketable title is somewhat less obvious. Marketable title means, in essence, that the seller has the power to convey the property free of any unreasonable risk of litigation concerning the state of the title. Examples of defects in marketable title include: property that was acquired through adverse possession that has not yet been quieted through a judicial decree; property encumbered by a remainder interest where the remaindermen have not consented to the sale; the existence of a private encumbrance like a mortgage, covenant, purchase option, or easement; or a violation of the applicable zoning ordinance. As the court in *Lohmeyer v. Bower*[108] explained, the substance of a zoning ordinance cannot be the basis for a breach of marketable title, but a condition on the property actually in breach of existing zoning can be. This is true even if the seller offers to cure the defect by conveying an additional strip of land that would bring the property into conformity, because this would "compel the purchaser to take something he did contract to buy."

Title defects, if any, typically will come to light through the process of a title search, usually conducted by a title search company. That search will look back through the applicable land records to ensure there are no clouds on title, and will also disclose whether the property complies with existing land use regulations.

In addition, the seller in many jurisdictions has a duty to disclose known defects on the property. This can include things like underground storage tanks that might create environmental liability, excessively noisy neighbors, a leaky roof, or other problems that materially impact the value of the property. In one case, a court even permitted rescission when the seller failed to disclose ghosts "living" on the property![109] Although the court was clearly amused by the claim, it accepted the buyer's contention that the seller had spread tales about encounters with poltergeists, that this reputation had materially affected the value of the house (regardless of whether the haunting was real), and that the seller had a duty to disclose this reputation to the buyer. Failure to do so allowed the buyer to rescind the contract.

Rescission is a typical remedy for a breach of a land sale contract, but is not the only one. Remedies also include retaining (or returning) the buyer's down payment, damages, or specific performance. Even if the seller changes her mind, or receives a better offer after going into contract, the buyer may be able to compel performance under the land sale contract. Where there is a defect in marketable title, the buyer may simply rescind the contract and recover her down payment. The buyer may also sue for breach. Finally, the buyer may bring an action for specific performance, but seek a judicial abatement of the purchase price.

Assuming both parties meet their obligations under the land sale contract, the next step in the transaction is the closing. The closing involves the transfer of payment in exchange for the deed to the property. The typical closing will also include the buyer's bank

---

108. 227 P.2d 102 (Kan. 1951) [DKA & S, p. 548].

109. See Stambovsky v. Ackley, 572 N.Y.S.2d 672 (1991) [DKA & S, p. 553]; [S, p. 864].

that is providing the financing (of which more below), and the seller's bank as well if the property is subject to an existing mortgage, which will then be paid off at the closing.

The seller will convey one of three kinds of deeds, as specified in the land sale contract: a general warranty deed, a special warranty deed, or a quitclaim deed. Each contains different representations about what interests the seller is conveying, and different warranties about challenges to the title in the future. In many jurisdictions (and subject to some exceptions), once the closing occurs, the covenants in the land sale contract are extinguished by the doctrine of merger, which holds that the contract is replaced by the deed. At least in the absence of fraud, buyers' remedies are then limited to suing on the deed itself, and the contract is extinguished.

The broadest deed, as the name implies, is the general warranty deed. This deed contains both present covenants and future covenants. The present covenants amount to representations that the seller has the ability to convey good title to the property, and that it is not encumbered by undisclosed mortgages, liens, or servitudes (discussed in Part III). These present covenants are really representations about the state of the property at the time of the conveyance. If the seller breaches them, they are breached at the moment of the conveyance, and the statute of limitations begins to run then.

Future covenants are different. They commit the seller to defend the buyer against lawful claims of superior title against the property that may arise in the future. The difference between the two can be slippery and is easiest to see in the context of an example. Imagine that a seller conveys property to a buyer that is encumbered by an undisclosed mortgage. That is a breach of a present covenant, and the buyer may be able to recover damages. But if the holder of the mortgage then attempts to foreclose on the property, seeking to oust the buyer from possession, that foreclosure action had not commenced at the time of the sale and therefore would not be subject to any of the present covenants. But the future covenants in a general warranty deed would obligate the seller to defend the buyer against a lawful foreclosure action.

A special warranty deed is considerably more limited. It provides warranties only against encumbrances on the property or defects in title that arose during the seller's ownership. Therefore, it would extend to an undisclosed mortgage that the seller herself had taken out on the property, but not to an undisclosed mortgage of a previous owner.

The least protective is the quitclaim deed, which contains no warranties at all. It amounts to a sale on the following terms: "I make no representations that I own this property, but to the extent that I have any interests in the property, I convey them to the buyer." If someone tries to sell the Brooklyn Bridge on these terms, then buyer beware!

Once the deed has been transferred to the buyer, the last step is recording the deed in the relevant—usually county—records office. This simply means filing the deed with the clerk. That deed will then be listed in a large volume—sometimes still a physical book, with a complicated index—so that anyone searching the index can find out that the transfer took place. Recordation, however, is conceptually richer than it might seem, and is taken up in some detail next.

B. Recordation

Recordation, fundamentally, is about creating certainty in ownership of land. It is at once technical and tedious, but also vitally important for the alienability of real property. Real estate markets depend on buyers being able to identify who owns what, and on the security of ownership. A centralized system of land records allows a potential buyer to investigate claims of ownership against property, and to reassure herself that the seller has the power to convey good title. Contrast the "modern" recordation systems—actually dating back to the seventeenth century—with practices in the Middle Ages. In Germany, a young boy would be required to witness land conveyances, and the parties would punch him in the head to solemnize the deal.[110] The idea was to create an episode sufficiently memorable that the child would be able to testify about it years later, and to have that memory held by someone who was likely to live a long time. Judged against this baseline, recordation statutes are a tremendous improvement.

It is critically important, however, to understand that recordation is not required to effectuate a land sale transaction. Once a deed has passed from the buyer to the seller, the deal is done, whether or not the buyer records. Recordation does not affect the rights of buyers and sellers against one another. Recordation's promise is different. It plays a central role in protecting the rights of third parties, and the rights of buyers against claims by third parties. It comes into play in the following situation: Seller conveys

---

110. See James Lindgren, *The Fall of Formalism,* 55 ALB. L. REV. 1009, 1033 (1992).

Blackacre to Buyer One. Seller then purports to convey Blackacre to someone else, Buyer Two. In this example, there is no doubt that Seller does not have the right to re-sell the property to Buyer Two. If Seller no longer owns it, she cannot sell it again. Nevertheless, Buyer Two may (or may not) have known that; Buyer Two therefore may (or may not) have reasonably believed that she bought Blackacre. As between Buyer One and Buyer Two, then, who has a better claim to the property?

The answer seems obvious, but it is not. Viewed ontologically, Buyer One owns Blackacre. She acquired it when Seller had the power to sell, and Buyer Two bought nothing but an empty promise. The problem, from the perspective of the property system, is that no one buying property necessarily knows whether she is Buyer One or Buyer Two. No one knows, that is, whether the seller actually conveyed away property beforehand to someone else.

Recordation requirements, then, are designed to provide certainty in land transactions, certainty that is essential for the easy marketability of land. Therefore, at least in some situations, the law will protect subsequent buyers from earlier ones. Buyer Two may actually win against Buyer One, depending upon the requirements of the local recordation statute. And, the idea extends beyond outright purchases. Many interests in property are subject to recordation: mortgages, easements, covenants, options, to name just a few. Recordation will also determine whether a purchaser is bound by a pre-existing encumbrance on the property, and even whether someone seeking a new easement or covenant is bound by pre-existing ones. While the discussion below is framed in terms of buyers—for the sake of simplicity—they are stand-ins for this broader range of potential interest holders.

There are three basic kinds of recordation statutes in the United States: (1) race; (2) notice; and (3) race-notice. Each specifies the requirements for a subsequent purchaser to take as against a prior one.

By far the most straightforward kind of recordation statute is a pure race statute. Under a race statute, people with an interest in land are literally in a race against each other to file their paperwork first because the first to file wins. If a subsequent purchaser files her claim to the property first, then she wins against a prior unrecorded interest, whether or not she knew about it, and whether or not she was acting in good faith. This is not only the simplest of the three recordation systems, it is also the cheapest to administer. There is only one question: who got to the records office first? But it is also the rarest of the three systems, presumably because of the opportunity it creates for inequitable results. A buyer who knew of an earlier but unfiled encumbrance can still take the property free and clear if she records first.

In contrast, a notice system will award property to a subsequent purchaser only so long as she had no notice of the pre-existing claim to the property. That is, a good faith purchaser for value will win, and a purchaser with knowledge of the earlier conveyance will lose, regardless of who actually filed first. This system does not make recordation superfluous, however, because recording an interest in property puts subsequent buyers on constructive notice (specifically, record notice) of the pre-existing claim. That is, a buyer will take subject to pre-existing claims if she knew *or should have known* of their existence. Recordation prevents subsequent purchasers from claiming they had no notice of the previous interest in the property.

A race-notice system essentially combines the two other systems. It awards property to subsequent purchasers only if they had no notice of the prior claim, *and* they filed first. To see how these systems differ, consider the following example:

O conveys Blackacre to B1, who does not record her interest. O subsequently conveys Blackacre to B2. After the second sale, B1 records her interest, and B2 records her interest shortly thereafter. Who wins?

In a race jurisdiction, B1 wins. She filed first. End of story. In a notice jurisdiction, B2 will win because she was a good faith purchaser with no notice of the pre-existing claim to the property. And under a race-notice statute, B1 would again win, because B2 cannot show *both* that she had no notice of the prior claim *and* that she filed first.

Interesting questions sometimes emerge about who should be entitled to benefit from a recording statute. Most courts hold that recording acts can only apply to protect purchasers *for value,* and then only to the extent of what they actually paid. It therefore does not protect someone who inherited property without notice of prior claims, or who otherwise received the property through a gratuitous transfer. Lest this seem unfair, recall that the justification for recording acts is to protect buyers who might balk if the status of pre-existing claims was relatively unknowable. That concern is not present where the transfer is gratuitous.

C. Mortgages

Most people do not have enough cash on hand to buy property outright. They therefore need to borrow money to buy the property, typically in the form of a mortgage, which can be from a bank or from anyone else. The lender (called the mortgagee) lends money to the borrower (called the mortgagor) who agrees to pay it back over time, with interest. Conceptually, however, a mortgage actually contains two separate components: (1) a note with an obligation to repay; and (2) a security interest in the real property.

If everything goes well and the mortgagor meets her repayment obligations, the mortgagee will be repaid in full and the security interest in the property will disappear. But if the mortgagor does not meet her repayment obligations and defaults on the note, then the security interest may give the lender the right to foreclose on the property. From a property perspective, this is where the action is. The mortgagee's property interest in the underlying asset creates the opportunity to seek repayment as if from the underlying collateral itself. Foreclosure can be a drastic remedy, dispossessing the borrower from the property and putting it up for sale in order to satisfy the outstanding debt. The history of mortgages is important for understanding current doctrine.

An early form of mortgages involved an actual property conveyance from the borrower to the lender. This could happen in the context of a land sale transaction, or simply as a loan to a property owner (think, here, of the many eighteenth and nineteenth-century English novels where the land rich are money poor and use their property to borrow money, often ending badly). In the original form of these transactions, the borrower would actually transfer title to his property to the lender in exchange for money upfront. It looked, in other words, like a sale of the property. However, the lender took title to the property subject to an "equity of redemption," which meant that the lender promised to convey the property back to the borrower so long as the borrower repaid the loan by a predetermined date. Of course, if the borrower did not repay the loan in time, the lender was already holding title to the property, and he would then own the property outright. Stepping back, this is the transaction in a nutshell: the owner-borrower conveys title to his property to the lender in exchange for a loan, and the lender promises to convey the property back to the borrower so long as he repays.

The problem with this structure was the potential for unfairness to the borrower. Typically, the loan in this arrangement would be worth far less than the underlying property. Failing to repay therefore meant that the lender was receiving something of a windfall; he would have acquired full ownership of the property for only the money originally loaned to the borrower. Courts eventually stepped in to prevent this outcome, allowing borrowers to redeem their property even after the date the loan repayment was due. They held that a borrower could exercise his "equity of redemption" after—indeed, even long after—he was supposed to have repaid the loan, and reclaim his property. This, in turn, created a problem for the lender, because it left the title to the property profoundly unsettled. A lender would have trouble selling the property after a borrower's default because of the cloud created by the borrower's equity of redemption.

To deal with this problem, courts began permitting lenders to terminate the borrower's right of redemption. A court, sitting in equity, could give a borrower a fixed amount of time to repay, after which the equity of redemption would be "foreclosed" and the lender would own the property outright. This process was eventually codified, giving rise to modern mortgages, and to mortgagees' remedy of foreclosure.

Today, jurisdictions take one of two approaches to mortgages, adopting either a lien theory or a title theory. A title theory jurisdiction most closely resembles the original form of mortgages because the mortgagee (lender) holds the title to the property for the life of the mortgage. In a lien theory jurisdiction, by contrast, title to the property remains with the mortgagor (borrower). The mortgagee instead has a lien on the property, which is a recordable security interest and creates a right to foreclose. Most jurisdictions also recognize a deed of trust as an alternative to a mortgage. With a deed of trust, a third party holds title to the property, in effect acting as an escrow agent. If the borrower fails to meet the obligations under the mortgage, the third party is instructed to transfer title to the mortgagee. Of course, if the borrower does repay the loan, the agent transfers title to her. In theory, this avoids the need for a judicial proceeding for the mortgagee to take title to the property after default and foreclosure.

The different approaches can have important doctrinal consequences. For example, if a joint tenant unilaterally mortgages her interest in a joint tenancy, this is likely to count as a conveyance under a title theory or with a deed of trust; both will sever the joint tenancy and convert it into a tenancy in common. But in a lien theory jurisdiction, the mortgage is merely a lien and not a conveyance at all, and so the joint tenancy is likely to survive the mortgage.[111] Moreover, foreclosure is thought to be somewhat easier in a title theory jurisdiction because the mortgagee already holds the title to the property.

Regardless of the approach—whether a lien or title theory—a mortgagee's remedies take the same basic form. Once a borrower has defaulted on the loan—stopped making payments—the mortgagee can initiate foreclosure proceedings. That will allow the mortgagee to take good title to the property, typically to sell it to recover the balance of the loan. Any money left over—any "equity" in the property over and above the value of the outstanding mortgage—goes back to the mortgagor.

The mortgagor retains an important protection, however. Although details vary state by state, a mortgagor retains a right of redemption after default but prior to foreclosure. That is, even after a borrower has stopped paying and defaulted on a loan, she can avoid foreclosure by repaying the note in full, a kind of fallback protection consistent with the long-standing equity of redemption. More powerfully, some states have also created a statutory right of redemption that remains in place even after foreclosure for some fixed amount of time. In states with such statutes, a borrower can repay the loan and reclaim title to the property even from a third party purchaser.

As with all other property doctrines, seemingly pro-consumer protections have a dark side. The harder it is for mortgagees to foreclose and the more post-foreclosure protection that consumers have the more expensive mortgages will be. If the seller is not able to convey unencumbered fee simple title to the property immediately, it will be less valuable to potential buyers. Any bid by a potential buyer at the foreclosure sale will presumably be discounted by the risk of the original owner exercising a right of redemption. This, in turn, reduces the value of the property as a security interest. If the fair market value of property is, say, $250,000, a bank may take a haircut off that value for purposes of valuing it as collateral, to reflect both the costs of foreclosure and the reduction in value for the property if it has to be sold in foreclosure. All of this means that a bank will be willing to lend less money, or will charge higher interest rates, because of the reduced value of the collateral in foreclosure.

Mortgages implicate many doctrinal complexities. They also intersect with the law of commercial paper (in ways and for reasons discussed briefly below). A mortgagee seeking to foreclose must

---

111. See Harms v. Sprague, 473 N.E.2d 930 (Ill. 1984) [DKA & S, p. 330]; [M & S, p. 611].

follow specific procedures, with detailed notice requirements and other procedural protections. This is all vitally important to banks and property owners alike but does not implicate core property issues or concepts. From a property perspective, the interesting aspect of mortgages and foreclosure is the possibility of multiple parties with an interest in the same property, and how the law mediates between their claims.

Today, thanks to sophisticated financial markets, a single piece of property can be subject to multiple mortgages and liens. For example, someone buying property in a homeowner's association may take out an initial mortgage to purchase the property, may later take out a second mortgage to finance a home renovation, and may also be subject to a lien by the homeowner's association for nonpayment of annual dues. All three creditors will need to be paid off before the mortgagor can recover money left over (if any). And, they will be paid off according to their priority, which depends again on recordation.

As noted above, a mortgage includes a recordable security interest in the underlying property. Therefore, when a mortgagee issues a mortgage, it should record that mortgage in the relevant records office. That way, if the owner seeks to sell the property or take out additional mortgages, subsequent buyers or creditors will take subject to the original mortgagee's prior claim to the property. Consider the following common situation. A buyer takes out a mortgage of $200,000 to buy property worth $300,000. Subsequently, the buyer seeks to take out a second mortgage. In deciding how much to lend, the second mortgagee will need to assess the property's value as a security interest. Assuming it still has a market value of $300,000, a title search by the new lender will determine that the buyer only has $100,000 of equity in the house (because it is subject to the original $200,000 mortgage). Moreover, the mortgagees will be paid back in order, not proportionately with their loans. The first mortgagee will be paid back in full before the second mortgagee will take anything. The second mortgagee will therefore be willing to lend based only on collateral valued at $100,000.

This highlights an interesting circularity problem that can arise in race-notice jurisdictions. Imagine that an owner takes out a $200,000 mortgage with Bank A, which does not record its interest. The owner then takes out an additional $100,000 mortgage with Bank B, after telling the bank about the prior mortgage. Bank B records. The owner then takes out a third mortgage for $50,000 with Bank C, which does not know of the prior two mortgages. Bank C records. If the owner defaults, and the property is sold in foreclosure for $250,000, how should the proceeds be distributed in a race-notice jurisdiction?

The problem is this: Bank A has priority over Bank B, because Bank B had actual notice of the prior mortgage. Bank B has priority over Bank C because Bank B recorded first. But Bank C has priority over Bank A because Bank C had no actual notice of Bank A's mortgage, and Bank C recorded first. Although courts and commentators disagree about the reasoning, the best outcome seeks to fulfill each mortgagee's expectations as fully as possible. The key is to work backwards. Starting with Bank C, it knew only that its security interest was junior to Bank B's $100,000 mortgage. Therefore, when the property was sold for $250,000, it reasonably expected there would be enough equity in the property to satisfy its claim, and it should therefore be paid back in full. Likewise, Bank B knew its $100,000 mortgage was subject to Bank A's $200,000 mortgage. When the property was sold for $250,000, Bank B should only have expected to receive $50,000. That leaves $150,000 for Bank A. And, while Bank A expected to be repaid in full—there were no prior mortgages—Bank A also did not record and so bears the risk of other mortgagees' claims. And this is, in fact the likely outcome: Bank A gets $150,000; Bank B gets $50,000; Bank C gets $50,000; and the borrower gets nothing.

Mortgages raise many other issues and problems that fall outside core property doctrines. The important conceptual takeaway from the material is simply this: mortgages create security interests in property that simultaneously allow people to borrow money, but that confer to the lender property rights in the underlying collateral.

D.   Mortgage Markets and the Problem of Securitization

Today, looking at mortgages from the perspective of a single bank lending money to an individual borrower is as quaint as examining the problem of acquisition from the perspective of fox-hunters. Mortgages are now part of an incredibly complex web of financial transactions. And, while the details of those transactions are topics for advanced study in other areas of law, understanding their broad outlines is nevertheless useful for seeing how mortgages work in practice, and the risks they represent.[112] But that first requires understanding banks and how they make money.

---

112. Increasingly, too, this material is presented in first year property classes because it is particularly topical following the collapse of the housing market in

In their simplest form, banks take in deposits and put that money to work by extending loans. Banks then make money by charging higher interest rates to borrowers than they pay to depositors. Someone opening a savings account might receive 1% interest from the bank, but the bank will take that deposit and lend it to a homebuyer who has to pay 6% interest back to the bank. That interest rate spread (here, the difference between 1% and 6%) is revenue for the bank.

At one time, banks were highly local institutions. Money for banks came from local depositors, and borrowers were primarily local mortgagors. This worked well enough for small stable communities—think Jimmy Stewart in "It's A Wonderful Life"—but came under increasing pressure when development began extending in earnest to new parts of the country, like the South and the West. Local banks in newly developing communities, or in communities facing a housing boom, did not have the depositor base to fund demand for mortgages. A bank, after all, has to have the cash on hand to lend out to borrowers who will repay slowly over time. Once a bank is out of money to lend, it must either stop lending until it gets paid back, or find new sources of money to raise capital.

Enter securitization. Starting in the 1930s, the federal government created agencies and, later, private but federally backed corporations—Fannie Mae and Freddy Mac (together, Fannie & Freddy, or "F & F")—to recapitalize local banks by buying their loans.[113] In the traditional model, a bank would take $100,000 of its deposits, and extend a $100,000 loan in exchange for a promise to repay at, say, 6% over 30 years, secured by the underlying property. The loan would actually pay the bank approximately $215,000 (for its initial investment of $100,000), but over 30 years. Under the new model, F & F would simply buy out the income stream from the bank for a fixed amount upfront. F & F would pay, for example, $110,000 today for the right to collect the 6% interest payments into the future. In additional, F & F would pay the bank to continue "servicing" the loan (collecting payments, dealing with delinquencies and even foreclosures, etc.). Now, instead of receiving monthly payments on its loan for the next 30 years, the bank would receive a fresh pile of cash (including a modest profit) that it could turn around and lend out all over again.

2008. What follows is only one of several possible narrative accounts of the mortgage meltdown.

113. For another version of this general account, see [M & S, p. 846–49].

This looks like a win-win situation for everyone involved. F & F make money on their own interest rate spread. They borrow money to buy up mortgages and make money on the difference between the interest rates on their debt, and the mortgage income coming in. But, unlike traditional banks, F & F are not dependent on local depositors for their money. Instead, they can access much more money than local banks by issuing bonds to investors. What's more, because they are government supported enterprises, investors traditionally viewed the debt as particularly safe and therefore allowed F & F to borrow money at very low interest rates (i.e., F & F's bonds pay very little interest). The banks benefit by securing an immediate profit upfront, and replenishing their capital to enable them to make more loans. And borrowers benefit because this process increases the availability of mortgages generally, and keeps prices down. Moreover, Congress imposed limits on the loans that F & F were allowed to buy. The loans had to contain certain pro-consumer terms, like fixed interest rates and no pre-payment penalties. They also were capped at loan-to-value (LTV) ratios of 80%, meaning that the loan could not be for more than 80% of the appraised value of the property, which required borrowers to provide an equity "cushion" of 20% themselves. Because banks wanted to resell their loans to F & F, their off-the-rack mortgage agreements contained these terms, making 30–year fixed prime rate mortgages something of an industry standard.

The federal government's involvement in mortgage markets has not always been for the good, however. There is a long history of racial discrimination in mortgage markets. From the 1930s to the 1960s, the federal government, through the Federal Housing Administration (FHA) was complicit in this discrimination. Banks engaged in a practice known as redlining—literally, drawing a red line around certain predominantly minority communities in which they would not lend. Reinforcing that practice, the FHA had a program to guarantee certain kinds of residential loans, but not in most of those redlined areas. The result was to starve these minority communities of access to credit, which in turn suppressed property values. After all, if traditional mortgages are not available to buy property in a certain area, the cost of borrowing goes up, and the purchasing power of buyers goes down. This, in turn, made it more difficult for minority owners to attain economic stability because their property did not increase in value very much. It also led to disinvestment in the communities, and to a troubling cycle of poverty.

To confront this history of discrimination, Congress, in 1977, passed the Community Reinvestment Act, which was intended to stimulate bank lending to minority and traditionally underserved communities. As mortgages slowly became available in communities that had traditionally been denied access to ready credit, property values began to increase dramatically.

Banks suddenly saw increased opportunities to make money in these formerly credit-starved communities. While many of the borrowers did not have credit scores allowing them to take out prime rate mortgages, the underlying property was increasing in value so quickly that banks perceived little risk in the loans. Even if a borrower defaulted, banks viewed their security interest in the underlying property as very safe. This was a potential goldmine for banks that could charge higher interest rates to borrowers with less than perfect credit, but still underwrite loans that were very safe because of the increasing property values. Banks were not the only ones to notice this business opportunity; Wall Street noticed, too.

Wall Street had traditionally been shut out of the mortgage securitization market. Because F & F were government sponsored entities, with an implied guarantee by the federal government, they could borrow money more cheaply than almost any other private investors. As a result, no one could compete with them meaningfully in the market for prime real estate loans—the loans Congress authorized F & F to buy. But F & F were not allowed to buy subprime loans, that is, loans to borrowers too risky to receive the prime rate. Wall Street was not subject to this limitation. Wall Street bankers therefore realized that they could buy subprime mortgages from the banks without competition from F & F. All Wall Street needed were investors for these mortgages.

The problem for Wall Street, then, was figuring out how to sell subprime mortgages to investors, and specifically to large institutional investors (the ones with the most money), who were often required to invest in financial instruments with a AAA credit rating (reflecting the safest investments). Creative investment bankers came up with the following plan. They would buy up a large number of subprime loans and bundle them together in a special purpose vehicle (SPV) that owned the entire pool of mortgages. They would then divide that pool into "tranches," defined by which loans continued to perform. To take a hugely simplified and stylized example, the investment bank would bundle together 100 loans, worth, say $10 million. It would then create 3 tranches. The best would be whichever 30 loans continued to perform. The next would be the 40 loans that continued to perform after that. And the last—and worst—would be the first 30 loans to fail. Notice, then, that the top tranche consisted of whichever 30 of the 100 loans continued to perform. The investment bankers did not need to know which particular loans those would be; all they needed to know was that, on average, at least 30 loans in any pool of 100 would continue to perform. In this case, that top tranche of loans suddenly looks quite safe, safe enough, in fact, to receive a AAA rating from the credit rating agencies. Voilá. The investment banks transformed subprime mortgages to borrowers with poor credit ratings into AAA-rated securities that could be sold to institutional investors.

They did not stop there. After the investment banks sold off the top tranche (the income from the top 30 of the loans in their pool), they were left with two other tranches with less than AAA ratings. The solution was to rebundle and retranche. That is, take the middle tranche from 10 different SPVs, bundle them up together, and retranche into a high, middle, and low category. While the banks may not have been able to predict which of the loans in those middle tranches were likely to go bad, they believed they could predict with some measure of certainty that some percentage would continue to perform, and by defining the top tranche by that percentage they generated a new AAA-rated security. The process could be iterated and reiterated, leading at times to rebundling and retranching ten or even twelve times.

This created a new appetite for subprime loans. And it was precisely subprime loans that Wall Street most wanted because F & F were boxed out of that market and because those loans paid higher interest rates. Moreover, the banks' financial models all viewed those loans as safer than borrowers' credit ratings suggested because property values were increasing. If a borrower was at risk of default, she could always refinance based on the new, higher value of her property, or could sell. The risk of actual default was therefore minimal, or so banks thought. Banks began to originate loans with 100% or even 110% loan-to-value ratios, because within a few years—or even sometimes within a few months—the property values would catch up and transform them into relatively conservative 80% LTV loans.

Everyone now knows that this did not end well. As the economy slowed, people stopped being able to make their loan payments. The banks' financial models contemplated such defaults for some number of borrowers, but defaults started happening on a far wider scale than financial analysis has anticipated. Buyers grew scarce, and banks stopped refinancing loans based on earlier models' aggressive assumptions. Faced with loans they could not repay, and banks unwilling to refinance, homeowners began to default even more. This, in turn, generated an increase in foreclosures, which put additional downward pressure on property values. Suddenly, an over-collateralized pool of loans in an SPV was under-collateralized because of the drop in home values. Loans stopped performing, so SPVs stopped generating their anticipated income, and investors, banks, and insurance companies—most notably, AIG—were left holding the bag, either as investors in SPVs, or as holders of sophisticated financial instruments based on those SPVs. All of this had a spiral effect, as further economic decline further depressed property values, leading to the monumental collapse of the real estate market in 2008 and the general economic crisis that followed.

This is more than an interesting and sobering economic history, however. As an account of economic collapse, it contains a number of hidden property concepts and problems, and so a property lens helps to make sense of it all, even if it does not generate specific prescriptions.

A pressing question raised by this recent history is why the banks allowed borrowers to go into default, precipitating a foreclosure crisis, instead of modifying the loans to work with borrowers to keep them in their homes. Conventional wisdom is that everyone loses with foreclosure. It imposes tremendous administrative costs on banks, and usually requires them to sell the property at a discount because foreclosure sales rarely yield the value of a voluntarily private sale. For loans with aggressive LTVs, this might result in a substantial loss on the loan for the bank. The borrower, of course, is harmed by foreclosure, which will usually take away her property and hurt her credit rating, making it harder to buy again in the future.

Core property concepts provide some hints at answers. First and foremost is a problem of fractionated ownership. Bundling, rebundling, and tranching loans through multiple SPVs makes it very difficult for the loan servicers—typically, the originating banks—to know who will be harmed and who will benefit from a work-out instead of foreclosure. Investment bankers sliced and diced the actual economic value of mortgages in an SPV to an extent that real economic interests became abstract and difficult to discern. Someone might own the first 20 loans to be foreclosed, someone else the income stream from a number of loans for the first 5 years, someone else the income stream from the next 5, and so on. The loan servicer might reasonably worry that working out a loan—redefining the interest rate, the length of the loan, or writing down some of the principle—might well affect certain classes of investors in unpredictable ways, and open the loan servicer to legal liability. True, any decision—including the decision to foreclose—will affect those economic stake-holders in unpredictable ways, but the procedures for foreclosing on property require much less discretion than working out a loan. In short, then, the foreclosure crisis is partly the result of overly fragmented ownership—economic interests that are hard to rebundle into a well-functioning unit of property.

Furthermore, banks do not internalize all of the costs of foreclosure. While foreclosure does impose costs on banks, as noted above, it also imposes significant costs on neighboring property and the entire community. Even a single foreclosure can have a detrimental impact on neighbors' property values. During the foreclosure process, the property may be inadequately maintained. And, since foreclosed property often sells at something of a fire-sale discount, it can drag down values for all similarly situated properties. Add several foreclosures to a neighborhood and the effect can be devastating. It can destabilize communities and lead to a long-term downward spiral. If a foreclosing bank holds the mortgages on other properties in the area, it will internalize at least some of these costs because the collateral securing its other loans will decrease in response to the foreclosure. But there are still likely to be costs—and significant ones—that are borne by other neighbors and that the foreclosing bank does not internalize. Therefore, when comparing the relative costs and benefits of foreclosure versus workouts, banks may choose foreclosure too often.

There are also serious transaction costs associated with working out loans, perhaps the most important but least obvious of which is the effect on other borrowers. If banks were to begin making loan modifications for borrowers in default, more borrowers might go into default. Distinguishing good-faith but struggling borrowers from strategic borrowers seeking to capitalize on the situation might impose considerable information costs on banks. If those information costs are high enough, banks might actually prefer the suboptimal outcome of foreclosure for individual loans in order to prevent a cascade of delinquencies and threatened defaults.

There are undoubtedly additional pressures complicating both the causes of, and potential responses to, the wave of foreclosures instead of loan modifications. But regardless of the causes, courts have come under added pressure to handle the unprecedented number of foreclosure cases working their way through the system. And, interestingly, some courts have been relying on consumer protection laws, and technical requirements from the law of commercial paper, to protect borrowers from foreclosure. For example, in *Commonwealth v. Fremont Investment & Loan*,[114] the state Attorney General claimed that loans with specific characteristics

---

114.   897 N.E.2d 548 (Mass. 2008) [DKA & S, p. 630]; [S, p. 84].

violated state consumer protection laws because they were essentially doomed to end in foreclosure unless real estate prices continued to rise.[115] The state Supreme Court upheld a trial court order that those loans were unfair under state law. Therefore, prior to foreclosing on such loans, banks were ordered to attempt to work with the Attorney General's office to restructure the loans and, if that failed, to obtain judicial approval before commencing a foreclosure action.

The defendant, a bank holding a number of mortgages with the proscribed characteristics, objected that the state was changing the standard of "fair" lending practices retroactively, and that this would have a chilling effect on future lending. The state Supreme Court disagreed, finding that the defendant should have known its practices were unfair at the time it initiated the loans. Furthermore, the court pointed out that its remedy did not preclude foreclosure, but instead required banks to jump through certain hoops before foreclosing. In other words, it made foreclosure more expensive, but not impossible. The Court was therefore skeptical about any chilling effect on future lending, although it is almost certainly true that increasing the cost of foreclosure will make loans marginally more expensive in the future.

An even more dramatic remedy has emerged in some of the challenges to foreclosure actions based on the law of commercial paper. In another case out of Massachusetts, the state Supreme Court invalidated two foreclosure actions on grounds that the foreclosing banks could not demonstrate that they actually held the mortgages at the time of the foreclosure.[116] The problem came from the process of securitization. The court described the series of transactions surrounding the mortgages. After a mortgage company originated the loans, they were held by the Option One Mortgage Corporation. That corporation then assigned the mortgages to an investment bank, which pooled the mortgages and sold securities based on those pools. When the loans defaulted, the investment bank then assigned the loans to another bank as a loan servicer in order to foreclose on the property. At least, that is what was supposed to have happened. The problem for the loan servicer was that it could not demonstrate that the assignments of the loans had actually taken place. The loans were supposedly listed in a large

---

115. Those characteristics included loans with an adjustable rate mortgage (ARM) beginning at a low teaser rate before resetting to a higher rate; that have a debt-to-income ratio of greater than 50% after reset; that required no down payment; and that had either a loan-to-value ratio of 100% (or greater) or a substantial prepayment penalty.

116. See United States Bank Nat'l Assoc. v. Ibanez, 941 N.E.2d 40 (Mass. 2011) [M & S, p. 849].

index of loans transferred from the originating bank and to the investment bank, but no one could produce the index. Nor could anyone produce any other paperwork demonstrating that the mortgages had actually been assigned. Since only the holder of the mortgage has the right to foreclose on the property, an inability to establish ownership is fatal to a foreclosure action. The state Supreme Court therefore held that the foreclosing entity could not demonstrate that it had actually been assigned the mortgage, and therefore did not have a right to foreclose.

If no one has the ability to foreclose on the property, the borrowers would appear to be off the hook for their mortgage payments. This is a dramatic outcome because no one disputed that the mortgagors in fact originated mortgages that they had not yet repaid. Perhaps banks could bring something like unjust enrichment actions to try to collect on the mortgage payments still due, but their security interest in the underlying property disappears if they lose the right to foreclose.

Although the dust from this and other similar cases is still settling, it implicates very important issues. It appears increasingly that many banks' record-keeping practices were more than a little bit sloppy. And this is an area of law in which records matter. While the common law of property is often governed by general standards, and implicates broad issues of social policy, it is important to remember that compliance with the law's technical requirements remains critically important. In at least some, if not many cases, banks are unable to establish that they have the right to foreclose. Courts must therefore decide whether to forgive the banks' non-compliance with the technical requirements for assigning mortgages, or allow borrowers to escape the threat of foreclosure. Either is a harsh result.

On the one hand are borrowers who really do owe money that they promised to repay. On the other are banks with such shoddy paperwork that they cannot even demonstrate who owns the mortgage. Neither party has clean hands, and courts are having to navigate this terrain with the fate of banks, and the economy, hanging in the balance. If it turns out that banks cannot establish who has the right to foreclose on many loans, then borrowers may stop repaying and banks, without recourse to their security interest in the property, will take enormous losses. But, of course, if banks are excused for their poor paperwork and weak, if not predatory, lending practices, then the wave of foreclosures they may precipitate could crush property values—and individual property owners— even more.

We do not yet know how this story ends, but there can be little doubt that the global economy balanced, for a time, on the transferability of mortgage interests, and on the application of property recordation.

* * *

Land sales and mortgages implicate a host of core property concepts, and not just because they involve that most basic and familiar form of property: land. Fundamentally, they raise interesting new questions about the divisibility of property rights. Where there have been serial buyers of the same property (i.e. Buyer One and Buyer Two), their rights against each other will depend on recordation and notice. Even though it may seem that the "first" purchaser should win—consistent with the over-arching principle of first-in-time—recordation and notice may actually provide superior title to the purchaser who was second-in-time.

Likewise, mortgages create simultaneous rights to the underlying property in both the mortgagor and mortgagee. Dividing property in this way, and allowing mortgagees to lend based on a security interest in the underlying collateral, unlocks tremendous economic value. Banks and other mortgagees are willing to extend loans because of their recourse to the underlying property. Dividing mortgages further, and securitizing pools of mortgages through complex financial transactions, unlocks even more value and liquidity . . . to a point. But past that point, as we have seen, the property interests become so fragmented and esoteric that they are difficult and costly to reassemble, to the detriment of borrowers, banks, and the entire economy.

Part III

SERVITUDES

The law of servitudes, which includes easements, covenants, and equitable servitudes, serves as a useful bridge between the divisibility of ownership and land use controls. Fundamentally, this constellation of doctrines is about giving someone the right to use, or the right to restrict the use of, someone else's property. It is, therefore, about separating the right to use from the rest of the sticks in the bundle of ownership. But the effect is to control how people use real property. Covenants and equitable servitudes, in particular, have traditionally served as the basis for many private restrictions in land use developments like homeowners associations.

The law of servitudes also provides a particularly vivid example of common law evolution. Over time, the technical and complex rules for creating real covenants have largely given way to more flexible equitable servitudes, which in turn are now being replaced by a single, more capacious category: "servitudes." When feeling bogged down by the complicated doctrines governing this area of law, it is useful to look up at the light at the end of the tunnel—a legal landscape that today is far simpler and more straightforward than it once was. Still, understanding the history remains important both because it reveals ongoing doctrinal issues, and because the older categories remain good law in many jurisdictions. The law in this area is evolving, but—as with the law of estates and future interests—the transformation is not yet complete.

Chapter 9

EASEMENTS

A. Terminology

An easement, fundamentally, is a right to use someone else's land in a specific way. Classic examples include a right-of-way for a driveway, or access for power lines, telephone lines, or sewer pipes crossing over someone else's property. Any easement necessarily involves at least two parties: the owner of the underlying land, and the person with the right to use it. The following diagram demonstrates the use of an easement for a driveway to get from the public road (on the west side of the property) to a house on Lot B.

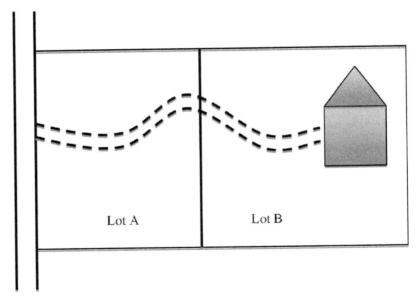

In this picture, the property subject to—burdened by—the easement is Lot A, and is called the "servient tenement". The property benefitted by the easement, Lot B, is the "dominant tenement".

Easements can be either appurtenant or in gross. That is, the benefit of an easement—like the right to cross over someone else's land—can be held either by an individual, or can run with specific property. In the picture above, the owner of Lot B has the right to cross over Lot A to access her house. But what if the owner of Lot B sells her house? Does she retain the right to cross over Lot A, or does that right transfer to the new owner of Lot B? It depends. If the easement is appurtenant, it transfers to the new owner. If it is in gross, it remains with the original owner. In this example, after the owner of Lot B sells her house, it does not do her any good to be able to cross over Lot A any longer, and the parties would almost certainly have created an appurtenant easement.

Easements in gross can be important in other contexts, however. For example, someone might obtain an easement, not to reach their own land, but instead to access a lovely fishing spot on a river, hiking trails, and the like. Those uses may not depend on living next door, and the owner of the dominant tenement might want to retain those use rights no matter where she lives. While the law will generally presume that easements are appurtenant, the parties can create easements in gross, if they want.

It is also important to distinguish easements from other interests that look like easements: profits and licenses. A profit is the right to enter someone else's land in order to remove something from it. A logging company, for example, would obtain a profit to come and remove trees from someone else's land; a mining company could use a profit to enter to take minerals.

A license, by contrast, is merely a short-term right to enter someone else's property, revocable at any time. When a plumber or a dinner guest comes over, they are subject to a license—a temporary right to enter, for a specific purpose. A homeowner is, of course, free to revoke that license any time, firing the plumber or ending the dinner party.

B. Creating Easements

Easements look superficially like plain vanilla contracts. Two parties, the dominant and servient tenement holders, agree to some right-of-way in exchange for consideration. But easements are, in fact, a special kind of contract because they can bind successive owners. The easement can remain in place even if the servient tenement holder sells her property, and an appurtenant easement can survive sales of both the servient and the dominant estates. That is unusual as a matter of contract law because third-party buyers are not in privity of contract with the original counterparties. The new servient tenement holder never entered into a contract with the original dominant tenement holder and yet remains bound by the easement if it runs with the land.

There is an obvious need for such a device. Where the beneficial use of some parcel of land requires access to someone else's land—whether for a driveway, power lines, or a sewer—it can be important to secure that right in a way that binds future parties, otherwise the dominant tenement holder will not be able to rely on the easement continuing into the future. Imagine someone wanting to build a house that required access over a neighbor's land. It would be easy enough but also entirely insufficient to enter into a contract that bound only the current neighbor. The neighbor could escape the contract simply by conveying to a third party. Moreover, the neighbor will sell or die eventually, at which point the dominant tenement holder would have to renegotiate access with the new owner. But this is now a negotiation on completely different terms, because the dominant tenement holder has already built a house relying on the right to access the property; the servient tenement holder will therefore be able to extract a substantial premium—in fact, every successive servient tenement holder will have this ability. The more likely outcome, then, is that the dominant tenement holder simply would not build in the first place. Without a mechanism for securing access into the future, the property will go under-used. By running with the land and binding future successors, easements can enable reliance into the future, and in the process make everyone better off.

A doctrinal consequence of this power is that easements are subject to the statute of frauds because they are interests in land and not personal contracts. Typically, then, an easement must be in writing, and is governed by the relevant recordation act. Explicit, negotiated easements are usually unproblematic. So long as the parties execute and record a written agreement, successive owners will be bound.

There are, however, a number of exceptions to the writing requirement for an easement, and this is where the doctrine becomes considerably more complicated. The question, then, is when a court will find an easement in the absence of an explicit, written agreement between the parties. This can occur in four different ways, by estoppel, implication, necessity, or prescription.

Estoppel

An easement by estoppel exists when it would be inequitable to allow the servient tenement holder to cancel a license on which the dominant tenement holder reasonably relied. More specifically, if the dominant tenement holder expends significant resources in reliance on the continued existence of a license, then that license may eventually become irrevocable through estoppel. This doctrine shares a rationale with the purpose of easements more broadly; it permits reasonable reliance on a servient tenement holder's representations about a right to continued use of the property.

Holbrook v. Taylor[117] demonstrates both how this can work, and also some of the complexity lurking behind the doctrine. In *Holbrook*, the Taylors bought property and built a house, gaining access to their land by using a road that crossed over the Holbrooks' land. The Taylors claimed that the Holbrooks had given them permission to improve the road, to use it for access to build their house, and even to continue using it after their house was built. Approximately 5 years later, however, the Holbrooks sought to commit the agreement to writing—in what the Taylors claimed was an effort to extort a purchase of the underlying property—and the parties could not agree. In response, the Holbrooks closed off access over their property by putting a steel cable across the road, and the Taylors sued.

According to the *Holbrook* court, a license can become irrevocable if the licensee reasonably relies on it to make improvements "at considerable expense." Here, the Taylors improved the right-of-way and built a house, relying on their ongoing ability to access their property. Because the Holbrooks did not enforce their right to exclude, watching as the Taylors spent money to develop their land, they were estopped from terminating the license.

Viewed *ex post*, this ruling makes perfectly good sense. After all, if the Taylors could not access their house, it would become effectively worthless to them, either because it could not be used at all, or because the Holbrooks would be able to capture most of its value. The Taylors had spent approximately $25,000 building their house (this was the 1960s, remember). Faced with the option of either losing their investment, or paying for an easement, they should be willing to pay nearly the full value of the house, if not more, for the easement. This would seem unfair to the Taylors. It is somewhat surprising, then, that the Holbrooks appeared ready to sell the easement to the Taylors for only $500; it is incredibly surprising that the Taylors refused!

But viewed from a different temporal perspective, the equities start to look quite different. There was, of course, no reason that the Taylors had to wait until after their house was built to try to negotiate a permanent easement over the Holbrooks' land. While they may not have known they needed such an easement—perhaps assuming that the road was public, or that they already had an easement—that cost of that mistake should perhaps be on them.

---

117.   532 S.W.2d 763 (Ky. 1976) [DKA & S, p. 774]; [M & S, p. 997]; [S, p. 427].

They had the capacity to search the land records and otherwise engage in the diligence necessary to ensure that they had access to their own property. And upon finding they did not, they should have negotiated for it up front before investing so much in building a house. In a sense, the court is bailing out the Taylors for their lack of diligence *ex ante*.

It is therefore clear enough what the Taylors could have done to avoid the problem, securing their rights ahead of time. The Holbrooks, however, faced a different kind of problem *ex ante*. Assume, for a moment, that they had wanted to be neighborly— that they had no problem allowing the Taylors to use the road to build their house and even thereafter, but that they wanted to retain the right to stop the use sometime in the future. It is not as clear what they could have done. Perhaps granting an express license, with a clear right to revoke in the future, might have prevented the Taylor's estoppel claim. But that puts a significant burden on the Holbrooks to draft a document and present it to their neighbors as a formal but limited grant of permission to use the roadway. While this is certainly intelligible, and would have been the safest course for the Holbrooks, it is not obvious why the burden should have been on them to protect their rights instead of on the Taylors to secure theirs. It was certainly more neighborly to rely on informal understandings rather than go to the lawyers up front.

As an equitable doctrine, there is no hard-and-fast rule about when an easement by estoppel will arise. Imagine that the Holbrooks had told the Taylors explicitly that they could use the roadway forever, but had never put it in writing. This would not create an express easement by grant because it would not satisfy the statute of frauds. But an estoppel claim is easier to justify if the Taylors had then relied on that explicit but otherwise unenforceable representation to invest in their own property. It is, of course, possible to imagine that a servient tenement holder's inaction in the face of an obvious mistake about the status of a right-of-way could justify the same outcome; sometimes silence communicates a misrepresentation almost as effectively as an affirmative lie. And that is perhaps the best way to understand *Holbrook*. For an easement by estoppel, the servient tenement holder must make some kind of representation about future access, either affirmatively or tacitly, on which the dominant tenement holder then reasonably relies. In that situation, the revocable license may become irrevocable despite the absence of a writing.

Implication

Easements by implication—or, more precisely, easements implied by prior existing use—are a second exception to the writing requirement. They arise, if at all, when property is divided. If, at the time of the division, a pre-existing use of one part of the property benefits another part, that use might give rise to an easement by implication. This is best explored by returning to the diagram at the beginning of this Chapter.

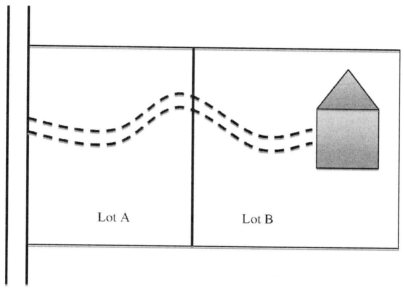

In the new example, though, Lots A and B start with a single owner. The public road and nearest access is on the west side of the property, and the owner uses the driveway (represented by the curved, dotted lines) to get from the road to her house. If the owner then divides the lots in two and sells Lot B, retaining Lot A for herself, can the buyer continue to use the driveway to get to the house *in the absence of an explicit written easement*? The answer depends on the availability of an easement implied by prior existing use.

It is important to understand that, prior to the division of the property, the homeowner could not have had an easement to access her house. You cannot have an easement over your own property. It is incoherent to separate the right to use from the other sticks in the bundle of ownership if they are all retained by the same person.

When someone crosses over part of her property to get to another part of her property, that is not an easement; that is simply ownership. Nevertheless, a court may characterize that use as a *quasi*-easement. The term is more evocative than analytically helpful, however; it simply means that there is some prior existing use of part of the property that benefits another part. The problem is deciding when that prior existing use—the driveway in the example above—should ripen into a full-blown easement once the property is divided.

Why should an easement ever arise by implication in this situation? The overriding goal of this doctrine of easement implied by prior existing use is to satisfy parties' expectations (actual, or objectively reasonable). If the parties had notice of the *quasi*-easement, and the easement was sufficiently important to the use and enjoyment of the benefitted property, a court may presume that the parties intended for the use to remain in place after the transaction, even in the absence of a written agreement. In the example above, any buyer might reasonably expect that the house came with the use of the driveway to access it. Failure to secure that right formally and in writing might reflect sloppy lawyering, but courts are sometimes willing to allow the easement to exist by implication if it appears consistent with parties' reasonable expectations.

The equities look a little bit different, however, if the seller retained the house, and tried to claim an implied easement over Lot A. The law distinguishes between two situations: an easement by implied grant, and an easement by implied reservation. The difference between the two is simply whether the original owner retained the dominant or the servient tenement. If the original owner retained the servient tenement—as in the example above where the seller retained Lot A—then the claimed easement would come from an implied grant. The claim is that the original owner, when selling the dominant tenement, impliedly granted an easement over the property she retained (the servient tenement). But if the original owner retained the dominant tenement—say, selling Lot A, and keeping Lot B—then the easement must arise through implied reservation. That is, the original owner impliedly reserved an easement for her own benefit and thereby burdened the land she sold.

Courts have traditionally been more hostile to implying easements by reservation than by grant, in some jurisdictions prohibiting easements by implied reservation altogether. If an owner wanted to retain the right to cross over property she was selling, she should have reserved it explicitly. Courts have long held that

162

buyers can be forgiven more easily than sellers for thinking that a pre-existing *quasi*-easement will be allowed to continue. Underlying this difference is the intuition that a seller has an informational advantage over a buyer. Even after conducting due diligence, a buyer may not fully appreciate the significance of, or need for, securing a particular right-of-way or other pre-existing use of the property.

While the hostility to easements by implied reservation remains, many jurisdictions have followed the Restatement (Third) of Property, and treated this merely as one factor to consider when deciding whether to recognize an easement by implication.[118] Other factors include the terms of the conveyance, the necessity of the easement for the reasonable use of the benefitted property, and whether the parties knew or should have known of the pre-existing use. All of these again go to the parties' likely intent in the transaction, and are worth considering in order.

Obviously, if the conveyance itself expressly reveals the parties' intent, that will carry significant weight. But assuming the conveyance is silent, necessity is an important factor. The more necessary a use, the more likely the parties intended for it to continue. A driveway is one thing, a zip-line as part of a child's jungle gym may be something else altogether.

Parties' intent can sometimes also be discerned from the consideration paid by the buyer. Someone might intend to sell property with no driveway or utility access, but that should be reflected in the purchase price. In at least some cases, purchase price can reveal what the parties intended.

The parties' actual or constructive notice of the prior use is somewhat more complicated because it relates to both the creation of the easement at the time the property is divided, and whether the unrecorded easement will run against successors. Take *Van Sandt v. Royster*.[119] There, a single owner, Laura Bailey, subdivided her property into three separate lots, conveying two of them to purchasers and retaining the third for herself. At the time of the subdivision, a sewer line ran across the entire property, providing modern (as of 1904!) plumbing to the house that Bailey retained. Bailey did not, however, expressly reserve an easement for the sewer line crossing over the lots she sold.

---

118. Restatement (Third) of Property, Servitudes § 2.12 (2000) ("Although grantors might be expected to know that they should expressly reserve any use rights they intend to retain after severance, experience has shown that too often they do not.").

119. 83 P.2d 698 (1938) [DKA & S, p. 779].

The two buyers built houses on their lots and connected them to the sewer line. At that point, the lot nearest the road—Lot 19, in the opinion—was the servient tenement; the sewer line passed through that Lot to the benefit of the other two lots. The middle lot—Lot 20—was both a dominant and servient tenement: dominant as to Lot 19, and servient as to the lot Bailey retained.

Eventually, the sewer pipe backed up and began to overflow on Lot 19, the servient tenement, prompting litigation over the continued use of the pipe. The issues, specifically, were whether Bailey created an easement by implied reservation for the sewer pipe over Lot 19, and then whether that easement ran to the current owners.

The court had relatively little trouble concluding that Bailey had created an easement by implied reservation. The court pointed out that the original purchasers knew the sewer pipe existed—they connected their own houses to it—and that it was reasonably necessary for the comfortable enjoyment of the dominant parcels. This is precisely the situation that easements by implication are intended to remedy; the original parties appear to have expected that the sewer line would remain in place, and would be available to the new buyers as well.

By the time the litigation commenced, however, none of the lot owners were the original parties to the subdivision. It was therefore a different question whether the easement should run against successors. While the power of easements is that they can run with the land, an unwritten easement interferes with the law's protection for *bona fide* purchasers. Recall from the discussion of recordation that a good-faith purchaser can take property free and clear of unknown clouds on title.[120] Quite simply, an easement will be unenforceable against the servient tenement if a buyer did not know, and should not have known, that the easement existed. Recordation will typically provide that notice, but in *Van Sandt*— where the easement was implied and never the subject of a written grant—the easement had never been recorded.

Nevertheless, the *Van Sandt* court held that the sewer easement was sufficiently obvious to have put the current owner on notice of its existence. It was not "obvious" in any visible sense; it was, after all, buried under ground. But the court found that the buyers had adequate notice of the existence of the sewer pipe, because "[t]hey knew the house was equipped with modern plumbing and that the plumbing had to drain into a sewer." This seems like a bit of a stretch. It is one thing to know you have toilets, and

---

120. See Chapter 8(B).

another to know there is a sewer easement running across the property.

Perhaps more than anything, the court viewed utility access as both routine and unnoticed. Even if most parties would not *actually* be aware of utility access across their property, they would be unlikely to object if they were. Or, to put it differently, sewer and utility easements are perhaps so ubiquitous and—generally—inoffensive that courts will impute knowledge of them to buyers. This is no sure thing, and utility easements are routinely recorded, but courts may be willing to bail out parties who fail to do so, as in *Van Sandt*.

Ultimately, courts will imply easements from prior existing uses when the persistence of the easement is consistent with the parties' imputed intent.

Necessity

Easements by necessity occur in only one circumstance: when a property conveyance landlocks a parcel. When that happens, the law may recognize an easement by necessity to create access over the last lot sold, creating the landlocked parcel.

It is important to distinguish easements by necessity from easements by implication, which include necessity as a factor. In reality, the two doctrines have little to do with one another and rely on very different justifications. Instead of focusing on parties' intent, easements by necessity are based on a broader concern that parties not be allowed to make property inaccessible. Intent has nothing to do with it. Instead, society loses if property is inaccessible, and the law will not permit it.

Several consequences follow. First, it does not matter whether a *quasi*-easement existed prior to the conveyance. Easements by necessity are not based on a claim of a prior use. Nor does the law particularly care whether the original owner was attempting to convey away a landlocked parcel, or retain it for himself. There is no distinction, in other words, between reservations and grants. In both respects, the doctrine is more powerful than easements implied by prior existing use.

On the other hand, courts have traditionally required strict necessity to imply an easement by necessity. Mere inconvenience is not enough. No sewer? Too bad. No telephone cable? Tough luck. Access only through a swamp, over rugged terrain filled with wild boars? That is still access, and an easement by necessity for a more convenient location will not arise. Under the strict necessity standard, the dominant tenement holder (the owner of the landlocked parcel) must demonstrate that there is no access to the property by any other means. Failure to do so will defeat the claim.

That standard has loosened up in some jurisdictions. Some courts have adopted a reasonable necessity standard, instead of the traditional higher bar. Deciding where to draw the line involves trading off the servient tenement holder's right to exclude against the inefficiency of requiring truly inconvenient, expensive, and maybe even heroic efforts to gain access by another route.

Is there any reason to continue limiting easements by necessity to strict necessity, even if it results in imposing dramatic costs on the dominant parcel? Perhaps there is something qualitatively different about landlocking property; it is not just making it expensive to develop, but actually impossible to use. But that claim is too strong by half. There is nothing to prevent the owner of the landlocked parcel from negotiating for a right-of-way. It might be prohibitively expensive, if the neighbors do not want to grant access, but building an inconvenient driveway might be prohibitively expensive too. If the underlying concern is with preventing the cost to society of landlocking property, there is also a social cost to building overly expensive roads in truly inconvenient places. The doctrinal point is nevertheless clear: there is some degree of necessity—strict or reasonable—that will allow a court to create an easement to provide access to property that would otherwise be landlocked.

Prescription

Easements by prescription are the final exception to the requirement that easements be in writing. They are closely related to adverse possession, and all of the same justifications apply.

Conceptually, a prescriptive easement arises when someone adversely possesses a right to use someone else's property. Unlike adverse possession, this does not involve a claim to own the underlying property, but merely a right to use it. If someone cuts a path through someone else's field, and uses it without permission every day, it will eventually ripen into a prescriptive easement, even if it would not ripen into ownership. If a utility line is in place for long enough, a utility company may have a right to keep it there, although the company does not become the owner of the underlying land.

The elements for a prescriptive easement are essentially the same as for adverse possession. The use must be open and notorious, adverse, and continuous for the statutory period. One difference, however, comes from the exclusivity requirement. Adverse possession requires that the adverse possessor's use be exclusive.

Several people cannot maintain separate adverse possession claims for the same piece of property simultaneously. The lack of exclusivity will defeat an adverse possession claim. Not so with prescriptive easements. If two different neighbors regularly use a private road to access their respective properties, they may both be able to claim prescriptive easements.

There is an exclusivity requirement for prescriptive easements; but it means something different. Exclusivity in this context means that the prescriptive right being claimed does not depend on the rights of others. Or, to put it differently, the claimed use has to be individual and not based on a group. If, for example, a bird-watching group crosses over someone's property every morning for the statutory period (that is a lot of birding!), no individual birder will gain a prescriptive easement. Similarly, even if someone walks through Rockefeller Center every day on the way to work, she will not obtain a prescriptive easement because her access is not sufficiently distinct from the public's.

It is possible, though, for the public itself to obtain a prescriptive easement. If the public regularly uses property—cuts through a courtyard, uses a path through the woods, and so forth—then the public may obtain an easement by prescription. For that reason, the owners of Rockefeller Center close the gates and do not let the public enter on one day every year, in order to stop the statute of limitations from running and to prevent the public from obtaining an easement.[121]

This highlights an important question about how to stop a prescriptive easement claim. How can an owner prevent regular use from ripening into a prescriptive easement? The most common answer is that the owner must actually stop the use. It is not enough to put up a sign asking people to keep out. It may not even be enough to erect a fence if the fence is inadequate to keep people out. The owner has to do more, and actually keep people off the property. Lest this seem a recipe for conflict, the owner can presumably bring a legal action to stop the use in order to forestall physical confrontation and thereby stop the statute of limitations. Alternatively, the owner might be able to make the use permissive. As with adverse possession, hostility is an essential element of a prescriptive easement claim. If the owner explicitly grants a revocable license to the users, this may well prevent the creation of a prescriptive easement (although it might, of course, give rise to an easement by estoppel if the owner is not careful).

* * *

---

121.   [DKA&S, p. 798].

Stepping back from all of these doctrinal details, exceptions to the writing requirement for easements satisfy a number of different purposes. Estoppel, like all equitable doctrines, seeks to prevent unfairness and also to prevent the loss of reasonable investments in property made in good faith reliance on a revocable license. Easements implied from prior existing uses are quite different and seek to give effect to parties' reasonable expectations about the continued use of one piece of property to benefit another. But the purpose is different, still, for easements by necessity, which are about preventing the costs to society of making property inaccessible and effectively removing it from the marketplace. Finally, prescriptive easements validate expectations around the use of property that develop over time. If parties become sufficiently accustomed to using property—for access or for some other purpose—and the owner fails to object, the law will eventually recognize and protect that ongoing use.

As distinct as these doctrines are, they frequently come together in a single set of facts. Someone might plausibly be able to claim an easement under more than one of these theories. *Othen v. Rosier*[122] provides a useful springboard for examining these relationships. There, someone named Hill owned almost 2,500 acres of land. Over time, and long before the litigation, he sold off bits and pieces. Critical to this case, he sold off 100 acres of land in 1896, fronting on the only access road to the property. That property eventually wound up in Rosier's hands. In 1897 (one year after the first sale), Hill sold 60 acres of land further in, and separated from the access road by the parcel he had sold the year before. This latter lot found its way to Othen. A few more parcels were bought and re-sold, but the basic facts were simply these: the Rosier lots were sold first, and were between the Othen lots and the public road. For years, this caused no problem because Othen used a small road—the court referred to it as a lane—passing over the Rosier's property, connecting the public road to a tenant's house on the Rosier land, and then continuing to the Othen property. A conflict arose, however, when flooding prompted the Rosiers to build a large levee, which rendered the lane impassible for long periods of time. Othen sued, claiming interference with his easement over the Rosier property.

There is no doubt that, at the time of the litigation, the Othen lot was entirely landlocked. For Othen to access his property, he had to cross over someone else's land. This immediately implicates the easement by necessity doctrine, which would prevent Othen's

---

122.   226 S.W.2d 622 (Tex. 1950) [DKA & S, p. 786].

lot from becoming inaccessible and therefore unusable. It is one thing, however, to say that Othen should be able to access his land; it is quite another to say that he can cross Rosier's land to do so. According to the *Othen* court, it was unclear whether the sale of the Rosier lots landlocked Othen's land. It is entirely possible that when Hill originally sold the Rosier lots, Othen's lots were still accessible from some other road, from some other direction. Recall that an easement by necessity will only be implied over the lot that finally landlocked a parcel, and the burden is on the party seeking the easement to show the lack of access anywhere else. Othen, in other words, was entitled to an easement by necessity somewhere, but he had the burden of demonstrating which sale landlocked his parcel; unable to meet that burden, Othen lost.

Why not an easement by prescription? Othen himself used the lane over the Rosier property for over 40 years before the levee blocked his access. An easement by prescription would have been consistent with his expectations of continued access, and the owners of the Rosier land had slept on their rights for over four decades. The problem, said the court, is that Othen's use was not adverse. Starting in 1906, the lane was fenced, with gates on either side. By letting Othen use the gates, the Rosiers were implicitly granting him permission to use the lane, and permissive use cannot ripen into a prescriptive easement. Nor could Othen claim a prescriptive easement prior to 1906, because he was unable to demonstrate the precise location of the path he used before the lane was fenced.

There are two other possible bases for establishing an easement, although the *Othen* court did not consider them. First is an easement by estoppel. If the Rosiers (or their predecessors) sat by while Othen built a house on his property, relying on continued access over their property, fairness and equity might demand that the permissive license become unrepealable. In *Othen*, this claim was a non-starter, however, because Texas did not recognize easements by estoppel. In a different jurisdiction, this could have been a successful claim. It would, however, be in some tension with the prescriptive easement claim, which is based on non-consensual use. Othen claimed that he did not have permission to use the lane prior to 1906, making his use adverse. But the estoppel claim requires a permissive license that becomes unrepealable through reliance. If there was no permissive use to begin with, there could be no license, and therefore not estoppel. Of course, these arguments can work in the alternative, and a party can plead both claims, but at the end of the day a court will have to rely on one or the other.

Othen might also have been able to claim an easement implied by prior use, but it too faces factual and doctrinal hurdles. Because Hill sold the Rosier land first, this would have been an easement by implied reservation. That is, Hill would have to have reserved an easement over the Rosier lots for the benefit of the land he retained, and courts are generally more hostile to these claims than to implied grants. But it is also unclear whether the lane actually existed when Hill originally sold the Rosier lots. If it did not—if there was no *quasi*-easement in the form of a prior use *at the time the property was originally divided*—then there could be no easement implied by prior existing use.

If nothing else, *Othen* demonstrates the limits of the various exceptions to the writing requirement for easements. Each doctrine has its own specific requirements, and failure to prove them defeats an easement claim, even on facts where it looks like the claimant should have *some* relief. Here, Othen was left with no choice but to bargain for access to his own property, and the Rosiers were under no obligation to sell.

C.   Remedies: Property and Liability Rules

Most of the discussion so far has implicitly assumed that injunctions are the appropriate remedy for disputes over easements. Someone should either be allowed to cross over someone else's land, or not. But introducing a damages remedy expands the range of possible outcomes. In fact, this turn to remedies introduces a range of possibilities that extends far beyond the law of easements, and introduces a critical concept in the private law more generally: the difference between property and liability rules. This requires a bit of a detour into more general observations about remedies, but ultimately it relates squarely to the easement problem, as well as to a number of additional doctrines, like nuisance, still to come.

In an incredibly influential paper, Guido Calabresi and Douglas Melamed divided the range of remedies for legal conflicts into what they termed property and liability rules.[123] Protecting a legal entitlement with a property rule means allowing or forbidding the challenged conduct. Property, after all, traditionally lets owners set their own terms for using or accessing a resource. Protecting an entitlement with a liability rule means, instead, court-awarded damages.

A useful way to conceptualize the difference between property and liability rules is to ask who gets to set the price for a legal

---

123. Guido Calabresi & A. Douglas Melamed, *Property Rules, Liability Rules, and Inalienability: One View of the Cathedral*, 85 Harv. L. Rev. 1089 (1972).

entitlement. Property rules allow the parties themselves to set the price. The entitlement holder can demand as much as he or she wants, and cannot be forced to sell for any particular price. With a liability rule, however, the court sets the price in the form of damages. The fundamental question, then, is who will be better at setting the price in a particular context: the parties (i.e., the market) or the courts?

Either party can be protected with either form of entitlement. This is easiest to see in the context of a specific example, like *Othen v. Rosier.*[124] Protecting Othen's entitlement with a property rule would mean recognizing the easement and allowing Othen to cross over the Rosiers' land. Protecting the Rosiers' entitlement would mean the opposite: finding no easement, and forbidding Othen from crossing the Rosiers' land without permission (what the court actually concluded). But there are two additional remedies that are at least conceptually available. First, Othen could be allowed to continue using the property, but would have to pay court-awarded damages to the Rosiers. Or, Othen could be prohibited from using the property, and the Rosiers would have to pay *him* for the loss of access. Calabresi and Melamed presented this in the form of a 2 X 2 matrix, which reveals the range of options.

		Method of Protecting Entitlement	
		Property Rule	**Liability Rule**
Entitlement Holder	**Dominant Estate**	Easement exists.	Easement does not exist, but servient tenement pays damages for loss of access.
	Servient Estate	Easement does not exist.	Easement does exist, but dominant tenement pays damages for access.

Why choose one box over another? From an economic perspective, the optimal outcome is for the resource to end up in the hands of the party who values it the most. Different choices increase or decrease the likelihood of an efficient outcome, depending on the setting and the nature of the dispute.

It is important to understand that neither markets nor courts are likely to set prices in a way that ensures the efficient allocation of resources. The choice is really among the less bad of two alternatives. Courts are obviously imperfect at assessing damages. No matter how extensive parties' evidence, courts cannot measure harm, or the value of property, with any real precision. Judicial

---

124. *Supra.*

determinations of damages are filled with assumptions and guess-work that may or may not approximate the parties' actual prefer-ences. Whether this is worse than the market's valuation—through voluntary transaction between the parties—depends in large part on the extent of transaction costs.

According to Ronald Coase, parties in the absence of transac-tion costs will bargain to the efficient outcome.[125] Of course, we do not live in a world without transaction costs. Instead, information and coordination costs, free riders and the possibility of holdouts, can prevent parties from bidding the true extent of their prefer-ences (or from bidding at all). Where transaction costs are likely to be high, then, liability rule protection, with court-assessed damages, may be preferable. Typically, when there are many parties involved, or when they have very limited ability to coordinate or to negotiate with each other, liability rules may actually be better than the market at setting the price for an entitlement.

Imagine, then, that Othen valued being able to access his house at $25,000, and the Rosiers valued preventing flooding over their crops at $15,000 (and had no other interest in excluding Othen). The efficient, welfare maximizing outcome from society's perspec-tive is for Othen to be able to get to his property, because it means that the resource (here, the right to use the Rosiers' land) ends up in the hands of the person who values it the most. Protecting either party with property rule protection is likely to lead to that result. If Rosier is given a right to exclude Othen from his property, Othen should be willing to pay up to $24,999 for the easement, and the Rosiers should be willing to accept anything more than $15,000. There is a deal to be struck and, in the absence of transaction costs, the parties will strike it. Of course, if Othen is given the right to cross the Rosiers' land, the Rosiers will not be willing to offer Othen enough money to stop. Again, this is the efficient outcome. The initial allocation of the rights between the parties does not affect their ultimate distribution.

But add some more parties, and the outcome becomes less certain. Imagine that Othen was not the only person who used the fenced lane over the Rosiers' property but that others used it too. On the Rosiers' side, imagine that others also benefitted from the new levee, like abutting property owners whose land it also protect-ed. Now, transaction costs make it less likely that the parties will bargain to the efficient outcome. The costs of organizing the parties, and the possibility of free riders and holdouts means there

---

125. See Ronald Coase, *The Problem of Social Cost*, 3 J. OF L. & ECON. 1 (1960), discussed in Chapter 1.

is a real chance that the parties will not necessarily bargain to the efficient outcome. By protecting the entitlement with a liability rule—in the form of damages—a court may more accurately reflect the actual value of a legal entitlement to the parties.

A liability rule has another distributional consequence, too. It pre-specifies the division of the economic surplus between the parties. Instead of allowing the Rosiers to capture as much as they can of the value of the easement to Othen, the court will specify the damages. Or vice versa. The risk here, of course, is that the court will get this valuation quite far wrong. Instead of dividing the surplus, the court's award might amount to undervaluing the legal entitlement and actually result in an inefficient outcome.

The important insight—and one that will now recur throughout the rest of the material here and in the chapters that follow—is that legal entitlements can be allocated to either party, and protected in one of two ways. It is therefore always important to ask both how rights should be allocated, and then also how they should be protected. This is particularly relevant to the remaining discussion of easements.

D. Modifications: Terminating or Expanding the Scope of an Easement

Creating an easement is only one source of conflict between dominant and servient tenement holders. An existing easement may come under additional pressure from either the servient tenement holder seeking to limit or terminate it, or from the dominant tenement holder seeking to expand its scope. Although these are very different doctrines, they are usefully considered together as modifications of existing easements.

Termination

All of the doctrines for creating an easement come with an analogous mechanism for terminating one. The most important are release, abandonment, merger, estoppel, and prescription.[126]

Release is the easiest. Just as an easement can be created through an express writing that complies with the statute of frauds, an easement can be terminated in the same way. The dominant and servient tenement holders can agree in a writing to terminate an

---

126. Some others exist as well, with details that vary by jurisdiction. Notably, destruction or condemnation of the easement—or of a structure that is the reason for the easement—can terminate the easement. Likewise, an attempt by the dominant tenement holder to sever an appurtenant easement from the land it benefits can also terminate an easement.

easement and, by recording the writing, eliminate the easement for successors as well.

Similarly, a dominant tenement holder can abandon an easement. After all, one of the usual sticks in the bundle of property rights includes the right to abandon, and an easement is no exception.[127] Abandonment can be hard to demonstrate, however. Mere non-use is typically not enough; nor are oral statements, because they do not satisfy the writing requirement. But an affirmative act demonstrating a clear intent to abandon the easement may be sufficient, for example the dominant tenement holder erecting a barrier blocking the path of the easement on his property or otherwise disconnecting the dominant tenement from the easement.

Termination through estoppel occurs where the servient tenement holder reasonably relies on a dominant tenement holder's representation that the easement has been abandoned. For example, a dominant tenement holder might give the servient tenement holder oral permission to build a structure in the path of the easement. Because the permission was not in writing, it would not satisfy the statute of frauds. But if the servient tenement holder erects a building in reasonable reliance on the representation, or otherwise takes steps that would be inconsistent with the ongoing use of the easement, the dominant tenement holder might be estopped from trying to reassert the easement in the future.

Easements by implication and the doctrine of merger look like flip sides of the same doctrinal coin. Just as dividing property will sometimes turn a *quasi*-easement into an easement, unifying ownership of the dominant and servient tenements will do the opposite: convert an easement into nothing more than a *quasi* one. The point is simple. An owner cannot possess an easement over her own property. Therefore, merging the burdened and benefitted parcels will eliminate the easement.

Finally, easements can be terminated by prescription. In effect, the servient tenement holder can re-take the right to use by adverse possession. This is easier said than done. Because an easement does not necessarily confer exclusive use, the mere use of the easement by the servient tenement holder will not be enough to

---

127. See Eduardo M. Peñalver, *The Illusory Right to Abandon*, 109 MICH. L. REV. 191 (2011); Lior J. Strahilevitz, *The Right to Abandon*, 158 U. PA. L. REV. 355 (2010). Land itself can often not be abandoned because of the hole in title such abandonment creates. This is one of the mysteries of abandonment, and the doctrine is far from straightforward. But easements present no such problem because abandonment, or any other form of termination, will simply extinguish the easement but leave title to the underlying property entirely intact.

terminate it by prescription. Something more is needed. If the servient tenement holder actually interferes with the easement—builds a fence across it, strews boulders over it, cuts the utility lines, and so forth—the easement will end at the expiration of the statute of limitations. The justifications are again the same as the justifications for creating an easement by prescription, although they probably focus more on the demerits of the easement holder than the merits of the servient tenement holder. After all, there may be little that is meritorious about cutting utility lines and interfering with roads.

Expanding the Scope of an Easement

A dominant tenement holder can try to expand the scope of an easement in one of two ways, either increasing the intensity of use, or using the easement to benefit additional property. Each implicates a slightly different analysis.

In general, the dominant tenement holder can only use an easement consistently with the terms in the original grant. An easement for a bicycle path cannot be used for cars; an easement for a telephone line cannot be used for a natural gas pipeline. Hard cases are easy to imagine. Can an easement for a right-of-way be used for parking? Can an easement for power lines be used for cable television? Or, as in *Preseault v. United States*,[128] did the transformation of easements for railroad tracks into public walking trails expand the scope of the easement? In that case, the court answered, "yes," even though, by many measures, a train would appear to be a more intensive use than hiking. But these are factual questions and, while courts and juries may disagree, the overall inquiry is whether the use is consistent with the original easement. It is, in general, a matter of contract interpretation.

The situation is somewhat different in the absence of an express easement. There is no original document to interpret in the case of an easement by prescription, for example. Instead, the baseline for the scope of the easement is the use that formed the basis of the prescription claim. As the First Restatement of Property put it, "[t]he extent of an easement created by prescription is fixed by the use through which it was created."[129] This is not as rigid as it might seem, however. Otherwise, an easement for a right-of-way obtained with a 4–cylinder Honda Civic might not be expanded to allow access to a 6–cylinder Audi. Obviously, some line needs to be drawn, and they will be difficult to draw precisely. Courts usually rely on a number of factors for their analysis, chief

---

128. 100 F.3d 1525 (Fed. Cir. 1996) [DKA & S, p. 821].

129. Restatement (First) of Property § 477 (1944, updated 2011).

among them: whether the new use materially increased the burden on the servient tenement holder, whether the new use was a reasonably foreseeable evolution of the original use, or whether the new use was consistent with the general pattern of the old.

Stepping back from the specifics of these factors, the original justifications for adverse possession shed some light on the appropriate analysis for expanding the scope of a prescriptive easement. A servient estate holder who does not stop people walking over her property is not necessarily consenting to—or sleeping on her rights to exclude—ATVs, cars, or other motorized vehicles. Imagine the servient tenement holder making a reasoned calculation when she notices her neighbor crossing over her lot every day on foot. She could seek to enforce her rights, but this comes with costs, both literal and neighborly. She might well be willing to tolerate what she views as a minor and inoffensive trespass in the interests of good relations. But the equation changes if the trespass had been less minor: noisier, smellier, or otherwise more offensive. Had that been the prescriptive use, the servient owner would have taken great pains to stop it. In this scenario, it would be unfair to allow pedestrian access to serve as a foot in the door for allowing other kinds of more intensive uses. Focusing on the parties' reasonable expectations goes a long way towards making sense of the doctrine.

This is less true of the other "scope of the easement" problem. The dominant tenement holder might seek to expand the scope of an easement, not by changing the intensity of the use of the servient estate at all, but instead by trying to benefit an additional parcel. In *Brown v. Voss,*[130] for example, owners of a lot had an express easement over an adjacent lot in order to access their land. They then purchased an additional lot, and sought to build a house on it, still using the servient tenement to access the new land. This, said the court, was an impermissible expansion of the scope of the easement. The express easement was for the benefit of a specific parcel of land; the easement could not be used for the benefit of a different one. It did not matter that the intensity of use of the easement itself would be entirely unchanged.

There is something rigid and formalistic about the rule forbidding expansion of the scope of the easement in this way. The reasoning is simply that an appurtenant easement is for the benefit of a particular lot. Use of the easement to benefit a different parcel is outside the scope of the original contract, and is therefore impermissible, whether or not it would have any effect on the

---

130.   715 P.2d 514 (Wash. 1986) [DKA & S, p. 820]; [M & S, p. 1025]; [S, p. 473].

intensity of the use of the easement. That is, in fact, what the *Voss* court held.

This is a curious doctrine. From the perspective of the servient estate, it should be a matter of indifference whether the house was located on an adjacent parcel, or on one behind it. In fact, it is easy to imagine that the servient estate owners would prefer if their neighbors' house was located as far away as possible. It should be the intensity of the use that matters, not the identity of the dominant tenement.

Perhaps for this reason, the court in *Voss* declined to enforce the rights of the servient tenement holder with property rule protection. So, while the use of the easement to benefit a parcel other than the original dominant parcel was impermissible, the remedy was not an injunction but was instead damages. And because the servient tenement had not actually been harmed by the use of the easement to benefit a non-dominant parcel, it awarded only nominal damages. So, while the decision was a victory of sorts for the servient tenement holder, it actually permitted the expansion of the easement for only $1. In fact, this award is functionally indistinguishable from protecting the dominant tenement with a property rule.

The remedies for impermissibly expanding the scope of an easement or otherwise misusing one are actually quite complex. Courts can obviously enjoin the dominant estate from misusing the easement, and this is the typical remedy. But courts have sometimes held that misuse of an easement results in forfeiture, at least where the use of the easement cannot be reduced to its original scope.[131] Some courts have even held that misuse of an easement constitutes trespass, which can be subject to an injunction and damages including, potentially, punitive damages if the trespass is egregious.

When a court awards damages instead of an injunction, there are a number of ways of valuing compensation. Conceptually, a court might award damages based on the value of the right-of-way. Alternatively, a court might calculate damages based on the diminution in value of the servient estate. A misuse of an easement might consist of excessive noise and congestion that detrimentally impacts the value of the servient estate.[132] That loss in value could be substantially higher than the fair market value of a right of way. Where the misuse of an easement results in physical damage to the easement or surrounding land, compensation might also be based

---

131. *See e.g.* Crimmins v. Gould, 149 Cal.App.2d 383, 308 P.2d 786 (1957).
132. *See, e.g.,* Burke–Tarr Co. v. Ferland Corp., 724 A.2d 1014 (R.I. 1999).

on the costs of restoring the property to its previous condition. No one approach is necessarily correct. But, as the nominal $1 award in *Voss* makes clear, the measure of damages can determine the scope of property rights just as surely as the original allocation of the rights.

E.   Negative Easements

All the easements considered so far involve a dominant estate benefitting from a right to use the servient estate. But the benefit might take a different form: a restriction on the servient tenement holder's right to use her own property. That is, some easements grant the dominant estate the right to *restrict* uses on the servient estate. This is a powerful concept, but traditional limits on the content of negative easements have severely curtailed their utility.

Early common law courts permitted only four kinds of negative easements: light, air, water, and support. That is, a dominant estate could obtain a negative easement that would prevent the servient estate from: obstructing windows on the dominant estate; interfering with air or water flowing through a defined channel on the dominant estate; or digging in a way that removed support for a building on the dominant estate.

This is a somewhat anachronistic list of permissible restrictions. Courts traditionally refused to expand this list, both because they had trouble conceptualizing easements as rights to *restrict* use and, more functionally, because they worried about encumbering servient estates with restrictions that would be difficult to detect. Most affirmative easements, like paths or roads, are easy to spot (sewer lines notwithstanding). Not so with negative easements. That someone has not, in fact, interfered with his neighbor's windows does not signal to the rest of the world, nor to buyers, an obligation to refrain from blocking the windows in the future. The more non-obvious restrictions that exist, the higher the information costs for prospective buyers, creditors, or others with an interest in the servient estate to understand restrictions on the title. Furthermore, if negative easements can arise by prescription, not interfering with a neighbor's property for long enough might actually ripen into an obligation not to interfere.

These various objections to expanding the available forms of negative easements should not have had particular traction in American courts, however. With a comprehensive recordation system, and a rule prohibiting the creation of negative easements by prescription, there were no obvious policy objections to allowing negative easements to come in more flavors. Nevertheless, American courts did not expand the menu, perhaps because the law of covenants and servitudes—discussed next—stepped in to fill the gaps, and so there was little pressure on the law to evolve.

Given the ascendance of these other doctrines, it is perhaps surprising that state legislatures have added some new forms of negative easements in recent decades. Many states now recognize solar easements to prevent obstruction of solar panels, view easements to protect scenic views, and, most importantly, conservation easements to prevent development on the servient estate. Conservation easements have become widespread and are worth considering in some more detail.

A conservation easement amounts to a restriction on the ability to develop the servient estate. Conveying the development right to a third party does not give that third party—now the dominant estate holder—the right to develop the servient estate; instead, it gives the dominant estate holder the right to *prevent* the servient estate holder from developing her own property. It is a veto right only, just like any negative easement.

In the typical transaction, the owner of undeveloped land—often farmland, but it could be any kind of relatively undeveloped property—creates a conservation easement on her own property, and then conveys that easement to a third-party not-for-profit conservation group (or the government) to hold. That third party, now the dominant tenement holder of a negative easement in gross (because it does not benefit specific land), can prevent the property from being developed, in effect ensuring the conservation of the land. Importantly, this easement consists only of a right to veto development, not an affirmative right to develop the property.

Sometimes, the government or conservation group will pay for the easements, effectively buying preservation rights in the property without buying the property itself. More often, though, the servient tenement holder simply donates the conservation easements. This is not purely altruistic, however, because the donation can count as a charitable donation for tax purposes. Moreover, conservation easements reduce the value of the burdened property, often substantially, which can result in significant savings on property taxes.

Conservation easements have been widely embraced by property owners and by the environmental and preservation communities generally. The benefits are obvious. It is far less expensive to buy conservation easements over property than to buy the property itself. Far more property can therefore be conserved using conservation easements than by acquiring it outright.

There are costs, however. Conservation easements are only as strong as their enforcement. Today, in many states, many different entities hold conservation easements, from national conservation groups, to small statewide and local ones, and from the state to local governments. Not all have equal capacity to monitor, let alone to enforce, the terms of a conservation easement. Easements, after all, are not self-executing. The costs of monitoring and enforcement are exacerbated by diversity in the content of conservation easements. The donor—the owner of the servient parcel—can tailor the content of the easements to her specific needs. Some donors retain the right to build small numbers of additional buildings; others, the right to expand farming operations, and the like. For the group holding the negative easements, this diversity increases enforcement costs by making it more difficult to know what uses are actually permitted on the servient parcel.

Moreover, conservation easements are not free. Even when a property owner donates the conservation easements *gratis*, the tax benefits—from the charitable deduction and the decreased property taxes—amount to an expense to the government. In essence, the private conservation easement donors are able to direct foregone tax revenue to the preservation of their property. This may or may not be consistent with the state's broader conservation goals, and may or may not involve individual property that the state has any particular interest in conserving. Foregone tax revenue is not a budget item for the state, however, so taxpayers do not typically view conservation easements as an expenditure (although they should!). The relative invisibility of the costs of these easements means that there is little political pressure to limit their use despite the very real costs they impose.

Finally, conservation easements represent a guess by the current landowner (and conservation group) that the property will be appropriate for conservation in the future. As interests in land, conservation easements will run in perpetuity. In one hundred years, a new highway or rocket ship launch pad nearby may well make the property entirely unsuited for conservation, and yet the easement will persist. In other places in property law, donors are limited in their ability to control the future. The rule against perpetuities is the most notable example, but many others exist as well, from the *cy pres* doctrine allowing for modification of charitable trusts, to the changed conditions doctrine in the law of covenants.[133] There are no such obvious mechanisms for preserving future flexibility when it comes to conservation easements.[134] In theory, the holder of the easements could relinquish them. Conservation groups will occasionally sell conservation easements, allowing them to raise money to conserve property they deem more important to protect. This is a flexibility of sorts, but it is likely to be idiosyncratic in its application, and many conservation groups are constrained in their ability to waive or sell conservation easements, either by reputational concerns or by actual limits in their corporate structure.

It is still too early to know how this story will end. Conservation easements are now widespread. They promise large-scale conservation, and may protect vital natural resources for generations to come. However, they may prove too porous: too expensive to enforce, and therefore little protection after all. Or, they may prove too rigid, locking in contemporary views of conservation that may prove misguided far into the future. But at the very least, they reveal a recurring tension in the law of property: free alienability today versus flexibility in the future. And they also demonstrate how old property concepts, like common law negative easements, can be given new life as policy levers for facilitating private transactions to achieve public benefits.

* * *

The law of easements is important both practically and conceptually. Practically, easements are a crucial mechanism allowing people to secure rights over others' land. Easements are therefore commonplace for driveways, utility poles, and other rights of way where ownership of the underlying land is unnecessary and, perhaps, undesirable.

Conceptually, easements are important because they demonstrate how the right to use can be severed from the other sticks in the bundle of property rights. Typically, that right to use is an affirmative right to cross over someone else's property. But occasionally it is a negative right to prevent someone from using his own property in a certain way. So-called negative easements, including conservation easements, are examples of the latter. There are only limited forms of negative easements, however, because a

---

133. The rule against perpetuities was discussed in Chapter 4, and the changed conditions doctrine is discussed in Chapter 10.

134. For an account of the doctrinal opportunities for crafting flexibility, see Gerald Korngold, *Solving the Contentious Issues of Private Conservation Easements: Promoting Flexibility for the Future and Engaging the Public Land Use Process*, 2007 Utah L. Rev. 1039, 1054.

different body of law has developed to create rights to other people's property: covenants and servitudes, taken up next.

Chapter 10

COVENANTS

The limited forms of negative easements put substantial pressure on the law to innovate new ways of imposing obligations on other people's property. Covenants filled that role. As contracts that could—under the right conditions—run with the land, they offered nearly unlimited flexibility in the obligations they could create. Like easements, they could also be affirmative or negative, but now including affirmative obligations to perform some action on the property, or more varied restrictions on the uses of property. But why was the law in such hurry to innovate in this way? Why did property owners care so much about restricting the use of each other's property, or creating other kinds of burdens and obligations?

The answer, suggested already above, is that placing restrictions on neighbors' property may be vitally important to protecting investments in one's own land. Someone considering the perfect spot to build a new house might worry about where a neighbor might build on her adjoining lot because of the potential to block a scenic view. Someone seeking to preserve the value of his own house might want an enforceable commitment by neighbors to build big, fancy houses and, at the very least, to exclude mobile homes, for goodness sake! But an affirmative covenant might also create obligations to care for and maintain certain property, to keep a garden in good flower, or, perhaps, even to pay a share of plowing or other expenses. Covenants can create these kinds of obligations.

The history of covenants is unfortunately full of formalism and doctrinal complexity. Today, the law is being simplified. The relatively new Restatement (Third) of Property eliminates some long-standing distinctions, and otherwise streamlines the enforceability of promises running with the land. That transformation is not complete, however, and so it remains important to understand the origins of the doctrine and its common law rules.

A. The Evolution of Covenants

Contract law has traditionally adopted a narrow vision of privity. Subject to a few exceptions, only the parties to a contract can sue to enforce it. Covenants are one of those exceptions, and the law surrounding them can be a dense thicket of confusing doctrine. It is therefore important to demystify covenants, and to understand the important role they can play in allowing property owners to order their affairs.

Fundamentally, a covenant is simply a contract. One party promises to undertake or to forego conduct on her land for the benefit of another party (although the benefits and burdens can be reciprocal, as we shall see). There have traditionally been two separate ways to seek enforcement of such contracts, either at law or at equity. The former were called covenants at law or legal covenants, and the latter were equitable servitudes. And, while law and equity have largely merged in this country, the distinction between legal covenants and equitable servitudes remains. Focus first, however, on the relationships between the potential parties.

Imagine a valid contract between two neighboring property owners, Adam and Barbara, in which Barbara promises to use her property for single-family residential development only. If she breaches that contract by developing a commercial use on her land there is no doubt that Adam could sue her. They were in privity of contract with each other, and Barbara breached. It is as easy as that. The complexity arises when either or both Adam and Barbara have sold their property to third parties. If Adam sells to Charlie and now Barbara breaches, can Charlie sue her? Charlie and Barbara were not in privity of contract, after all. The question, formally, is whether the *benefit* of the covenant can run to Adam's successors. And what if Barbara is the one who sold? If her successor, call her Delia, is the one to develop a commercial use on the property, can Adam sue Delia? Again, Adam and Delia are not in privity of contract, so the question here is whether the *burden* of the covenant can run. And if both Adam and Barbara have sold, do both the benefit and burden run so that Charlie can sue Delia? This is all represented through the following diagram: a standard figure in the law of covenants.

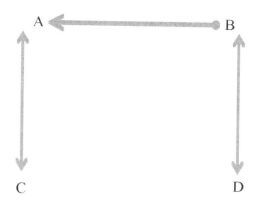

Since plain-vanilla contracts do not run to successors, something special is needed for covenants to run with the land. The requirements differ slightly depending on whether the burden or benefit is at issue, and whether the plaintiff sought enforcement at law or equity. The requirements are more stringent for the burden to run to successors (here, for D to remain burdened by B's promise), than for the benefit to run (for C to be benefitted by B's promise to A). B, after all, made the promise herself and so should be bound to A as well as to A's successors. But B's successors only inherit B's promise, and courts have traditionally viewed continuation of such restrictions with skepticism.

For the burden to run to successors at law, the covenant must be in writing, the parties must have intended it to bind successors, the successors must have had notice of the covenant (typically through recordation), there must be both horizontal and vertical privity between the parties, and the covenant must touch and concern the land (each of which is considered in a moment). The law imposes fewer requirements for a benefit to run at law than a burden, omitting the need for notice and horizontal privity. Therefore, the benefit running requires a writing, the intent to bind successors, vertical privity, and that the covenant touch and concern the land. If the requirements for the burden to run are satisfied, then the benefits will definitely run to successors.

The writing, intent, and notice requirements are largely self-evident. Typically, a properly recorded written covenant displaying the intent to bind successors would satisfy these requirements. Vertical privity is also straightforward. It simply requires a sufficient nexus between the successive owners, which can be supplied by any conveyance to a successor, whether through purchase, inheritance, or gift. Vertical privity is lacking only when the grant-or conveys something less than her entire interest in the property—say a life estate—or when the successor takes title through adverse possession.

The latter two requirements—horizontal privity and touch and concern—are considerably less obvious.

Horizontal privity is required for the burden of a covenant to run to successors at law. Horizontal privity refers to the relationship between the original parties to the transaction—here, A (Adam) and B (Barbara). In England, horizontal privity was satisfied only by a landlord-tenant relationship. Only a landlord could impose restrictions on the use of property that would run to tenants and tenants' successors (assignees).[135] American courts adopted a more capacious definition of horizontal privity to include grantor-grantee relationships. A grantor could include a covenant as part of a conveyance of land, and that covenant could be enforceable against successors (if all the other requirements were also met). In the example above, then, Barbara's successors would be bound only if Barbara originally acquired her property from Adam subject to the covenant at the time of the acquisition.

There has always been a relatively easy way around this restriction. If two neighbors wanted to create a covenant that would bind successors, they could not do so directly because they were not in the relationship of grantor-grantee. That is, if Barbara and Adam were simply neighbors, Barbara could not make a promise that would bind her successors because Barbara and Adam lacked horizontal privity. However, the eventual promisor (Barbara) could convey her property to the eventual promisee, who could then grant it right back to her subject to the covenant. In other words, parties could easily manufacture a grantor-grantee relationship through a straw transaction.

The horizontal privity requirement was much maligned by courts and commentators alike, who saw little reason to prevent parties with other relationships from entering into covenants. And, as discussed below, the Restatement (Third) of property does away with horizontal privity altogether. Much earlier, though, the horizontal privity requirement was significantly undermined by the possibility of equitable instead of legal enforcement of such promises.

The famous case of *Tulk v. Moxhay*[136] broadly opened the door to equitable enforcement of promises running with the land despite

---

135. For the law of assignments, see Chapter 7.

136. 2 Phillips 774 (Court of Chancery 1848) [DKA & S, p. 854]; [M & S, p. 1026]; [S, p. 476].

the absence of horizontal privity. There, Tulk sold Leicester Square in London to Elms, with a requirement that Elms would maintain the garden in the square for the benefit of neighboring property owners. Elms, however, conveyed away the property, and it ended up in the hands of Moxhay, whose deed did not include the obligation to maintain the garden. However, Moxhay admitted that he had actual knowledge of the obligations in the covenant that Elms had entered.

There is no doubt that the covenant was unenforceable at law. The horizontal privity requirement in England was limited at that time to landlords and tenants. Tulk and Elms therefore lacked the requisite horizontal privity for the covenant to run to successors—at least, to run *at law* to successors. The *Tulk* court held, however, that it would be inequitable to release Moxhay from his predecessor's obligation when Moxhay had actual knowledge of the covenant. The court noted that this would have resulted in something of a windfall for Moxhay, who bought the property subject to the covenant. Therefore, although unenforceable at law, the covenant was enforceable at equity.

A promise can therefore run against successors as an equitable servitude, instead of as a legal covenant, if the following conditions are met: it must be in writing (or part of a common scheme or plan, discussed below); the parties must have intended for the promise to run to successors; the content of the obligation must touch and concern the land; and the burdened party must have actual or constructive notice of the promise. Since plaintiffs will usually prefer injunctive relief to damages, and since equitable relief is actually *easier* to secure than damages, the requirement of horizontal privity required for legal covenants is much less important than it might otherwise seem.

The touch-and-concern requirement, for both real covenants and equitable servitudes, is perhaps the most cryptic of the elements. It is meant to distinguish mere personal obligations from those that run with the land. If courts and commentators have agreed on one thing, it is that the meaning of "touch and concern" is vague. A leading formulation asks whether the covenant affects the value of the land itself, although there is something circular about the definition, because a covenant can only affect the value of land if it is, in fact, enforceable.[137] Another way to think of the

---

137. See James Krier, Book Review, 122 U. Pa. L. Rev. 1664, 1678–79 (1974) (reviewing Richard Posner, Economic Analysis of Law).

requirement is that the obligation must relate, in some way, to the legal relations among owners of land.[138]

If this seems imprecise—and it is—a more helpful approach is to consider the easy and hard cases of the touch-and-concern requirement to get a sense of the limits of the doctrine. An easy case is any negative restriction on the actual use of property. A covenant to build only single-family residential housing, or to leave parts of the land undeveloped, undoubtedly touches and concerns the land. The hard case, and simultaneously the most important, involves the affirmative obligation to pay money. A grantor may well want to sell property subject to a condition that the buyer pays money every year to the grantor. This is not farfetched; it is, in fact, the basic covenant at the heart of homeowners associations.

Consider *Neponsit Property Owners' Association, Inc. v. Emigrant Industrial Savings Bank.*[139] There, the defendant bank bought at a judicial sale property that was part of an early form of a homeowners association. The property was encumbered by a covenant to pay money annually to help pay to maintain roads, paths, beaches, and other "public purposes" as determined by the association. The covenant also provided that the charge would be a lien on the property. When the bank failed to pay, the plaintiff homeowners association tried to foreclose on the lien. The bank defended itself, in part, on grounds that the covenant was unenforceable because it did not touch and concern the land, and so did not run to it as a successor to the promisor.[140]

The bank's claim seemed like a strong one. Under a traditional English rule, affirmative covenants—requiring the owner of the burdened parcel to undertake some affirmative conduct on her own property—did not run with the land, subject only to some minor exceptions. That rule, however, had been widely criticized in the United States, in part because it is very difficult to distinguish negative restrictions from affirmative obligations. A covenant to mow one's lawn might look like an affirmative obligation, but a covenant to prevent one's lawn from growing longer than 4 inches could look like a negative one. Obviously, the two are substantively identical. So, despite courts' unease with the possibility of a covenant forcing the burdened owner to undertake some affirmative act, most states abandoned the traditional English rule.

---

138. Alfred L. Brophy, *Contemplating When Equitable Servitudes Run With the Land*, 46 St. Louis U. L.J. 691 (2002).

139. 15 N.E.2d 793 (NY 1938) [DKA & S, p. 864]; [M & S, p. 1031]; [S, p. 509].

140. The bank also argued that the plaintiff lacked standing, a point set aside for purposes of the present discussion.

Permitting affirmative covenants to run with the land is one thing; extending that to cash payments is something else entirely. And there, the *Neponsit* court found that the touch-and-concern requirement is often a matter of degree. On the facts before it, the court concluded that the payment of money was for the specific purpose of maintaining the easements that came with the property for roads, parks, beaches and the like. Those easements could obviously run with the land, and so too could the obligation to pay to maintain them.

This seems, perhaps, like a commonsense conclusion, and it certainly represents the majority approach today. But the mere payment of money, by itself, may still not satisfy the touch-and-concern requirement. Imagine the sale of property that included an obligation to pay the seller $1,000 per year for no apparent reason. If such an obligation could run with the land, it would suppress the market value of the property forever, amounting to a diversion of the value of the property to that original promisee. This, courts will generally not permit.

The challenge, then, is to distinguish the naked obligation to pay cash from the kind of dues that will fund a homeowners association or other private ordering to share the burdens of maintaining property. The *Neponsit* court offered one approach, focusing on the purpose of the payment, and demonstrating how it remained connected to the use and enjoyment of land. The holding could perhaps also be justified by looking at the problem *ex ante*. Cooperative arrangements by neighbors to fund easements in their community might be mutually beneficial for everyone. In the absence of transaction costs, everyone would presumably agree to this kind of funding mechanism. Allowing a covenant to run with the land achieves this result without requiring all of the parties to enter into costly negotiations every time property in the neighborhood is bought or sold.[141] In other words, a court should enforce a covenant when doing so would result in an agreement that subsequent parties would have agreed to ahead of time, in the absence of transaction costs. This is as compelling an account as any, but touch and concern remains contested.

In 2000, the American Law Institute published the Restatement (Third) of Property, which substantially modified the law of covenants. Although most states have yet to adopt it, and courts have yet to follow it, the new Restatement is bound to exert significant influence on the development of the law in this area.

---

141. See Krier, *supra.*

Among the Restatement's innovations is the elimination of the discrete categories of negative easements, legal covenants, and equitable servitudes. Instead, all three are called, simply, "servitudes running with the land." More substantively, the Restatement does away with privity requirements, and with the requirement that the servitude touch and concern the land. Instead, the Restatement generally presumes that any contract can, if the parties wish, be enforceable and run with the land so long as it is in writing (or otherwise complies with the statute of frauds), and does not violate public policy.

Chief among the obligations that would violate public policy are racially restrictive covenants, which have a long and sordid history that deserves separate treatment, taken up next in an important doctrinal detour.

B. Racially Restrictive Covenants

The first third of the twentieth century witnessed a significant migration of southern African Americans to northern cities. The response in the north was often not very welcoming. Indeed, many white communities sought to exclude African Americans, using violence and threats as well as legal mechanisms to achieve their exclusionary aims.

Some cities tried racial zoning as a first line of "defense" against this migration. Zoning, as discussed below, seeks to segregate incompatible uses of land, and in the early twentieth century, some local governments sought to use zoning to segregate people by race. The Supreme Court invalidated racial zoning in 1917, however, and so communities turned to racially restrictive covenants.[142] As a kind of private law substitute for race-based zoning, property owners in a neighborhood would agree to covenants that required the sale of their property to white buyers only. Each lot was therefore both burdened and "benefitted" by the restriction, meaning that each neighbor had the ability to sue to enforce the covenant—and could presumably seek injunctive relief as well.

Notice, however, that to prevent African Americans from having access to a community, most if not all property owners would have to agree to put racially restrictive covenants on their property. A single defector could begin the process of integration. This kind of community-wide coordination should have posed serious collective action problems. Free riders, to say nothing of organizational

---

142. See Buchanan v. Warley, 245 U.S. 60 (1917) [M & S, p. 427; 1062]; [S, p. 1098].

costs, would seem to make large-scale adoption of racially restrictive covenants unlikely. And yet, the incentives for individual homeowners were evidently strong enough that racially restrictive covenants became widespread, blocking African Americans from buying property in a majority of communities in cities like Chicago, St. Louis, and Detroit.

Racially restrictive covenants posed a real challenge to the legal system. As private contracts, they did not appear to involve any obvious state action, and so the Fourteenth Amendment did not seem to apply. *Shelley v. Kraemer*[143] changed that, holding that judicial enforcement of a racially restrictive covenant was sufficient state action to trigger the Equal Protection Clause. The covenants themselves were not unconstitutional after *Shelly,* but judicial enforcement of them was. This case remains *sui generis.* Courts have generally not extended the ruling, and judicial enforcement of private agreements is usually not enough to trigger constitutional limitations.[144] But even if it is the high-water mark for state action, it is an important one; one that invalidated a truly pernicious practice with widespread social consequences.

Importantly, though, the Court's ruling did not end the practice of imposing racially restrictive covenants. Property owners continued to place racially restrictive covenants on property even after they were no longer enforceable. There are two troubling explanations. First, racially restrictive covenants continued to serve a signaling function about the nature of the community. This may have dissuaded African American buyers from purchasing some property because the racial covenants expressed the community's racist attitudes.[145]

Even more troubling, the Federal Housing Authority (FHA) actively supported the use of racially restrictive covenants. The FHA guaranteed certain residential loans, making credit more readily available to buyers. The FHA, however, refused to insure mortgages for African Americans buying property with racially restrictive covenants, *even though such covenants were unconstitutional to enforce.* The FHA also viewed the presence of racially restrictive covenants as a favorable characteristic when assessing the credit risks for a particular mortgage.[146] There can be little

---

143. 334 U.S. 1 (1948) [DKA & S, p. 876]; [M & S, p.424]; [S, p. 541].

144. One possible exception comes from judicial takings claims, discussed in Chapter 14.

145. See [DKA & S, p. 880] (citing unpublished paper by Richard Brooks); [M & S, p. 431] (same).

146. For further discussion, see the material on mortgages and bank lending practices, *supra* Chapter 8(D).

doubt that such federal policies contributed to the continuation of housing segregation even after *Shelly v. Kraemer.*

The use of racially restrictive covenants did not itself become illegal until Congress passed the Fair Housing Act in 1968. That statute made it unlawful to "make, print, or publish ... any notice, statement, or advertisement, with respect to the sale or rental of a dwelling that indicates any preference, limitation, or discrimination based on race...."[147] Courts held that a recorded covenant is a "statement" within the meaning of the statute.

Ultimately, then, when the new Restatement of Property presumes the enforceability of covenants subject to a public policy exception, it is referring most directly to racially restrictive covenants.

C. Subdivisions and Homeowners Associations

Residential subdivisions are at the heart of much of the modern law of covenants. A close look at this form of ownership reveals both the power and limits of covenants running with the land, and also explains an important exception to the writing requirement for a common scheme or plan.

Traditionally, to create a residential subdivision, a landowner would subdivide a single piece of property into a number of individual parcels. As he sold off the parcels, he would place covenants on each lot for the benefit of all the other lots in the subdivision. The covenants would typically restrict the property to single-family residential use, and, as in *Neponsit,* would also require payment to a common fund to pay for services shared by all the lots: roads, utilities, garbage pickup, and the like. The covenants could do more. A subdivider could try to ensure an upscale subdivision by imposing covenants restricting the choice of building materials (requiring expensive ones!), mandating minimum house sizes, forbidding above-ground swimming pools, and the like.

If all went well, everyone would be happy. People would build expensive houses on their lots, and property values would remain high. But trouble often arose if sales started to soften. Then, a predictable conflict arose between the early buyers into a subdivision and the subdivider who still had unsold lots to unload. Faced with flagging demand, the subdivider might start to loosen the requirements in the later covenants, or forego altogether putting covenants on remaining lots. This presented a substantial risk to the people who bought in early. If even one lot was sold without the

---

147. 42 U.S.C. § 3604 [DKA & S, p. 432]; [M & S, p. 435]; [S, p. 926].

covenants in place, the buyer of that lot might put in multi-family housing, a grocery store, or—gasp—even a gas station, any of which could decrease property values within the whole subdivision. A similar problem also sometimes arose through sheer inadvertence; the subdivider might simply fail to record covenants on all the property, or otherwise forget to encumber some of the lots.

In response to this very real problem, courts developed an exception to the writing requirement, implying an equitable servitude from a common scheme or plan. The existence of a common scheme in a subdivision can be sufficient to put the buyer on notice of restrictions on the property, even in the absence of a properly recorded covenant.

That was exactly the situation in *Sanborn v. McLean*.[148] On a very modern-sounding set of facts, owners of a lot in a residential subdivision sought to build a gas station. Neighbors sued, seeking to enforce what the court called a reciprocal negative easement, but what it should have called a reciprocal equitable servitude. There was just one problem: there was no covenant limiting the use of the defendants' land. The *Sanborn* court nevertheless implied a restriction on the defendants' lot, and found that the residential character of the neighborhood was sufficient to put the defendants on inquiry notice of the restrictions.

The decision imposed a burden on the defendants. Even if they had noticed the residential character of the neighborhood before buying their property to build a gas station, what should they have done? The most thorough title search on the world would not have disclosed any restrictions on their property. Under the court's ruling, they should have looked at title to their neighbors' property as well, but this would hardly have resolved the problem. Had they found restrictions on others' property, they would still have been hard-pressed to predict whether a court would imply a similar restriction on their apparently unrestricted lot.

Perhaps, though, this takes an overly rigid view of notice. Is it really so implausible to think that the defendants should have known they could not build a gas station in a residential neighborhood? Courts' willingness to imply reciprocal equitable servitudes may simply be a mechanism for giving voice to settled community expectations, at least when those expectations take the form of recorded restrictions on many people's land.

In fact, though, the doctrine is quite narrow. Courts will only imply reciprocal restrictions in the following situation: the property

---

148. 206 N.W. 496 (Mich. 1925) [DKA & S, p. 859]; [M & S, p. 1046]; [S, p. 506].

must all have started with a single owner (the subdivider), who must have sold property subject to a general plan. When this occurs, lots retained by the original owner are reciprocally burdened by implication, and that burden then runs with the land if and when the lots are eventually sold. Evidence of such a plan might come in the form of advertising documents, oral declarations, or the deeds themselves. But when does that general plan emerge? In *Sanborn*, the original owner subdivided his property into 91 lots, only 53 of which contained express restrictions on the use of the property. Moreover, the original owner had sold only 21 lots before the defendant's lot. For an equitable servitude to have been implied on the defendant's property, it must have arisen at or before that time. The common plan, then, must have been based on the covenants governing the 21 lots sold first—less than one quarter of the total lots in the subdivision. At the very least, *Sanborn* was not a case involving a single unrestricted lot in an otherwise restricted subdivision. Many of the lots were unrestricted. Still, the court there was willing to find a common plan, and sufficient notice.

It is worth asking why any of this should matter. Although the *Sanborn* court implied a residential-only restriction on the defendant's land, the parties were free to negotiate around it. If the gas station is the more valuable use of the property, the defendants should have been able to buy their neighbors' permission to build. And, if the court had refused the injunction, the neighbors could have bought out the defendants if the gas station was sufficiently objectionable. The problem, of course, is transaction costs. If the neighbors had the right to prevent the gas station from being built—as the court held—holdout problems may well have prevented the parties from striking even a welfare-maximizing bargain. With 90 residential neighbors, the defendants would have faced an expensive negotiation over the right to build a gas station. If the court had ruled for the defendants, the neighbors would have faced high organizing costs and free rider problems that may well have prevented them from bidding the full extent of their preferences *not* to have a gas station. In other words, the gas station may still have been built, even if it caused more harm to the neighbors than it benefitted to the defendants. Relying on *ex post* private ordering through negotiations over individual land uses is complicated, expensive, and unlikely to substitute for more effective *ex ante* limits.

Against this backdrop, common-interest communities evolved to provide simultaneously more reliable, and more flexible *ex ante* protection for homeowners in a residential development. Common-interest communities can take many different forms, but all share some central features. Authorized by statute in most states, common-interest communities—which generally include a homeowners association in some form or another—provide a streamlined mechanism for imposing restrictions and obligations on property.

Instead of placing a covenant on each lot individually, the developer of a common interest community can file a single Declaration of Covenants, Conditions and Restrictions (CC & R, sometimes called the Declaration, or Master Deed) that governs all the lots in the development. Buyers, then, can look to the CC & R for the affirmative and negative obligations running with each individual lot. These generally include restrictive covenants on the uses of property, as well as affirmative obligations to join the homeowners association and pay dues, as well as specifying the powers of the association.

CC & Rs frequently impose detailed restrictions on property owners. They can include limits on the color of one's house and even one's car, gardening requirements, limits on signs and decorations, and so on. This can make for complicated conflicts when the burdens become particularly onerous. In the famous case of *Nahrstedt v. Lakeside Village Condominium Association, Inc.*,[149] a condominium owner challenged application of the association's "no pets" policy to her "noiseless" cats. After much hand-wringing about the therapeutic benefits of pets, the court nevertheless upheld the restriction, finding that it was reasonable. The court held that a restriction is only unreasonable if "the burdens it imposes on affected properties so substantially outweigh the benefits of the restriction that it should not be enforced against any owner." The standard, in other words, requires that the restriction be inefficient for everyone, and not simply as applied to a particular property.

Is this the right result for poor Nahrstedt and her silent cats? Comparing the costs to her of enforcing the restriction, versus the benefit to the association of not having cats, the case appears wrongly decided. The burden to her is acute and the costs to her neighbors are trivial or non-existent. But this may be the wrong comparison.

If individual owners could challenge the reasonableness of restrictions *to them*—what amount to "as applied" challenges— then the costs of enforcing restrictions in the CC & R goes up for everyone. Litigation becomes both more likely and more expensive, because each challenge would require evaluating the impact of the restriction to the burdened property owner and comparing it to the benefits to the community. Expanding the frame to include enforcement costs, the *Nahrstedt* court's rule begins to make more sense.

---

149. 878 P.2d 1275 (Cal. 1994) [DKA & S, p. 900]; [M & S, p. 752]; [S, p. 579].

There are basic reliance interests at stake, as well. While Nahrstedt herself may have reaped untold but idiosyncratic benefits from having cats, her neighbors may include people with an idiosyncratic hatred of cats—people who derive genuine if subjective use-value from living in a pet-free community. One does not automatically trump the other. The point is an important and generalizable one: Nahrstedt, of course, has a property interest in using her home as she wants. But her neighbors have settled expectations over the use of their property, too. Because of the covenants running with the land, or the restrictions in the CC & R as the case may be, those expectations—actually, an enforceable property right!—include being free of neighbors with pets. And just as we do not generally demand that property owners justify their idiosyncratic preferences for the use of their property, here the neighbors should not have to justify their preferences, either.

Homeowners associations are governed by statute and by state-specific rules. Details of their operation fall far outside the standard introduction to property. But they do highlight the important evolution of common law covenants. Homeowners associations exist largely because of deficiencies in the law of covenants, and CC & Rs are both more powerful *ex ante* and, potentially, more flexible *ex post*. Homeowners associations can modify the terms of a CC & R through pre-determined voting rules, instead of requiring consensus by the covenant holders. Indeed, the inflexibility of common law covenants gives rise to another set of problems, taken up next.

D.   Terminating or Modifying Covenants

The strength of covenants running with the land is also their potential weakness. Their permanence risks encumbering land with out-of-date, inefficient, and even perverse restrictions far into the future. As a result, an important set of doctrines has developed for modifying and even terminating covenants. These doctrines generally reflect a tension permeating this area of law between protecting reliance, on the one hand, and preserving flexibility in the face of changed conditions on the other.

At the most general level, there are two ways to modify or terminate a restrictive covenant: (1) voluntarily, or (2) over the objections of the benefitted property owner. As with easements, the benefitted party can always choose to waive a covenant, allowing it to terminate. The parties can also bargain for modification, and courts will not interfere with their consensual transactions so long as they conform to the requirements for creating a covenant in the first place. The interesting issues revolve around non-consensual termination and modification through the changed-conditions doctrine.

The principle behind the changed-conditions doctrine is simple enough: if conditions have sufficiently changed since a covenant was put into place, the restriction can be modified or removed. The conceptual problem is deciding when conditions have changed enough to grant this relief.

Case law traditionally sets a very high bar. Courts have held that covenants remain enforceable "so long as the original purpose of the covenants can still be accomplished and substantial benefit will inure to the restricted area by their enforcement,"[150] or, if "they are still of real and substantial value" to the benefitted parties.[151] But even this does not capture the limited scope of the rule, or the problems that it can raise.

Consider, first, *Rick v. West*.[152] There, Catherine West was an early buyer into a residential subdivision, and her land was both encumbered by—and benefitted by—a covenant restricting the land in the subdivision to single-family residential use. Unable to sell more than a few lots, the subdivider, Chester Rick, changed course and sought to sell the remaining unsold forty-five acres of land to a hospital. A number of the other early residential buyers agreed to release their covenants. West, however, refused and so Rick sued, alleging a change in conditions that rendered the covenant unenforceable.

There is no doubt that the hospital was the more valuable use of the property. The market had spoken and there was no demand for the residential property. The residential subdivision was a failure. And the hospital would, presumably, have been quite valuable—at least more valuable than West's "modest" single-family house. The court nevertheless upheld the covenant, refusing to find a sufficient change in conditions. As the court explained, "[i]t is not a question of balancing the equities or equating the advantages of a hospital on this site with the effect it would have on defendant's property." Changed conditions does not mean simply that the subdivision turned out to be a failure.

Western Land Co. v. Truskolaski[153] makes a similar point. Plaintiffs owned property in a residential subdivision and sought an

---

150. Western Land Co. v. Truskolaski, 495 P.2d 624 (Nev. 1972) (quoting West Alameda Heights H. Assn. v. Board of Co. Comrs., 458 P.2d 253 (Colo. 1969)) [DKA & S, p. 882].

151. *Id.*

152. 228 N.Y.S.2d 195 (1962) [DKA & S, p. 887].

153. Truskolaski, *supra*, 495 P.2d at 624.

injunction to prevent a corner lot in the subdivision from being converted to commercial use. Defendants claimed that the conditions of the property had changed—traffic had increased on the adjoining road, and additional commercial development had happened in the area—making residential use of the property inappropriate. But the court held that the relevant question is not whether the burdened property is more valuable without the restriction than with the restriction. It almost always will be. Nor is the question even whether the costs imposed by the restriction outweigh the benefits they confer. It does not matter, in other words, whether some alternative use would be more valuable. No—according to the court, the covenant will be upheld so long as it retains value to the benefitted party or parties, and here it did.

The more general question, then, is whether this is the appropriate standard to apply. It looks like a threshold test destined to ensure that outdated, inefficient covenants will continue to be upheld. But efficiency in this context is somewhat difficult to assess because the costs and benefits have a strong inter-temporal component. The easier it is to be released from a restrictive covenant, the less valuable that covenant is in the first place. While a more liberal standard for modification or termination might well result in a more efficient allocation of uses today, such a standard would make property owners less willing to rely on covenants in the future. Catherine West might not have bought into her subdivision at all if she had worried about the enforceability of the residential covenant in the future. And, while that might have been fine in her case— after all, the subdivision was a commercial failure—it would deter buyers in ultimately successful subdivisions as well, because no one can predict with certainty when a more productive use will come along.

Ultimately, then, *ex post* flexibility runs the risk of creating disincentives to invest in property *ex ante*. To combat this risk, subdividers and others seeking to restrict the use of property might want to create binding pre-commitments—promises that they will not, in fact, seek relief from restrictions in the future. But that is precisely what covenants themselves are meant to do! They are just such precommitments. By running with the land, and into the future, they provide a mechanism for inducing reliance by third parties.

In theory, however, restrictive covenants do not need to be protected with injunctions to be valuable to the benefitted property owners. Faced with a request to build a new hospital, or to erect a new commercial use on property covenanted residential only, a court could terminate the covenant but award damages to the benefitted party.[154] The *Rick v. West* court emphatically refused to take this approach. But imagine how that outcome would have looked. The hospital would have been built, and West would have been compensated for the reduction in value to her property as a result of terminating the residential-only covenant. West could have been made whole, future buyers would not discount the value of covenants, and yet the more valuable use of the property would have been permitted.

Of course, it is not quite that simple. If West—or any other benefitted party—had strong idiosyncratic preferences that would not have been reflected fully in the change in market price, then an award of damages would not have made her whole. But by allowing West to hold out—by enforcing the restrictive covenant with a property rule—there is a chance that even obsolete and grossly inefficient covenants will remain in place, if transaction costs prevent higher-valued users from bargaining for their removal. It is telling that in *Rick v. West* most but not all of the other property owners had agreed to release their covenants. Coordinating those last few holdouts could be prohibitively difficult.

All of this, of course, ignores the distributive consequences of enforcing covenants. Another way to conceptualize the changed-conditions doctrine is to ask who should be able to capture the economic surplus of releasing the restriction. If the covenant is protected by a property rule with an injunction, then the benefitted parties can set the price at which they will voluntarily sell, and so will be able to capture some if not most of that economic surplus. If the covenant is protected by a liability rule and damages, the benefitted parties may be compensated for their harm, but the owner of the formerly restricted property will capture any of the value above that. There is no reason in the abstract to prefer one over the other, but is important to understand the stakes in these economic terms.

The Restatement (Third) of Property offers something of a compromise. It provides for injunctive relief unless "a change has taken place since the creation of a servitude that makes it impossible as a practical matter to accomplish the purpose for which the servitude was created...." In that case, a court may modify the servitude and, if modification is impossible or impracticable, a court may terminate the servitude and award damages to the servitude's beneficiaries. To paraphrase: the Restatement provides injunctive relief up to the point that changed conditions make the restriction obsolete, and then substitutes a damages remedy instead. This

---

154. For the distinction between property and liability rules, see Chapter 11.

reflects deference to the original grantor, but also includes an escape valve when there is a real likelihood that the restriction no longer serves a purpose except to create strategic holdouts.

Notice, too, that one of the advantages of a homeowners association with a CC & R is the ability to modify obsolete restrictions. In a subdivision governed simply by reciprocal covenants, each lot is both burdened by and benefits from the restrictions. Each individual lot holder therefore has a right to enforce the covenants, and so someone seeking modification or termination will need to get consent from every covenant holder. This amounts to a unanimity requirement, and practically invites holdouts. At the very least, the transaction costs involved in seeking consent from every lot owner individually, where each has the right to refuse, can be impractically high. It can lead to a clear example of a tragedy of the anti-commons.[155] The voting rules in a homeowners association combat this by allowing a majority or at least a supermajority to modify a CC & R, eliminating the power of any individual owner to hold out. While it is popular to criticize homeowners associations for rigid adherence to nitpicky rules, flexibility is actually one of their greatest advantages over traditional reciprocal covenants.

* * *

Covenants and equitable servitudes mark a real break from the limited forms of negative easements. They provide mechanisms for creating burdens and obligations running with the land, overcoming limits from the requirements of contractual privity. They also offer a useful example of common law evolution of a property doctrine. The enforceability of real covenants was limited by various technical doctrines, from horizontal privity to "touch and concern." The former gave way with the rise of equitable servitudes, and the latter has been abrogated by the new Restatement. Ultimately, the value of imposing obligations that run with the land has resulted in increasing liberalization of the rules for their creation and enforceability.

---

155. For discussion of the anti-commons, see Chapter 1.

Part IV

LAND USE CONTROLS

Land use controls are the final overarching topic in the law of property. They take different forms, from nuisance law to public regulation, and consist of different restrictions on the use of property. The topic follows naturally from the discussion of servitudes above, where property owners through private agreement could create restrictions that run with the land. But it extends beyond the context of those voluntary transactions to involuntary restrictions based on community norms or political decisions.

It is important not to lose sight of the background rule animating this entire area of law: your home is your castle. You can do what you want with it. If you want to paint it purple, hang Christmas lights in May, fill it with ugly tchotchkes, or let it fall into disrepair, that is okay. It is your property to do with as you like. But that is only the background rule. It is not ironclad, and the exceptions are large and important. First, you cannot use your property in a way that unreasonably interferes with others' use of their property, and, second, you cannot use your property in ways that the government prohibits, subject to constitutional constraints on the governments' regulatory powers. Those exceptions are the topics of this Part, in order: nuisance, zoning, and constitutional limits on the government's regulatory power.

Chapter 11

NUISANCE

One inherent constraint on your right to do what you please on your property is your neighbors' right to do the same. When one person's use and enjoyment of land comes into conflict with someone else's, the law of nuisance mediates that conflict. It manifests the Latin principle *sic utero tuo ut alienum non laedas*, meaning, loosely, "that every person should use his property so as not to injure that of another."[156] Property lawyers often refer to the doctrine colloquially as *"sic utero"* and toss off the phrase as shorthand for nuisance.

According to the classic definition, a nuisance is a non-trespassory invasion that interferes with another's use of her property. In its medieval origins, nuisance law provided nearly absolute protection against any such interference. Modern courts now prohibit using property in a way that *unreasonably* interferes with other people's use of their own property, and the test for unreasonableness will occupy much of the discussion in this chapter. But it is important to understand up front that the nuisance-making activity does not have to involve any wrongdoing or any inherently unreasonable behavior; the litmus test is simply whether the activity causes an unreasonable interference.

The underlying intuition is captured by familiar examples everywhere. When a student's use of her laptop distracts others in class, her use of the computer is not inherently wrongful (probably!). There is nothing *per se* inappropriate about playing solitaire, messaging friends, shopping, or watching movies on one's computer—in the privacy of one's home. But do those activities in class, and they may suddenly be unreasonable because of how they distract classmates. Or, when someone reclines an airplane seat all the way back, this is not an unreasonable use of the seat; it was, after all, designed to recline. But if someone tall is sitting directly behind, the rights of the recliner to use her seat as she wants conflict with the rights of the person in back to sit comfortably. Neither person is doing anything "wrong," but their property rights nevertheless conflict. These examples obviously do not involve land—and nuisance remains stubbornly although not exclusively linked to uses of land—and are intentionally tongue-in-cheek.

---

156. Morgan v. High Penn Oil Co., 77 S.E.2d 682 (N.C. 1953) [DKA & S, p. 731]; [M & S, p. 959].

But they illustrate the important conflict at the heart of nuisance law. And they highlight the two conceptual problems that arise in any nuisance dispute: defining a nuisance, and assigning a remedy.

A. The Doctrine: An Overview

Nuisance law is a broad topic and covers a wide swath of conduct. Mastering it requires, first, developing a general sense for its doctrinal contours. That is taken up here, with a more detailed analysis following in the section below.

A nuisance can be either intentional or unintentional. An unintentional nuisance arises from conduct that is negligent, reckless, or ultra-hazardous. If someone keeps tigers on her property, and the tigers regularly escape and eat the neighbors' dogs, that would be an unintentional nuisance. Unintentional nuisance claims are better examined through a tort lens as they implicate strict liability for certain kinds of dangerous activities.

Intentional nuisance fits more squarely within the law of property. A nuisance is intentional when the nuisance-maker acts for the purpose of causing harm or, more typically, knows or should have known that harm would result from her conduct. The harm need not be intentional in the sense that, "I want to shower you with noxious gases." As the court in *Morgan v. High Penn Oil Co.* explained, it is enough that I intentionally engage in operations that I know generate noxious gases and odors, which then interfere with your property.[157]

Of course, not every interference with someone else's use of property is a nuisance. Neighbors' uses come into conflict all the time—loud music, bright lights, bad smells, etc.—but do not rise to the level of a nuisance. A nuisance, then, requires that the interference be unreasonable and substantial.

There are two general doctrinal approaches to defining an unreasonable and substantial interference: the common law, and the Restatement.

The traditional common law approach is a threshold test. If the alleged nuisance-making activity interferes with others' use and enjoyment of land past a certain threshold, it is a nuisance and violates the neighbors' property rights. That threshold is typically quite low, and the presumptive remedy is an injunction. After all, the neighbors are entitled to use their own property free from

---

157. Morgan, *supra.*

interference—*sic utero,* recall—and that entitlement is usually protected through injunctive relief.

Remedying a nuisance with an injunction, however, risks giving neighbors veto power over activities that actually generate a substantial benefit to society as a whole. To prevent this outcome, courts in many jurisdictions will "balance the equities" and may then award damages, instead of an injunction. If, after balancing the equities, a court determines the activity is generating important benefits that outweigh the harm to the plaintiff, then it may allow the activity to continue and award damages instead.

That balancing is intended to protect the public's interest in the nuisance-making activity, however, and not the nuisance-maker. This is an important point, because it affects the equities that courts will include in their balancing. For example, in *Estancias Dallas Corp. v. Schultz,*[158] plaintiffs complained about the noise from an air conditioning unit for a nearby apartment building. It sounded like a jet airplane or helicopter only feet from the plaintiffs' property. The noise reduced the value of plaintiffs' property by approximately $15,000 (from $25,000 to $10,000), but it was going to cost up to $200,000 for the apartment building to abate the noise. The harm to the defendant of stopping the nuisance therefore appeared much higher than the harm to the plaintiff of the nuisance continuing. But the *Estancias* court nevertheless awarded an injunction, finding that the critical comparison was between the harm to the plaintiff and the harm *to the public*—not the harm to the defendants—of the activity stopping. Because there was no evidence showing that the *public* would be harmed by an injunction—no evidence of a housing shortage in Houston, for example— the court granted an injunction. It might seem jarring for a court to consider local housing markets in deciding the remedy for a private nuisance claim between two parties, but balancing the equities seeks to protect the public from the effect of injunctive relief; it is not about protecting activities that are more costly to stop than the costs they impose.

The Restatement (Second) of Torts offers a somewhat different approach, although it has more in common with the common law than it might initially seem. Under the restatement, a nuisance is defined by a balancing test and not a threshold. Courts are asked to decide whether "the gravity of the harm outweighs the utility of the actor's conduct." If the costs of stopping the conduct are higher than the costs it imposes, then the activity is not a nuisance.

---

158.   500 S.W.2d 217 (Tex. Ct. Civ. App. 1973) [DKA & S, p. 739].

The Restatement does not focus purely on economic costs, however. Its definition of "gravity of the harm" includes, among other factors: "the character of the harm involved; the social value that the law attaches to the type of use or enjoyment invaded; [and] the suitability of the particular use or enjoyment invaded to the character of the locality"[159] In other words, even an activity that is economically beneficial might be outweighed by harms that society holds out as especially important to protect: the quiet enjoyment of one's home, the ability to raise a family safely and in comfort, and the like.

There is something of an apples-to-oranges comparison here, and courts following the Restatement approach may find themselves balancing "the social value of the use invaded" against the "impracticality of preventing or avoiding" the harm to the plaintiff. Nevertheless, the Restatement's provisions offer a one-step calculus for weighing the costs to society of stopping a beneficial activity, and the unfairness to affected neighbors of denying them compensation. It also protects these competing values by providing money damages as the ordinary remedy, acknowledging only that injunctions may be appropriate as part of the Restatement's general provisions regarding equitable relief.[160]

Both the common law and Restatement tests raise as many questions as they answer. What interests should courts balance, and how should they be valued? What remedy should courts award? With an understanding of the doctrine's rough outlines, these deeper questions still need answers—answers that require a more solid theoretical footing.

B. A Closer Look

1. Assigning Liability

Stepping back, a nuisance constitutes an externality. By engaging in an activity, the nuisance-maker is imposing a cost on a neighbor. One way of conceptualizing the goal of nuisance law, then, is to force the nuisance-maker to internalize the costs of the activity. But there is an important twist. The costs of a nuisance are in some sense reciprocal. A tannery (or factory, gas station, disco, or bar) is only a nuisance if someone else is nearby to be bothered. Who is really imposing a harm upon whom? In a sense, it

---

159. Restatement (Second) of Torts § 827.

160. Restatement (Second) of Torts § 822 Comment (d).

is the neighbors in these examples who are imposing a harm on the commercial or industrial use nearby.

The classic illustration of this reciprocal nature of nuisance involves red cedar rust, a fungus that can occur on cedar trees.[161] This rust is entirely harmless, except to apple trees. If fungus-infected cedar trees end up near apple trees, which one is the nuisance? The answer may seems obvious. The cedar trees are the carriers of the rust. The cedars are the trees that are *doing* something; they are creating the harm. But that harm only occurs because of the proximity of the apple trees. No apple trees, no harm. Why should the cedar trees (or their owners) be punished just because there are apple trees nearby?

A more recent application is *Hendricks v. Stalnaker*.[162] Defendant drilled a well on his property and plaintiff sued, alleging that the well was a nuisance because it interfered with his ability to install a septic system. A rule prohibited him from installing a septic system within 100 feet of his neighbor's well. There is nothing inherently harmful about wells or septic systems; both are appropriate uses of property. But when they are too close together, they come into conflict. As the court noted, "either use, well or septic system, burdens the adjacent property." The septic is a burden because its discharge can contaminate ground water. And the well is a burden because it requires "non-interference" by neighbors. The *Stalnaker* court found that the septic system was the "more invasive burden" but the basic problem remains: where neither use of property is inappropriate, and yet each interferes with the other, which one should be allowed to continue?

These are not overly contrived examples. The conflict is inherent in the nature of most nuisance claims. True, some activities are so inherently harmful that they are considered a nuisance *per se*—really, a nuisance wherever they occur—things like a brothel, a factory emitting poison gas, an illegal casino, and the like. But these are very rare. In all other cases—and, frankly, in the more interesting cases—the activity at issue is a nuisance only because of its effect on a neighboring property owner. So which "activity" is responsible for the nuisance?

The conventional problem with nuisance is now starkly presented. Nuisance law, then, is best seen as a framework for evaluating the interaction of conflicting uses of property, and not just about stopping "harmful" activities. But in a relationship without

---

161. See Miller v. Schoene, 276 U.S. 272 (1928) [DKA & S, p. 1103]; [M & S, p. 1277]; [S, p. 1106].

162. 380 S.E.2d 198 (W.Va. 1989) [M & S, p. 23].

inherently wrongful conduct, how should rights be allocated? And, to add even more complexity, how should those rights be protected, with an injunction or with damages?

From a law and economics perspective, the goal of nuisance law should be to maximize social welfare by minimizing nuisance costs. Costs, however, are not just the harm imposed by the activity. According to Professor Robert Ellickson, any kind of nuisance in fact generates three different kinds of costs: nuisance costs, prevention costs, and transaction costs.[163] Nuisance costs are the most straightforward; they are the costs imposed by the activity on its neighbors. Prevention costs, in contrast, are the costs of preventing the imposition of nuisance costs on neighbors. But because of the reciprocal nature of nuisances, prevention costs can be borne by either party. A factory can stop creating a nuisance by shutting its doors, but neighbors can also prevent a nuisance by moving away. Prevention costs also need not be so all-or-nothing. A factory might be able to reduce but not eliminate nuisance costs by installing scrubbers, limiting its hours of operation, and the like. And neighbors can perhaps keep their windows closed, install air filters, or stop eating outdoors. Transaction costs, finally, are the costs of coordinating and organizing to respond to the activity.

Applying a traditional Law and Economics analysis, the goal of the legal system should be to minimize the sum of these three costs together. Of course, the law has little control over nuisance and prevention costs; they are the stuff of technological innovation (better scrubbers for the factory; better air filters for the neighbors), avoidance (moving away, shutting down the factory), or resignation (glumly enduring the pollution). What the law can affect are the transaction costs, and by minimizing them the law can increase the prevention costs that parties will voluntarily undertake.[164] That is, reducing transaction costs increases the money available for abating other kinds of costs, which will actually affect the amount and character of activity in the world.

If this seems somewhat abstract, view the problem from a different perspective. Instead of a cost that property owners impose on one another, think of nuisance as a framework for minimizing the costs of a joint enterprise.[165] Two neighbors are *together* growing both apple trees and red cedars (just each on their own individual land); or are together operating a factory and residential housing next to each other. The goal of nuisance law should be to

---

163. *See* Robert C. Ellickson, *Alternatives to Zoning: Covenants, Nuisance Rules, and Fines as Land Use Controls*, 40 U. CHI. L. REV. 681, 719–28 (1973).

164. *Id.*

165. E.g. A. Mitchell Polinsky, *Resolving Nuisance Disputes: The Simple Economics of Injunctive and Damage Remedies*, 32 STAN. L. REV. 1075 (1980).

maximize the value of that notional joint project. That might mean cutting down all the cedar trees, or letting the apple trees die. Or it might mean investing in fungus-inhibitors, in genetic modification, or other technological innovation. Whatever the answer, minimizing the costs of "cooperation" between the parties will maximize the value of the enterprise. The law can influence the costs of "cooperation" (i.e., transaction costs), by assigning legal entitlements and protecting them appropriately.

In a world without transaction costs, à la the Coase Theorem,[166] the allocation of legal entitlements should not affect whether or not the activity continues; nor should it affect the value of the joint enterprise. The apple trees will stay if they are more valuable; the cedar trees if not. This analysis is functionally identical to the discussion of servitudes in the previous chapters,[167] but a new nuisance-based hypothetical reanimates the underlying intuition.

Consider a factory emitting foul-smelling gases that harm its neighbors by $500,000. The factory, however, is worth $750,000 to its owner. If a court finds the smell to be a nuisance and grants an injunction, the factory should nevertheless be able to buy out the neighbors and continue operating because the $750,000 factory is worth more than the harm it is creating. The neighbors should be willing to accept anything more than $500,000, and the factory should be willing to pay up to $750,000. And, if the court finds that the smell is not a nuisance and denies the injunction, the neighbors will be unable to pay the factory to stop; they will be willing to pay a maximum of $500,000, and the factory will demand $750,000. Wherever the court places the entitlement, then—whether with the neighbors by finding and enjoining the nuisance, or with the factory by finding that it is not nuisance—the factory will be able to continue to emit its smelly gases, so long as there are no transaction costs.

This example, however, has the character of an open hand in a card game: it assumes omniscience and the values that each party assigns to the legal entitlement. The real power of injunctive relief is that it does not require courts to assign values to the parties' interests at all. The parties assign those interests themselves. Look at the same factory example but without numbers (still assuming zero transaction costs). If the court declares the gases to be a nuisance, and the factory is unable to buy its way out of an injunction, then, *by definition*, the factory was generating more harm than gain. And if the factory is able to pay to continue—that

---

166. For a discussion of Ronald Coase, see *supra* Chapter 1.

167. See supra Chapters 9 & 10.

is, if there is a price that the neighbors will accept and that the factory is willing to pay—then the factory is necessarily creating more gain than harm. Allowing parties to value legal entitlements themselves reveals the activities that are welfare maximizing. In the absence of transaction costs, in other words, protecting legal entitlements with a property rule will reveal at least whether an activity is creating a net benefit or net harm.

As before, transaction costs put a monkey wrench in this analysis. A legal entitlement will not necessarily wind up in the hands of the party who values it the most if transaction costs prevent efficient, welfare maximizing bargains from happening. If holdouts mean that neighbors demand too much, or if information and organizing costs mean they demand too little, the fact of the bargain (or lack of a bargain) between the nuisance-maker and her neighbors does not necessarily reveal whether the activity is creating a net benefit or net cost.

In a world with transaction costs, then, the initial allocation of legal entitlements matters. From the perspective of economic efficiency, the goal should be to assign responsibility for abating the costs of a nuisance on the party who can do it most cheaply. This is just like the intuition in torts that liability should be placed on the least cost avoider.

It is no easy task to specify the criteria for deciding where to place liability. But the goal of minimizing transaction costs at least provides some guidance. As a first pass, the best option is to assign the legal entitlement in a way that eliminates the need for bargaining and coordination altogether. This is possible when, for example, one party clearly values the legal entitlement more than the other. In that case, awarding the legal entitlement to the obviously higher-valued user will eliminate any need for bargaining; the other party will perceive the futility of trying to buy out the entitlement and will not even bother.[168]

If it is difficult to determine the high-valued user, then the law can minimize transaction costs by placing the risk of loss on the party facing the lower information and organizing costs—usually the party with better access to information about the relevant nuisance costs, and with the fewer members, respectively.[169] Essentially, allocating liability this way will minimize prevention costs—actions taken to prevent nuisance costs—at least when those costs require coordinated action.

---

168. *See* Polinsky, *supra.*

169. Ellickson, *supra* (identifying knowledge, organization, control, and simplicity of rules as appropriate factors to consider when assigning nuisance liability).

Distributional concerns make the nuisance problem even more difficult. In a Coasian world of no transaction costs, declaring an activity to be a nuisance will not affect whether the activity continues. But it will determine who pays. In the recurring factory example above, declaring the pollution to be a nuisance means that the factory owners will pay the neighbors somewhere between $500,000 and $750,000 to continue polluting. Declaring it not to be a nuisance means the factory gets to keep its money. Law and economics provides little help in deciding who should capture this money.

It is perhaps tempting to resort to "first in time" to resolve distributional questions. Make the newcomer responsible for the nuisance. If the apple trees were there first, the cedar trees are the nuisance. But if the cedar trees were there first, then the apple trees are the nuisance. People moving next door to a factory cannot complain about pollution. Some common law courts articulated that intuition with the "coming to the nuisance" defense. In essence, according to those courts, a neighbor cannot object to an activity that was in place and ongoing before she arrived.

Today, however, that rule has been roundly and almost universally rejected. Whether the plaintiff came to the nuisance—bought property knowing about the activity—may be a factor for courts to consider, but it is rarely dispositive. This modern view is entirely consistent with contemporary criticisms of first-in-time, discussed in Chapter 1. A "coming to the nuisance" defense threatens to lock in certain activities simply because they were there first, even long after they have become wholly inappropriate for an area. Imagine a slaughterhouse built on the outskirts of a city but that, over the decades, has been overtaken by residential development. Can that slaughterhouse really continue, simply because it was there first? Even if it is imposing far more harm on neighbors than it is worth to the owners? Even if it is stunting the growth of a city because of its effect on neighboring property values? No. If an activity is unreasonable for an area—or has become unreasonable—it can be a nuisance. The same goes for residential uses. If an area was once a pastoral setting but has become an urbanized industrial zone, homeowners may lose the right to object to the presence of a factory nearby. A use, once inappropriate and unreasonable for an area, may become perfectly well suited to that area over time.

There is, at the end of the day, a deep social judgment reflected in nuisance law about which uses are appropriate in a given area. What counts as a nuisance will therefore vary depending on local context. As Justice Sutherland famously observed, "A nuisance may be merely a right thing in the wrong place, like a pig in the parlor instead of the barnyard."[170] Professor Ellickson referred to this as "unneighborliness." The legal entitlement should be given to the party whose activity was neighborly according to community standards. If this all seems unsatisfyingly vague, that is the nature of nuisance liability. It is based on a standard of reasonableness and not a rule that can be mechanically applied.

2. Protecting the Entitlement

Law and economics' insights are again illuminating when it comes to deciding how to protect legal entitlements, whether through a property or liability rule. Many economists agree that property rule protection is preferable where transaction costs are low.[171] The parties can value the various activities for themselves— what it is worth to the factory to stay open; what is it worth to the neighbors to move, live with pollution, close their windows, and the like.

But where transaction costs are likely to be high, liability rule protection—where a court assess damages instead of ordering injunctive relief—offers a second-best alternative to generate the efficient outcome. If the damages approximate what parties would have negotiated *in the absence of transaction costs*, then a damages award will force the nuisance-maker to internalize the costs of her actions and generate efficient results. In effect, the court is assessing for itself the demand that the neighbors would have made absent transaction costs. Choosing between liability and property rule protection should, on this view, be motivated by the relative institutional competence of markets and courts to price the activity correctly. And that, in turn, depends largely on transaction costs.[172]

Liability rule protection can also address some of the distributional concerns identified above. It can allow an activity to continue but ensure that injured parties are compensated for the resulting harm. As we know from Professors Calabresi and Melamed, compensation can flow in either direction.[173] A nuisance maker might be forced to pay her neighbors for the harm imposed, or the neighbors

---

170. Village of Euclid v. Ambler Realty Co., 272 U.S. 365 (1926) [DKA & S, p. 930]; [M & S, p. 1064]; [S, p. 1100].

171. But see Polinsky, *supra* (arguing that liability rule protection can also induce bargaining and lead to more efficient outcomes even when transaction costs are low); Luis Kaplow & Steven Shavell, *Property Rules Versus Liability Rules: An Economic Analysis*, 109 HARV. L. REV. 713 (1996) (same).

172. For an exceptionally illuminating treatment of this analysis, see Ellickson, *supra*, at 719–28.

173. See Chapter 9(C) (discussing property and liability rules).

might be forced to pay the nuisance maker to stop. Nuisance cases, then, present useful examples of all four of the "boxes" in Calabresi and Melamed's 2 X 2 matrix.

For example, in *Estancias*, discussed above, the court found that the defendants' air conditioning unit was a nuisance and enjoined its use. That amounts to protecting the neighbors with a property rule. But any case in which a court finds that an activity is not a nuisance accomplishes the opposite: protecting the activity with a property rule. The activity is simply allowed to continue.

Boomer v. Atlantic Cement Co.,[174] is a good example of liability rule protection for neighbors. Neighbors of a cement factory sued, claiming that the factory was emitting dirt, smoke, and vibrations that damaged nearby property. The trial court found that the factory was, in fact, a nuisance, but denied an injunction. The trial court's resolution appeared sensible, but faced a significant doctrinal problem. Nuisance law in New York prohibited balancing the equities; it followed the older more traditional approach that property owners were absolutely entitled to be free from unreasonable interference with their property. If an activity was a nuisance, the neighbors were entitled to an injunction.

Enjoining the factory in *Boomer* would have been quite problematic, however. The factory represented an investment of close to $45 million, and had created permanent damages to the plaintiffs' property of only $185,000 (a number disputed in subsequent academic work[175]). Granting an injunction would have required the factory to pay potentially vast sums of money to its neighbors, since each neighbor could have demanded holdout value. It is even possible that the factory would not have been able to obtain voluntary consent from all the neighbors because of strategic holdouts and the resulting transaction costs. Not only might this have been an inefficient outcome, it might also have injured the public who benefitted in concrete (pardon the pun) ways from the having the factory nearby, since cement does not travel well over long distances and can be very expensive to move.

The New York Court of Appeals therefore crafted a creative solution. It awarded the plaintiffs an injunction—as New York law required—but then set a price for the factory to buy out the injunction. That is, the New York Court of Appeals remanded to the trial court to issue an injunction, but also to determine the

---

174. 257 N.E.2d 870 (NY 1970) [DKA & S at 743]; [M & S, p. 966]; [S, p. 380].

175. Daniel A. Farber, *Reassessing* Boomer: *Justice, Efficiency, and Nuisance Law, in* PROPERTY LAW AND LEGAL EDUCATION (Peter Hay & Michael H. Hoeflich eds. 1988) (noting that, on remand, damages came closer to $710,000).

amount of permanent damages that the factory could pay to lift the injunction. Ultimately, then, the court was valuing the plaintiffs' damages instead of letting the parties set the value themselves. It therefore amounted to liability rule protection for the neighbors.

The final "box" contains the famous case of *Spur Industries, Inc. v. Del E. Webb Dev. Co.*[176] There, Spur Industries' predecessor had opened a feedlot on relatively undeveloped land in Arizona. At that time, the feedlot was almost certainly not a nuisance; it was appropriate for its location and did not harm neighboring property owners. Over time, however, residential development began to encroach. Del Webb developed a large subdivision near the feedlot. With all the new residential units in the development, Del Webb sued, claiming that the feedlot—and it noxious smells—was both a public and a private nuisance. The court had no trouble concluding that it was; the feedlot was, after all, substantially interfering with the neighbors' property. The problem of remedy proved more difficult, however.

As a public nuisance (public nuisances are discussed at greater length below), the plaintiffs were entitled to an injunction. However, the court was disturbed by the equities of the case. After all, Spur Industries' feedlot had been there first. The court even went so far as to say that in a suit between Del Webb and Spur Industries, the coming to the nuisance defense might well preclude recovery for Del Webb. However, because the feedlot was also a public nuisance, injuring all the people who had bought into Del Webb's development, the court refused to bar Del Webb's suit simply on grounds that Spur Industries had been there first. Instead, the court awarded the injunction, but held that Del Webb was required to indemnify Spur Industries for the cost of moving its feedlot operations.

This is a startling conclusion. It looks as though the court is ordering the harmed neighbors to pay the nuisance-maker! But this is entirely consistent with the reciprocal nature of nuisance law. The feedlot only became a nuisance because Del Webb developed residential property next door. While the feedlot was responsible for the smells, Del Webb was responsible for the presence of people to be bothered by them. This case therefore fits neatly within Calabresi and Melamed's famous Box 4. The activity—here, the feedlot—was being protected with a liability rule. Instead of allowing it to continue, the court ordered it to shut down, but awarded damages assessed by the court.

A chart neatly captures all of these nuisance cases.

---

176. 494 P.2d 700 (Az. 1972) [DKA & S, p. 750]; [M & S, p. 975]; [S, p. 378].

	Property Rule	Liability Rule
Neighbor	*Estancias*	*Boomer*
Nuisance-maker (alleged)	No nuisance	*Spur Industries*

C. Public Nuisance, and the Leading Edge of Nuisance Law

Nuisance law has followed an interesting trajectory in the United States. It first came into its own with urbanization in the late nineteenth and early twentieth centuries. As people moved closer together and, more importantly, as people moved closer to industry, nuisance became a central mechanism ordering urban life. Nuisance law could be used to keep industry out of residential areas, and could mediate the inevitable disputes between close-packed activities. In truth, however, nuisance was not entirely up to this challenge. Even governed by an evolving standard of "reasonableness," nuisance often proved too blunt an instrument to address the complexities of modern urban life.

Legislative land use controls stepped in to fill gaps in nuisance doctrine, and the ascendance of zoning—starting in the 1920s and described in the following chapter—took considerable pressure off of the evolution of nuisance law. While nuisance remained—and remains—important, many of the property conflicts created by urbanization are now resolved through ever-more-detailed zoning ordinances and public land use controls.

More recently, however, creative lawyers have invoked nuisance law to address new social problems, although with at best middling success. Nevertheless, these hot topics, representing the leading edge of nuisance law, reveal that nuisance law remains a vital tool in property lawyers' toolkits. Most of these claims, however, take the form of public as opposed to private nuisance.

Public nuisance is closely related to its private cousin. A public nuisance is an activity that unreasonably interferes with the health, safety, or property of the community as a whole. Most importantly, a public nuisance claim may be brought by a member of the community without an individual private property interest at stake. This is very different from private nuisance claims, which require interference with the use and enjoyment of property. But not anyone can bring a public nuisance claim; the plaintiff must allege some kind of special injury. Still, the category of potential plaintiffs is far broader than private nuisance claimants.

The essence of a public nuisance suit is that an activity is harming the public generally. Recall that the court in *Spur Industries* sustained an injunction on grounds that a feedlot created a public as well as a private nuisance. Uses like feedlots, or polluting factories, are good examples because they may impose harms that are quite diffuse and relatively minor for any individual neighbor, but that are really burdensome for the public as a whole. Public nuisance claims can therefore fill an important role by making cognizable small diffuse harms that might not rise to the level of a private nuisance for any one property owner.

Lawyers in recent years have not limited these actions to claims against feedlots and polluting factories, the traditional objects of public nuisance claims. Instead, lawyers have used public nuisance claims to address broad social harms transforming them into something of an alternative to regulation when legislatures have failed to act. And claims have been brought to address some of the more pressing public policy issues of our time, for example against power producers alleging that their carbon emissions are leading to global warming.[177]

Such claims face a number of hurdles. First, it can be difficult to find appropriate plaintiffs—people who can allege that they suffered a harm distinct from the general harm to the community. Owners of property that might be submerged by sea level rise would be one category of potential plaintiffs. Second, they have to establish causation. When it comes to climate change, causation is a topic of fierce political debate at the highest levels of government. Of course, the power of a public nuisance suit—for good or bad—is that a court might well make a causation determination that the political process has not been able to produce. Finally, the plaintiffs will have to show that their claims are not pre-empted by federal or state law. In *American Electric Power Co.*, the United States Supreme Court remanded for a determination of the preemption issue, and it remains contested.[178]

Even more dramatically, some plaintiffs have sought to use public nuisance law to bring claims entirely divorced from real property. Suits against gun manufacturers for gun violence, tobacco producers for public health problems, and even banks for foreclosure actions, all ask courts to wade into complicated policy questions through the doctrinal hook of public nuisance. It may even be possible to argue that email spam is a public nuisance because of its

---

177. See Thomas W. Merrill, *Global Warming as a Public Nuisance*, 30 Colum. J. Envtl. L. 293 (2005) (discussing *Connecticut v. American Elec. Power Co.*, 406 F. Supp. 2d 265 (S.D.N.Y. 2005)).

178. 131 S.Ct. 2527 (2011).

interference with the public's use and enjoyment of their computers.[179] Most of these claims have so far proven unsuccessful, but they clearly represent the cutting edge of nuisance law, and the potential use of public nuisance to address broad public policy concerns.[180]

* * *

Nuisance imposes an inherent limitation on property because of the reciprocal nature of property rights. People's right to use their property as they wish is constrained by others' rights to do the same. And when those rights come into conflict, nuisance law governs the dispute. The doctrinal and conceptual challenge is to define a nuisance—using either the common law threshold test, or the Restatement's balancing approach—and then to select the appropriate remedy. Indeed, all four "boxes" of property and liability rules are on vivid display in this area of law, and the lawyers and economists have offered various approaches seeking to minimize transaction costs, minimize nuisance costs more broadly, and achieve distributional fairness.

---

179. See Adam Mossoff, *Spam—Oy, What a Nuisance,* 19 BERKELEY TECH. L. J. 625 (2004).

180. For an argument that this trend is entirely misguided, and the public nuisance should really be seen as a form of public action instead of tort, see Thomas W. Merrill, *Is Public Nuisance a Tort?*, 4 J. TORT L. 2 (2011).

Chapter 12

LAND USE REGULATIONS

Property rights frequently come into conflict. As the last chapter discussed, the urbanization of the Nineteenth Century fueled the development of nuisance law to address those conflicts. The law evolved to include an increasingly nuanced balancing of interests to protect the various stakeholders in nuisance lawsuits, including the public. Even so, nuisance remained and remains a relatively blunt legal instrument. It is triggered by conflicts that have already occurred, and then resolves the conflicts case by case.

As urbanization and industrialization continued to pick up steam in the early Twentieth Century, governments began searching for a more comprehensive way to deal with disputes over conflicting uses of land, and, ideally, to prevent the conflicts from occurring in the first place. Their solution was zoning.

Zoning today plays an important and indeed central role in development patterns throughout the United States. It plays an equally important role in the study of property because it represents a point of intersection between private property rights and governmental power. What justifies government efforts to regulate what people do on their own property? What legal doctrines exist to protect property from government encroachment? This Chapter explores those thorny issues.

A. Historical Evolution

Governments in America have regulated the uses of property since colonial times. To manage the risk of fire, Cambridge, Massachusetts prohibited certain roofing materials on buildings within the city. Some early governments limited where houses could be built, and still others prohibited "unsightly or irregular" buildings.[181] Nevertheless, land use controls did not fully blossom until the invention of zoning, a dramatic innovation in the history of property.

Today, the fact of zoning may seem quite uncontroversial. Reading early zoning cases from a contemporary perspective, the outcomes may seem obvious and all but predetermined. In the early

---

181. See, e.g., John F. Hart, *Colonial Land Use Law and Its Significance for Modern Takings Doctrine*, 109 HARV. L. REV. 1252, 1259 (1996).

twentieth century, however, zoning was extremely controversial, and it is important to understand the doctrinal hurdles that local governments had to overcome to implement comprehensive land use controls. And that, in turn, requires understand something about the nature of local governments.

Local governments' legal status has evolved over time. It is tempting to think of local governments as mini-sovereigns; the governmental unit at the bottom of the totem pole, but—like a fractal—identical in content to its larger relatives, just smaller in size. That is not, in fact, how local governments were viewed in the early twentieth century. Instead, the relationship between states and local governments was governed by Dillon's Rule (named for an influential nineteenth-century treatise).[182] Under this earlier conception, local governments were, effectively, agents of state governments. They possessed only those powers explicitly delegated by the state, and Dillon's Rule required that those grants of power be narrowly construed. Today, Dillon's Rule has been replaced in many states by Home Rule, which presumptively delegates the state's full regulatory authority to local governments. In a Home Rule state, local governments really are closer to mini-sovereigns than to their state-agent predecessors. But at the dawn of zoning, local governments were still subject to Dillon's Rule and did not have the power to regulate land use within their borders without explicit state authorization.

To encourage states to grant local governments the power to zone, the United States Department of Commerce, in 1924, promulgated the Standard Zoning Enabling Act (SZEA). The Commerce Department intended the SZEA to serve as model legislation, and encouraged states to adopt it wholesale. Almost every state did, and, to this day, almost all zoning in the United States can be traced directly back to this original document.

Under the SZEA, the overall purpose of municipal zoning was to separate incompatible land uses. Quintessentially, it provided a mechanism for segregating industrial and residential uses. It kept industry from moving into bucolic residential settings, and so prevented nuisances before they arose. But the SZEA anticipated that zoning ordinances would be much more finely tuned.

Early zoning ordinances typically divided a municipality into three or four broad categories of uses: Residential (R); Commercial (C); Industrial (I); and sometimes Agricultural (A). Each use was further subdivided to reflect different levels of intensity within each respective category of use. A zoning ordinance might have had six

---

182. John F. Dillon, Treatise on the Law of Municipal Corporations (1872).

different residential zones—R–1 through R–6—with R–1 allowing only single-family residential uses, R–2 two-family buildings, up to R–6 for apartment buildings.

In addition to separating different uses from each other, zoning ordinances also imposed bulk limits, including height, area, and set-back restrictions. Together, these constrained how high a building could be, how much of the lot it was allowed to occupy, and how far back from the property line it had to be sited. Combining both use and bulk limits could create relatively detailed control over the character of a zoned neighborhood, specifying both permitted uses and the general form that buildings must take.

It was immediately clear, however, that zoning had the potential to impose significant limits on individual property rights. An owner of a vacant lot who planned to develop a factory or an apartment building might suddenly find himself limited to building single-family homes worth much less money. And this had a substantial impact on land values. Properties that were otherwise identical were suddenly worth very different amounts of money if they were zoned differently.

To early opponents of zoning, this looked like too much governmental control. They therefore found a test case, *Euclid v. Ambler Reality Co.*,[183] to challenge the constitutionality of comprehensive zoning as envisioned by the SZEA. That case continues to provide a blueprint for zoning's constitutionality. (It also gives its name to Euclidean zoning, named after the Ohio town and not the Greek mathematician.)

It is crucial to understand what the plaintiffs were and were not alleging in *Euclid*. For the plaintiffs, the litigation was intended as a fundamental challenge to the government's power to zone. They did not claim that the zoning ordinance was an unconstitutional taking of property in violation of the Fifth Amendment (discussed in Chapter 14). Nor did they claim that the zoning ordinance was unconstitutional as applied specifically to them. Instead, the plaintiffs brought a facial challenge, alleging that the zoning ordinance was unconstitutional from the outset—no matter how it applied—because it reflected irrational and arbitrary distinctions that violated substantive due process. Broadly, they claimed that the very act of distinguishing between the permissible uses in a zone had no rational basis and so violated substantive due process.

---

183. 272 U.S. 365 (1926) [D & K p. 930]; [M & S, p. 1064]; [S, p. 1100].

To a modern ear, a substantive due process challenge might seem like a peculiar path for the plaintiffs to have pursued. In 1926, however, the plaintiffs' litigation strategy made good sense. Their goal was to invalidate zoning as a tool for municipal land use controls. And in this light, substantive due process looked perfectly suited to the task. *Euclid*, of course, was decided during the heart of the *Lochner* era, when the Supreme Court invalidated a number of laws for infringing on private rights. *Euclid* was therefore set up to be the next in that line of cases. But it was not to be. Instead, the Supreme Court affirmed *Euclid's* power to zone, and thereby broadly authorized comprehensive land use controls.

Euclid is more than a *Lochner*-era historical anomaly, however, and instead reflects the reciprocal nature of property rights. From the plaintiff's perspective, Euclid's zoning ordinance represented a significant infringement on their rights. Plaintiffs owned vacant land that they had been planning to use for industrial purposes. The new zoning ordinance restricted the property to residential use, diminishing its value from $10,000 per acre to $2,500 per acre. In effect, the government was diminishing the value of their property by 75%. The property rights stakes seem clear.

But viewed from another perspective, the story changes. Keeping industrial uses away from residential neighborhoods is an expansion of the neighbors' private property rights as much as it is an infringement of the regulated owners' rights. And that is, in fact, how the Court saw the conflict, with Justice Sutherland authoring an opinion recognizing that zoning was a tool for *protecting* property rights, not just limiting them.

If *Euclid* were only about separating industrial and residential uses, the story could end there. The opinion could be cited for its important but uncontroversial recognition that property rights are two-way streets, and it would be difficult to muster too much sympathy for property owners prevented from building industrial buildings wherever they want in a municipality. Zoning, in this view, really is just anticipatory nuisance prevention. Yes, the Court admitted that the zoning ordinance was broader than necessary— "it may thereby happen that not only offensive industries will be excluded, but those which are neither offensive nor dangerous will share the same fate"—but it held that prophylactic efforts to exclude industrial uses from residential zones were appropriate. The Court had little trouble upholding this aspect of Euclid's zoning ordinance.

More problematic, however, was the exclusion of commercial uses, and even apartment buildings, from lower-density residential zones. What, after all, is the government purpose of excluding apartment buildings or multi-family houses from R–1 (single-family) zones? What is the public harm of a small shop or bodega in a residential neighborhood? If the purpose of excluding industry from residential areas is to prevent pollution, noise, and the toxicity of factories, those justifications have little if any force applied to apartment buildings or low-intensity commercial uses. According to the plaintiffs, this kind of line-drawing was just irrational.

The Supreme Court disagreed, finding that commercial uses, and more intensive residential ones, increase traffic accidents, make access more difficult for emergency vehicles and, perhaps most importantly, decrease the "safety and security of home life." As the Court bitingly concluded in *Euclid*: "[V]ery often, the apartment house is a parasite, constructed in order to take advantage of the open spaces and attractive surroundings created by the residential character of the district."

It is difficult to ignore the nasty insinuations about class and, perhaps, race in this view of apartment buildings. While apartment buildings do not typically rise to the level of common law nuisances, the Supreme Court was nevertheless willing to defer to the legislative findings that apartment buildings were incompatible with detached single-family homes. Perhaps, more accurately, the Court saw zoning as a way of protecting middle and upper-class homeowners from neighborhood incursions by the poor. And it is ultimately this concern about protecting owners of single-family homes that appears to have motivated the Supreme Court's approval of the full panoply of restrictions in Euclid-style zoning.[184]

Whatever the Court's motivation—and whatever the class overtones—this much is clear: *Euclid* decisively held that zoning was not irrational or arbitrary on its face. Even when it goes beyond what nuisance law would achieve, and even when it includes detailed government control over the allowable uses of property, zoning is a permissible governmental function. It may still be susceptible to constitutional challenges as applied to any specific lot—if the designation of a particular parcel is irrational or arbitrary, or infringes on property rights too much—but after *Euclid*, the project of zoning could go on.

Go on, it did. In the ensuing years, zoning became ubiquitous in the United States. Nearly every metropolitan area adopted a zoning ordinance—with the notable exception of Houston, Texas—and zoning became part of the fabric of government regulation of

---

184. See, e.g., JOEL F. PASCHAL, MR. JUSTICE SUTHERLAND: A MAN AGAINST THE STATE (1951).

property. Significantly, Euclidian zoning has contributed to, and indeed substantially determined, the nature and shape of development in this country. Segregating uses by district, coupled with minimum lot sizes, has produced sprawling suburbs surrounding inner cities like concentric rings. Pushing commercial development into separate areas has often resulted in corridors of strip malls that service culs-de-sac filled with single-family detached homes. This is by no means an inevitable result of government land use controls, but it is one of the legacies of the Euclidian-style zoning approved by the Supreme Court.

Increasingly, planning professionals have pushed for new and more integrated forms of development, with mixed-use districts replacing traditional single-use ones. The so-called New Urbanists have developed plans for compact, walkable cities. A movement advocating sustainable development emphasizes transit-oriented development with decreased reliance on automobiles. All require integrating where people work and live, so that commercial uses are interspersed with residential ones. But these plans sometimes conflict with consumers' apparent preferences for living in low-density communities, accessible by car.

The evolution of land use planning is complex and contested terrain and the subject of advanced courses of study. Its importance for property is more limited and easily stated. The greater the government's authority over private property, the more capacity governments have to shape how land is used, for good and bad. Zoning therefore exists at this important intersection between public power and private rights.

Many of the deepest divisions in modern political life involve disagreements on precisely these terms: to what extent should private property trump government authority? Or, to put it differently, when should community preferences—expressed through the political process—be permitted to interfere with individuals' expectations about their property? This is not a question that should be answered in the abstract—even by ideological purists—but requires careful attention to context. It is therefore important, first, to understand what zoning is meant to accomplish, and then the mechanics of how it actually works. That will lead in turn to the persistent problem that land use presents for property law: what are the limits of the government's zoning power?

B. The Function of Zoning

If zoning were nothing more than the codification of nuisance prevention, it would be both uncontroversial and uninteresting for the student of property. But as *Euclid* demonstrates, zoning goes far beyond nuisance prevention. In many parts of the country, zoning ordinances have evolved into detailed blueprints about how and where people should be able to live and work: a kind of social and geographical engineering that operates through the built environment. To take one of the most extreme examples, New York City's zoning ordinance today spans over 3,000 pages, includes 150 different use districts, and defines buildings' permissible bulk in terms of Floor Area Ratios and Sky Plane Exposures. The complexity gives government planners tremendous control over the literal and figurative shape of the city.

This can seem at odds with that traditional conception of property as a protected sphere of liberty where owners are free to do as they please. In many municipalities, it is perhaps more accurate to say that owners are free to do what they want so long as—for example—it is to build a residence, with off-street parking for two cars, no more than 75 feet tall, and that conforms to the overall look and feel of the surrounding buildings. Land, in many of today's municipalities, is less of Blackstone's sole and despotic dominion than it is a locus for competing community pressures and directives.

But zoning is not something that happens to property owners. Property owners are themselves part of the community that benefits from, and so often demands, zoning. No one wants to be told what she can do on her own property, but everyone wants to be able to tell their neighbors what they can do on theirs!

From an economic perspective, land use regulations are efficient to the extent that they maximize the value of property. This is not just market value, but instead the use value of property—the value of property *to people*. But why are regulations necessary at all?

Here again, transaction costs loom large. In the absence of transaction costs (i.e. in some pure Coasian world) there would be no need for regulation. Imagine that someone wanted to build a gas station in the middle of a sleepy residential community. In the absence of regulation, neighboring property owners could express their preferences through voluntary market transactions. If that gas station were going to create more harm to the neighbors than benefits to its owner, the neighbors would be able to offer a price that the gas station owner would not refuse. The parties could reach an efficient result on their own.

In fact, however, there are a number of reasons that private market transactions may prove inadequate to the task. Organization costs and free rider problems may well prevent the neighbors from offering enough money to stop the gas station voluntarily, even if the gas station is, in fact, not worth the harm it is creating.[185] Even more profoundly, it will do no good for neighbors to pay one property owner not to open a gas station if a different neighbor next door may try as well. Neighbors would have to find a mechanism to stop not just one but all of their neighbors from opening gas stations; otherwise, they are paying money to secure no meaningful benefit.

Fortunately, as we saw in Chapter 10, the private law provides a mechanism for creating just such an arrangement: covenants and servitudes. But unfortunately, as we have also seen, covenants and servitudes can be very difficult to apply to existing communities. Every property owner would have to create a legally enforceable covenant running with the land. A single defector could build a gas station. And the covenants, once in place, might prove unfortunately inflexible. Sometime in the future, it may well be that a gas station is the highest and best use of property in the community, and the covenants would then be a formidable hurdle to overcome.

Nuisance law is unlikely to fare any better. Case-by-case litigation can prove unwieldy, costly, and insufficiently responsive to a community's reasonable expectations about the appropriate uses of land. And, as *Euclid* demonstrated, nuisance law may only prevent the friction of extremely incompatible land uses while doing nothing about more routine conflicts: between a bodega and its residential neighbors, or an apartment building and the nearby single-family residential neighborhood.

Zoning steps in to fill many of these gaps. It can be imposed through the normal democratic process and so can be applied to existing communities without the kind of unanimous agreement required to create comprehensive reciprocal covenants. And zoning can be changed through the normal democratic process as well, so that public land use regulations can evolve over time.

Zoning, however, replaces the risk of market failure with the risk of political failure. There is no guarantee that a government will, in fact, make efficient land use decisions. If planners and zoning officials simply judge people's preferences inaccurately, or—worse—use the zoning power to benefit favored constituencies at the expense of disfavored ones, then zoning can lead to grossly

---

185. The gas station may well create positive externalities, too, for drivers who will benefit from the business. And their preferences are especially unlikely to be represented in any deal between the gas station owner and her neighbors. For simplicity's sake, those positive externalities are set aside here.

inefficient results. Whether and when zoning is appropriate turns on the relative institutional competence of legislatures and markets. Neither is perfect. From an economic perspective, the question is which one is likely to lead to a more efficient outcome.

While land use controls are dominated by economic considerations, there are other important ways of justifying the zoning function. For example, zoning can serve an important expressive function, and help to create and not just reflect community norms. Forward-looking planners can put into place a vision for growth that individual consumers may not even know they want, but that—once achieved—will in fact make everyone better off. This is a paternalistic vision, or at least one that places more confidence in planning expertise than market mechanisms. But it may also sometimes be true.

While history is littered with the failures of plans and planners, there are also notable successes. New York City, Paris, and other planned metropolises exist as they do because of forward-looking land use plans. And, the new wave of planning features walkable, sustainable, mixed-use developments that consumers acculturated to their isolated *culs-de-sac* might actually prefer, but only if given the chance. "If you build it, they *will* come." The sufficiency of this justification for zoning obviously depends on your personal views about the relative competence of planners and markets—a dispute that implicates the most important political questions about whether and when government expertise should intervene to constrain markets.[186] But there is little doubt that zoning has the capacity to create expectations around land uses, and to shape—to some extent—long-term consumer preferences.

Closely related is the modern trend of using land use controls to encourage sustainable development. Traditional land use patterns, with car-dependent outer-ring suburbs supplying the labor for the urban core, have proven increasingly unsustainable from the perspective of resource consumption. These traditional development patterns—admittedly, partly the result of Euclidean zoning—consume more open space and foster greater dependence on fossil fuels than transit-oriented, mixed use and more dense developments.

In economic terms, traditional zoning patterns create externalities in the form of resource consumption that housing consumers do not entirely internalize. They internalize some of the costs in the

---

186. *See* JANE JACOBS, THE DEATH AND LIFE OF GREAT AMERICAN CITIES (1961) (criticizing zoning's rigid separation of uses, and advocating for more organic mixed uses).

price of gas, but unless and until the price at the pump accurately reflects all of the costs created by oil consumption—environmental costs, political costs, and the like, not to mention the infrastructure costs of road maintenance—then traditional suburbanites are imposing some costs on the rest of society.

You need not agree with the assumptions or the goals to see the broader point: society may have some objectives that markets are unlikely to produce. It is of course possible that the market will not produce them because people do not actually value them. Force people to pay, and their real preferences will win out. But as we have seen, markets can be imperfect, and regulatory land use controls might appropriately step in to achieve societal goals where markets fail.

Finally, zoning can embody communitarian values. Much of the recent property discourse in this country has focused on property as a locus of rights against the rest of the world. But increasingly, theorists have been pointing to the affirmative obligations that come with ownership. Property is not only about negative rights, but also reciprocal duties—duties that may include, for example, protecting important aesthetic, historical, or environmental resources, sharing some of the value of property with society, and contributing to the community more generally.[187] Zoning and land use controls can prevent people from building on their property unless they do so in ways that will contribute to some of these affirmative obligations, whether by preserving open space, creating some percentage of affordable housing, paying fees, and so forth.

The next question, then, is whether and how zoning actually works to accomplish these various functions.

C. The Mechanics of Zoning

Zoning varies state-by-state. Nevertheless, because of its shared origins in the Standard Zoning Enabling Act, the broad contours of zoning are almost always the same. Details and vocabulary will vary by jurisdiction, but the mechanics of zoning almost always share certain key features.

Zoning typically begins with a comprehensive land use plan for a municipality, appropriately called a Comprehensive Plan. That plan serves as something like a statement of principles; it sets out broad goals for development in the municipality. A zoning ordi-

---

187. See, e.g., Gregory S. Alexander, *The Social–Obligation Norm in American Property Law*, 94 CORNELL L. REV. 745 (2009); Gregory S. Alexander & Eduardo Peñalver, *Properties of Community*, 10 THEORETICAL INQUIRIES L. 127 (2009).

nance must then be in conformity with that plan. In reality, not all states require that the Comprehensive Plan and zoning ordinance be separate documents. Courts have sometimes been willing to infer a comprehensive plan from the zoning ordinance itself. But the basic principle remains. A municipality must set broad and relatively general land use goals, and then zone consistently with those goals.

Ideally, and as envisioned by the SZEA, the Comprehensive Plan serves as a kind of anchoring document. It frames expectations of property owners, putting everyone on notice of the municipality's land use goals for the future. But a Comprehensive Plan is not a permanent anchor. Time and time again, planners have confronted the limits of their ability to predict and plan for the future, and an inflexible plan can lock in ill-conceived land use goals. Plans are therefore mutable, and in many jurisdictions must be revisited at regular intervals.

The zoning ordinance is the detailed implementation of the Comprehensive Plan. It must be adopted by the local government's relevant law-making body, whether the city council, the town board of selectmen, or some other group. The ordinance then specifies the permissible use and bulk restrictions throughout the municipality.

Like the Comprehensive Plan, the zoning ordinance is also not rigid. Zoning includes a number of important mechanisms for creating flexibility, each subject to its own presumptions and legal protections. These devices are critically important, and not just for the operation of the zoning ordinance. With the government's power to zone firmly established, it is these various doctrines that determine how zoning actually applies to an individual parcel of land. And it is also against this backdrop that other constitutional limits on zoning apply—the topic taken up in the next section.

Consider these flexibility devices in order: variances, special exceptions, and rezonings.

A zoning variance is like a kind of escape valve. In theory, a variance is available when application of an otherwise acceptable zoning ordinance would impose an unfair burden on a particular property owner because of something unique or special about her parcel. The classic example is the application of a benign 50' setback requirement to an oddly shaped parcel—some kind of trapezoid, perhaps—leaving the property effectively undevelopable. In such a case, a property owner can seek a variance, permitting her to develop the property in a way that the zoning ordinance would not otherwise permit.

This was the situation in *Commons v. Westwood Zoning Board of Adjustment*.[188] Plaintiff's property was smaller than the minimum lot size, and so he requested a variance. The zoning board of adjustment (the local body with power to grant a variance) denied the application in the face of neighbors' opposition, and the plaintiff sued. The court ruled in favor of the plaintiff property owner, applying a two-part test: (1) whether the variance was necessary to avoid "undue hardship"; and (2) whether the variance would "substantially impinge upon the public good and the intent and purpose of the zoning plan". Importantly, though, this test can be invoked either by the property owner following the denial of a variance—as in *Commons*—or by the neighbors of a property owner if the variance had issued. In other words, if the zoning board in *Commons* had granted the property owner's variance, his neighbors may well have sued, alleging that the variance had been wrongly given.

A special exception—sometime called a conditional use permit—reverses the presumption. Instead of an escape valve for rare instances of unfair burdens, a conditional use is presumptively permitted in a zoning district, but only if certain pre-specified conditions are met. Conditional uses are therefore not permitted as of right—the developer must obtain some approval from the local zoning authority—but conditional uses are nevertheless presumptively allowed in the zone. Special exceptions are typically required for land uses that present some specific risks, or that may create burdens if grouped too closely together. Gas stations, night clubs, funeral parlors, and the like, may be permitted in a zone only after establishing that there are not too many already, and that they are not too close together.

The final mechanism for creating flexibility is the capacity of the local government to change the zoning classification of property. If an owner of a lot zoned residential wants to build a gas station, she can apply for a variance or she can simply seek to have the property rezoned for commercial use. The government, after all, can always change the law (subject to due process restrictions described below).

Variances, special exceptions, and rezonings, are not just spare doctrinal tools to be mechanically applied by zoning authorities, however. They highlight, instead, different competing visions of the nature of zoning and, therefore, different ways of thinking about the intersection of private property and public power.

---

188.   410 A.2d 1138 (N.J. 1980) [DKA & S at 955]; [S, p. 1046].

In an influential article, Professor Carol Rose argued that zoning can be seen either as a mode of planning or dealing.[189] From a planning perspective, zoning seeks to channel development into predetermined patterns. The municipality—through the political process, perhaps with the help of professional planners—decides what form development ought to take, and then drafts the zoning ordinance to achieve those forward-looking goals. From this perspective, variances, special exceptions, and rezonings, are simply a nod to the limits of the planning profession. They are an implicit acknowledgment that planners do not have perfect foresight, and cannot draft a plan that applies fairly and appropriately in every single case.

Through the dealing lens, by contrast, zoning establishes the framework for bargains between property owners (often developers) and municipalities. In this view, zoning is better seen as a kind of opening offer. It creates a bargaining moment with developers who might seek more intensive developments than the zoning ordinance allows, and the local government can condition approval on various concessions by the developer. In this view, flexibility is not a bug but a feature; it does not reflect society's inability to zone with perfect foresight, but instead creates space for bargaining between public and private interests.

Stepping back, the point is an important one for property law generally. Many of the common law property doctrines considered in this book implicitly view property in terms of enforceable and pre-specified rights. And that is the traditional interpretation of zoning as well. But the dealing model suggests something altogether different. It offers a vision of property as the product of negotiation—of an interaction between property owners and the community, mediated by the government. Whether this seems desirable or problematic depends entirely on your relative faith in local governments to regulate appropriately, and in markets and property owners to generate appropriate outcomes on their own.

Zoning does not just implicate property rights, however. A number of doctrines limit zoning because of its impact on other kinds of rights and interests. Those doctrines are still important for our understanding of property, however, because they reveal in stark terms how property rights relate to other protected interests, and can together constrain state power.

---

189. See Carol M. Rose, *Planning and Dealing: Piecemeal Land Use Controls and the Problem of Local Legitimacy*, 71 CAL. L. REV. 837 (1983).

D. Legal Limits of Zoning

Today, municipalities have quite expansive but not unlimited zoning powers. Property owners (and their neighbors) have a number of tools at their disposal to challenge unduly restrictive (or permissive) zoning changes. The discussion below highlights some of the most important, and in the process reveals some of the complicated relationships between property rights and other rights against the government.

As–Applied Substantive Due Process Challenges

While *Euclid* held that zoning was not an irrational or arbitrary exercise of the government's police power, the Supreme Court left open the possibility that specific applications of zoning might be. And, in *Nectow v. City of Cambridge*,[190] the Supreme Court invalidated the application of a zoning ordinance on precisely those grounds. Modern readers should recognize that substantive due process claims are a tough row to hoe. Conventional wisdom, post-*Lochner*, is that the deferential constitutional standard of rational basis review will never strike down economic regulations. However, land use is one context in which courts—and especially state courts—have shown a continued willingness to invalidate zoning that appears arbitrary or irrational.

This is particularly true in the face of spot zoning. Typically defined as a zoning or rezoning that singles out an individual or very small number of properties for preferential treatment, spot zoning amounts to a kind of epithet signaling likely political malfunction. The classic example involves a single parcel in an otherwise residential neighborhood that is granted an upzoning for commercial use. The rezoning might well create substantial economic value for the owner of the upzoned lot but at the expense of the community as a whole. Neighbors, then, can challenge the rezoning as impermissible spot zoning, alleging that it is irrational and arbitrary, inconsistent with the comprehensive plan, and intended primarily to benefit the individual owner. The power of the spot-zoning label is that it can trigger a more searching judicial inquiry than rational basis review. Although the challenge still sounds fundamentally in substantive due process, claiming that the rezoning is arbitrary or capricious, when the rezoning is "small" enough (affects a small enough area of land), courts may not be as deferential as they usually are to legislative determinations. Importantly, spot zoning can come in another flavor, too. Reverse spot zoning occurs when an individual or very small number of parcels

---

190. 277 U.S. 183 (1928) [DK & S, p. 940]; [M & S, p. 1290]; 1340–41].

are singled out for disfavored treatment. And it, too, can receive more than rational basis review.

The more general point is that legislative determinations regulating the use of land are entitled to broad judicial deference. Nevertheless, courts provide some oversight, either through rational basis review, or by applying a doctrine like spot zoning to trigger a more searching inquiry.

Purpose and Vagueness

Zoning is not all nuisance prevention, as *Euclid* made clear. And the legitimate purposes of zoning have continued to expand. However, there are still limits. An important example is zoning for purely aesthetic purposes.

Many municipalities have adopted some form of aesthetic regulations, requiring buildings to conform to design requirements or to go through an architectural review process. In general, however, those aesthetic restrictions must be justified on broader grounds than simply aesthetic preferences. In *State ex rel. Stoyanoff v. Berkeley*,[191] for example, property owners sought to build an "ultramodern" house on a street with more conventional architectural designs. They failed the architectural review process and sued, alleging that aesthetic preferences were an impermissible purpose for zoning. The Missouri Supreme Court rejected the argument, however, finding that the architectural review provisions were related to the "general welfare" of the community. In particular, the Court focused on evidence that the ultramodern building would decrease neighborhood property values. In other words, the architectural review provisions were not simply about regulating taste, but were instead about protecting neighborhood character and property values more broadly. According to *Stoyanoff*, architectural review is consistent with legitimate purposes for zoning, and is therefore entitled to substantial deference.

Notice, though, that essentially any architectural review provision can be justified on these terms. As a result, courts have seldom had to address whether aesthetic regulations, with nothing more than taste at stake, are valid purposes for zoning because it is easy enough for a government to find additional justifications.

But aesthetic regulations can run afoul of an entirely different problem: vagueness. The plaintiffs in *Stoyanoff* also claimed that the architectural review provisions in that case were void for vagueness. The regulations gave too little guidance to property owners and too much discretion to the architectural review board.

---

191.   458 S.W.2d 305 (Mo. 1970) [DKA & S, p. 969].

The *Stoyanoff* court rejected this argument too, finding that the standard of "conformity with the style and design of surrounding structures and conducive to the proper architectural development of the City" was constitutionally sufficient.

This contrasts with the holding in *Anderson v. Issaquah*.[192] As in *Stoyanoff,* the architectural review provisions required, in essence, consistency with the character of the neighborhood. In *Issaquah,* the architectural review board repeatedly rejected the plaintiffs' plans for a new commercial office building, each time demanding changes to make the proposal conform more closely to the neighborhood style. In contrast to *Stoyanoff,* the Washington Court of Appeals struck down the architectural review provisions as unconstitutionally vague, and was quite biting about the review board's findings. First, the court archly characterized the neighborhood as containing a "gasoline station that looks like a gasoline station" and a bank building in the "Issaquah territorial style" among others. The court was quite skeptical that the neighborhood had an aesthetic character with which the plaintiffs' plans could be in harmony. Moreover, the review board's findings did little to create precision, suggesting minor changes in color and design. One board member, in voting to reject the plaintiffs' plans, stated: "There is a certain feeling you get when you drive along Gilman Boulevard, and this building does not give that same feeling." This, said the court, was impermissibly vague.

It is no easy task, however, to balance the goals of notice and precision with the desire to allow for at least some flexibility in architectural expression. A zoning ordinance requiring that all houses be painted the same precise tint of ochre would be perfectly precise but not a good idea. And, there is a real question about who should be in the position to judge designs by whatever appropriate standard for architectural review a municipality adopts. Although architects often sit on such boards, they are not natural allies for the municipality in these decisions. Architects frequently chafe at the strictures imposed by architectural review, and resist the limits on their creative freedom.

At the end of the day, there may not be anything particularly special about aesthetic zoning if it is really about protecting neighboring properties from the externalities created by "offensive" land uses. It is at least plausible that living next door to an extremely ugly junkyard could depress property values independent of health and environmental concerns, and the difference between that and an offensively ugly home or other building may be just a matter of

---

192. 851 P.2d 744 [DKA & S, p. 978].

degree. However, provisions that vest too much discretion in architectural review boards can be impermissibly vague.

From a property perspective, the important point is that governments' regulatory powers go far beyond the power to control nuisances or harmful activities. Property owners, then, can find their property rights tempered by quite general community concerns and preferences. So long as the community is sufficiently clear, its preferences can limit even aesthetic choices owners make on their property.

Freedom of Expression

The First Amendment is another constraint on land use regulations, especially when governments attempt to regulate signs. This is not a trivial limitation, because signs are particularly likely objects of regulation. People often dislike billboards and other commercial signs in their community and try hard to keep them out. Simultaneously, sign regulations represent an interesting nexus between property rights and free expression. As the Supreme Court recognized in *City of Ladue v. Gilleo*,[193] signs present a particular problem for local governments. While signs are protected expression, they can "take up space and may obstruct views, distract motorists, displace alternative uses for land, and pose other problems that legitimately call for regulation."[194] Therefore, governments may be able to regulate signs, but they must walk a fine line. They may not restrict so much speech that signs become unavailable as a means of expression (total prohibitions on signs are not permissible); but they must not be drawn so narrowly that they discriminate based on content.

Gilleo is instructive. There, the plaintiff tried to erect several signs protesting the Gulf War. The signs were controversial in the community, to say the least, and the police eventually informed the plaintiff that the signs were prohibited by the Ladue sign ordinance. The plaintiff asked for a zoning variance for the signs, which the city denied, and so she placed a smaller sign in the window of her house, prompting the city council to adopt a new sign ordinance prohibiting that sign as well, but permitting signs for churches and schools, as well as certain commercial signs in some locations. Eventually the plaintiff sued and the Supreme Court invalidated the ordinance because it prohibited both too much and too little speech.

---

193.   512 U.S. 43 (1994) [DKA & S, p. 989].

194.   *Id.*

The Ladue sign ordinance was drawn so broadly that it made political speech—like Gilleo's—all but impossible, and so foreclosed an important medium of political expression. And, by exempting signs for churches, schools, and others, it began to look like a content-based restriction. At the least, these exemptions cast doubt on Ladue's assertions about its interest in minimizing visual clutter. In short, the regulation of signs—and especially billboards—is permissible, but it must be carefully done so as not to violate the First Amendment.

This raises a broader point for property. Property is often a vehicle for expression, even if less directly than through signs. People express their personalities through the property they own and how they display or decorate it. Restrictions on the use of property, whatever their source, can limit free expression. When those restrictions come from the government, they can even implicate free speech doctrine.

Religion and RLUIPA

The protection for religious land uses occupies a special place in property law, but understanding it requires knowing something of the conflict between Congress and the Supreme Court over the appropriate reach of constitutional scrutiny for regulations burdening religious practice.

In 1963, the United States Supreme Court decided *Sherbert v. Verner.*[195] The resulting *"Sherbert* test" applied strict scrutiny for burdens on religious exercise. In 1990, however, the Supreme Court changed course in *Equal Employment Division v. Smith.*[196] At its core, *Smith* held that rules of general applicability do not trigger strict scrutiny regardless of their incidental burden on religious practice. That case involved the denial of unemployment benefits to people who were fired for using peyote, even though peyote was part of their religious practice as members of the Native American Church.

Smith caused an immediate political backlash, and Congress reacted by enacting the Religious Freedom and Restoration Act (RFRA). That statute was designed explicitly to restore the *Sherbert* test, and so instructed courts to apply strict scrutiny "in all cases where free exercise of religion is substantially burdened."[197] In *City of Boerne v. Flores,*[198] however, the Supreme Court held that RFRA

---

195.   374 U.S. 398 (1963).

196.   494 U.S. 872 (1990).

197.   42 U.S.C. § 2000bb.

198.   521 U.S. 507 (1997).

exceeded Congress's powers under Section 5 of the Fourteenth Amendment, and was therefore unconstitutional as applied to the states. According to the Supreme Court, Congress only acts appropriately under its Section 5 enforcement powers when there is "congruence and proportionality between the injury to be prevented or remedied and the means adopted to that end."[199] In other words, RFRA was simply too broad, and the Court would not allow Congress to dictate the appropriate level of judicial scrutiny.

In response, Congress acted again. This time, it went back to the holding of *Smith*, which had limited the earlier *Sherbert* test to contexts involving both a history of discrimination, and "individualized government assessments." Congress found two areas that, in its view, met both criteria: prisoners, and land use. Hence, the frankensteinian Religious Land Use and Institutionalized Persons Act.[200] Congress found what it claimed was a long history of discrimination against religious land uses. It also concluded that land use regulation was an area in which government actors frequently made individualized determinations, raising the specter of religious discrimination. Therefore, under RLUIPA, any land use regulation that has a substantial burden on religious exercise is subject to strict scrutiny. Although the Supreme Court has yet to rule on the constitutionality of RLUIPA's land use provisions, a consensus has emerged in the lower federal courts that RLUIPA, unlike RFRA, is constitutional.

RLUIPA raises a number of difficult legal issues. First, what counts as an "individualized assessment" that triggers RLUIPA protection? In *Guru Nanak Sikh Society of Yuba City v. County of Sutter*,[201] the Ninth Circuit held that denial of a conditional use permit was an individualized assessment within the meaning of the Act. This is not an obvious conclusion, because conditional use permits do not vest very much discretion in government actors. If the use—here, a temple—satisfies pre-specified criteria, the permit must issue. Nevertheless, the standards for granting a conditional use permit often include subjective judgments about the character of the neighborhood. At least where such subjective determinations are required, courts, as in *Guru Nanak Sikh*, have often held that the individualized assessment prong is satisfied. The same reasoning applies to variances, which inevitably include a degree of subjectivity.

---

199. *Id.*

200. 42 U.S.C. §§ 2000cc–2000cc–5.

201. 456 F.3d 978 (9th Cir. 2006) [DKA & S, p. 1001]; [S, p. 1014].

Notice, then, how broadly RLUIPA applies to land use decisions. Imagine a community with an R1 zoning designation, flatly prohibiting all non-residential uses including churches. This would not appear to involve the kind of individualized assessment subject to RLUIPA. However, if a religious group were to apply for a variance to create a church in the community, the denial of the variance could very well constitute an individualized assessment and trigger RLUIPA's strict scrutiny. In other words, wherever a variance is available, RLUIPA might apply. Since variances are an inherent part of zoning, RLUIPA's reach is long indeed.

The second RLUIPA requirement, however, is that the government action "substantially burden" religious exercise. Religious exercise is defined to include the "use, building, or conversion of real property for the purpose of religious exercise," and this applies broadly. But "substantial burden" has proven more difficult to define. Some courts have interpreted it relatively narrowly, finding that excluding a religious land use in one part of a community does not substantially burden religious practice so long as it would be permitted somewhere else. But others have looked more broadly. In *Guru Nanak Sikh,* for example, the Ninth Circuit found a substantial burden because the County had denied several applications on very broad grounds, creating profound uncertainty about the plaintiffs' ability to develop anywhere in the community. Similarly, *in Sts. Constantine & Helen Greek Orthodox Church, Inc. v. City of New Berlin,*[202] the Seventh Circuit held that the denial of a rezoning was a substantial burden because the Church's choices were to search for a new parcel of land, or continue to file applications, both of which would have involved "delay, uncertainty, and expense."

While RLUIPA remains contested ground, and raises many issues of statutory interpretation, the important points for property law are more easily stated. First and foremost, the fact of RLUIPA highlights the existence of non-constitutional statutory protections for certain categories of land uses. The student of property should not leave the discussion of land use thinking that all disputes are constitutional; most land use disputes rest on more prosaic statutory grounds.

But RLUIPA again reveals how land use decisions can implicate more than property rights. After all, many religious practices are linked to real property (whether to a church, temple, or other religious site), or—for some religions—to personal property like a relic. If you have any doubt about the impact of property rights on

---

202. 396 F.3d 895 (7th Cir. 2005) [M & S, p. 1099].

religious freedom, simply consider the conflict in the Middle East and the violence spawned by disputed claims to land.

E. Affordable Housing and Impacts on the Poor

Land use disputes typically pit property owners against their neighbors, mediated through local governments and the land use process. But there is another interested party that has to be considered in any discussion of land use regulations: people excluded from a community because of regulatory restrictions on supply.

As traditionally practiced, zoning functions as a kind of growth control. It limits where development occurs and constrains density. It often also creates costly regulatory hurdles that developers must leap to obtain zoning approval. All of this has the tendency to increase the costs of housing. Sometimes this is an inadvertent side effect of local land use controls, and zoning officials seek to minimize its impacts. But other times it appears to be the purpose of land use regulation—so-called, exclusionary zoning—that is designed to keep property values high, and exclude the poor.

This dynamic is largely the result of property taxes and financing for public services, most notably public schools. And, while this may all seem somewhat far afield in a discussion of property, it is important to understand in order to make sense of the judicial efforts to require local governments to provide affordable housing.

Imagine a fictional and stylized Stepfordian village with only 10 families, each with two children, who live in identical houses on identical properties. If their 20 children are the entire population of the public school, the families will pay for their children's education directly through their property taxes. If each family pays $20,000 per year, the school will be able to spend an average of $10,000 per pupil. But what happens if a poorer family moves into town, and either buys property worth half what other families' property is worth, has four children instead of two, or both? This new family will contribute half as much in property taxes (because their house is worth half as much), and yet will consume twice as much in educational services because of the four kids. Suddenly, the school's per-pupil spending drops from $10,000 to $8,750. Families in town will either have to increase their property taxes or accept less in educational services from the town. The general point is this: when public services are funded through property taxes, owners of high-valued property will subsidize owners of low-valued property, and light consumers of local services will subsidize heavy ones.

This is by no means inappropriate. Indeed, our system of progressive taxation rests upon an assumption that it is, in fact, fair to ask the well off to pay a greater share of society's costs. Local governments fund services through taxes instead of fees in part because it spreads the obligation to society broadly, and to the people better able to pay. Moreover, education and other public services throw off positive externalities and so should perhaps be funded by everyone whether or not they have school-age children. But, whatever you think of the equities, the close relationship between property taxes and local services means that existing property owners—especially wealthier ones—benefit by minimizing the variation in local property values. The smaller the difference between expensive and inexpensive property in the municipality, the smaller the subsidy from high-valued owners to low-valued ones.

Zoning can be a tool for ensuring that property is not too cheap. Minimum lot sizes and bans on certain kinds of construction can, for example, prevent people from moving into town by putting a mobile home on a fraction-of-an-acre of land. And, while such zoning measures reflect self-interest on the part of well-to-do property owners, the effect is to exclude poorer people from the municipality by keeping prices out of reach, and thus constraining housing options for the less affluent.

The economic dynamic is easy to see, but the exclusionary effect is problematic. As a result, some courts have crafted a legal basis for prohibiting exclusionary zoning. The leading case is *Southern Burlington County N.A.A.C.P. v. Township of Mt. Laurel.*[203] There, a local chapter of the NAACP challenged Mt. Laurel's zoning ordinance, which zoned significant portions of the town for industrial use and imposed large minimum lot sizes in order to limit the supply of residential property. Tellingly, the town had recently approved a major residential development, but only after requiring the developer to restrict the number of units available to families with children, and to pay for any children above a certain number to attend the local public school.

The town represented to the court—and the court accepted for its decision—that its purpose was not to discriminate based on race or on any suspect classification. While some exclusionary zoning has more or less explicit racial overtones, here the town asserted that its interests were exclusively to protect the local property tax base. The question for the New Jersey Supreme Court, then, was

---

203.   336 A.2d 713 (1975) [DKA & S, p. 1037][M & S, p. 1088][S, p. 1014].

whether this was a permissible objective of local land use regulations. The Court held it was not.

The Court reasoned that a municipality's power to zone comes from the state's delegated police powers. Therefore, a municipality has an obligation to exercise its zoning power for the benefit of the state as a whole, and not just its own parochial self-interest. Exclusionary zoning, like Mt. Laurel's, shifts the burden of housing the poor onto neighboring municipalities. And this is an inappropriate use of the state's police powers. The New Jersey Supreme Court therefore famously concluded that every municipality in New Jersey has an obligation to make possible a variety and choice of housing, and to provide for its fair share of housing for low- and moderate-income people. As the Court concluded: "Municipalities must zone primarily for the living welfare of people and not for the benefit of the local tax rate."

There is a long and complicated postscript to *Mt. Laurel* involving subsequent litigation, legislation, and repeated efforts by municipalities and the state to change the Court-imposed fair share obligations. That story is a rich part of land use law, but involves more detail than is necessary for seeing the property stakes in the dispute. From the view of property law, *Mt. Laurel* is, first and foremost, a reminder that the right to exclude also implicates the rights of the excluded. Even if all property owners agreed among themselves to allow the most draconian restrictive zoning, property is a locus for others' interests too. And property—through the power of zoning—is a place for mediating those competing claims. As the New Jersey Supreme Court had written four years earlier in *State v. Shack*: "Property rights serve human values. They are recognized to that end, and are limited by it."[204]

And *Mt. Laurel* is also a reminder that property regulation comes with externalities, too. The private law, from servitudes to landlord tenant, restricts how people can structure their property arrangements, at least partly to protect the interests of third parties. The concern, again, is that bilateral decisions might impose unacceptable costs to society more broadly, either by increasing information costs or by imposing inter-temporal restrictions. In *Mt. Laurel,* the New Jersey Supreme Court offered a similar justification to restrict zoning—the public law of property—as well.

* * *

The pressures of urbanization and industrialization led states and local governments to anticipate and prevent property conflicts

---

204. See *State v. Shack, supra* Chapter 1.

before they arose by separating incompatible uses. But land use regulation has come a long way from its origins in nuisance law. The legitimate purposes of government regulation can extend even to aesthetic controls. This expansive regulatory power can interfere with a broad array of constitutional rights, from substantive due process limits on the purpose of regulations, to freedom of religion and expression. The appropriate limits on these powers depend entirely on one's view of the relative institutional competence of governments and markets and, ultimately, of courts that end up adjudicating the disputes.

Chapter 13

THE TAKINGS CLAUSE AND
EMINENT DOMAIN

The Fifth Amendment Takings Clause provides, "[N]or shall private property be taken for public use, without just compensation." This innocuous-sounding clause contains some of the thorniest problems in the law of property. When does a government "take" property? How should compensation be measured? And what counts as public use? This Chapter addresses the last two questions, while Chapter 14 focuses on the problem of deciding what counts as a taking in the first place.

Looking closely at its text, the Takings Clause does not grant the government the power to take property. The Takings Clause is, instead, a limitation on the power to take property—a power that is often said to come from the nature of sovereignty itself. Indeed, the power to take property—the so-called power of "eminent domain"—dates back to the earliest governments and is a consistent sovereign power throughout history. The American innovation reflected in the Fifth Amendment was to limit the power, and to provide property owners with some protection against government expropriation. According to the Fifth Amendment, those protections include a requirement that the government only take property for public use, and that it must pay for whatever property it takes.

These are relatively thin constraints. If the government wants to take your property, it almost certainly can. If the state wants to build a new road, a jail, or a park, it can force private property owners to "sell." By filing a condemnation action in state court, the state—or the relevant governmental subunit—can use its power of eminent domain to take title to private property upon payment of compensation. Condemnation amounts to a forced sale at a price determined by the court. First, however, the government must satisfy the "public use" requirement, the content of which is the first topic in this chapter.

A. The Public Use Doctrine

Given the nature of constitutional interpretation, the only certainty about the "public use" requirement is that it does not mean, literally, use by the public. Early Supreme Court case law interpreted "public use" to mean "public purpose." But this is hardly the model of clarity, either. And a sense of the historic uses of eminent domain helps to frame the interpretive problem.

There is no doubt that governments have the power of eminent domain to take property for a road, government building, or other actual use by the public. Similarly, courts have consistently held that the government may not take property from private person A simply in order to give it to private person B. Condemnation for no other purpose than redistributing property from one person to another is impermissible. The difficult cases, then, are those many in the middle, where the government is condemning property to effectuate some broad public goal but transfers the property to a private party along the way.

For example, the earliest widespread use of eminent domain in the United States was to build the railroads. Railroads, though, were usually private companies. As a result, states would often use eminent domain to take private property, and then transfer land—or sometimes an easement over the land—to private railroad companies to build tracks and necessary infrastructure. Courts generally did not object.

In the Twentieth Century, however, the purposes of eminent domain expanded beyond infrastructure development to broader economic development. Three famous cases lay the foundation, setting out the scope of government eminent domain power and culminating, ultimately, in a fourth decision: *Kelo v. City of New London.*[205]

In the first case, *Berman v. Parker,*[206] Washington D.C. sought to condemn a large swath of land as part of a program of urban redevelopment. It was a common if controversial approach to economic development at the time. The government would acquire and clear an entire neighborhood in order to facilitate large-scale redevelopment. These programs, sometimes referred to as "slum clearance" or, troublingly, as "negro removal" often involved the dismantling of whole communities. Governments justified them on grounds of blight remediation. In *Berman,* one of the properties subject to condemnation was a department store that was not, itself, blighted. The owner of the store sued, alleging that the taking of his non-blighted property for purposes of economic redevelopment was not, in fact, a public use.

The Supreme Court rejected the property owner's challenge. The Court held that economic redevelopment was a legitimate use

---

205. 545 U.S. 469 (2005) [DKA & S, p. 1065]; [M & S, p. 1223]; [S, p. 1074].

206. 348 U.S. 26 (1954) [DKA & S, p. 976]; [M & S, p. 1242].

of the government's police power, analogous in many ways to zoning. Having determined that the purpose of the government activity was permissible, the court then deferred to the use of eminent domain as the government's chosen means to accomplish its goals. The Court also deferred to the government's determination that the area needed to be planned as a whole, and that the blight in the community justified taking even the plaintiff's non-blighted store. Overall, the case reflects tremendous deference, both in deciding the scope of the government's police power, and then to the use of eminent domain to accomplish its goals.

This same dynamic was at play in *Poletown Neighborhood Council v. City of Detroit.*[207] There, General Motors threatened to leave Detroit because it was unable to expand some of its industrial operations. The unavailability of vacant land made relocating out of Detroit's urban core appealing to GM. Faced with this threatened departure of one of Detroit's bedrock industries, Detroit's mayor offered to assemble land adjacent to GM's existing plant in order to allow it to expand. Unfortunately, the only adjacent land was occupied by a relatively healthy and cohesive Polish community, in an area known as Poletown. Nevertheless, Detroit moved ahead with its condemnation, dismantling the entire neighborhood, and conveying the land to GM.

Some of the condemnees (the property owners whose property had been taken) sued, alleging that their property was not being taken for a public use. The Michigan Supreme Court disagreed and allowed the condemnation to proceed. Consistent with *Berman,* the Michigan Supreme Court deferred to the legislative determination of public use. As the Court held: "The determination of what constitutes a public purpose is primarily a legislative function, subject to review by the courts when abused, and the determination of the legislative body of that matter should not be reversed except in instances where such determination is palpable and manifestly arbitrary and incorrect." In the Court's view, Detroit's evidence of the economic stakes for the city if GM left was enough to demonstrate "public use." In essence, the Michigan Supreme Court held that "public use" was synonymous with "public need," which could include purely economic concerns, even if that meant taking private property and conveying it to General Motors.

The final case of the three is *Hawaii Housing Authority v. Midkiff.*[208] Hawaii has an usual distribution of land ownership

---

207. 304 N.W.2d 455 (Mich. 1981) [DKA & S, p. 1074–75]; [M & S, p. 1222]; [S, p. 1089].

208. 467 U.S. 229 (1984) [M & S, p. 1242].

tracing back to the early chiefs of the Hawaiian Islands. As of 1984, 47% of all land was owned by only 72 people, and on Oahu, in particular, 22 people owned over 72% of all land. This concentration of ownership distorted land markets in Hawaii, inflating prices and "injuring the public tranquility and welfare."[209] To remedy the problem, Hawaii enacted a statute requiring property owners, in some situations, to sell their property to residential tenants. These forced sales were effectuated through eminent domain.

Property owners sued, alleging that this use of eminent domain violated the public use requirement. The Supreme Court, in an opinion by Justice O'Connor, upheld the Hawaii statute. According to the Supreme Court, "[t]he 'public use' requirement is . . . coterminous with the scope of a sovereign's police powers." Therefore, if the government has the power to act—if its actions survive substantive due process review—the "public use" clause does not impose an additional restriction.

Ultimately, then, the public use inquiry is one characterized by deference to legislative determinations. Even when a government is exercising eminent domain to transfer property from one private property owner to another, as in *Poletown* and *Midkiff,* courts have traditionally deferred, at least so long as there was a colorable public purpose that justified the transfer.

Against this backdrop, the Supreme Court decided *Kelo v. City of New London* in 2005,[210] one of the more controversial decisions of the last few decades. In *Kelo,* the perennially distressed City of New London was engaged in active efforts to promote economic revitalization. Pfizer, the pharmaceutical company, announced plans to build a major new research facility adjacent to an area targeted for redevelopment. To leverage the opportunity that Pfizer's investment would create, New London authorized the use of eminent domain to assemble property in order to support the adjacent park or to provide parking or retail services. New London did not claim that the property was blighted, but only that it could be put to much more productive use as part of the overall plan for economic revitalization.

Several of the condemnees (including plaintiff Susette Kelo) sued, alleging that the taking was not for public use. In a sharply divided opinion, the Supreme Court voted 5–4 to uphold the condemnation. According to the majority, the decision followed naturally from *Berman* and *Midkiff.* Consistent with those earlier

---

209. Id.
210. 545 U.S. 469 (2005) [DKA & S, p. 1065]; [M & S, p. 1223]; [S, p. 1074].

opinions, the majority deferred to the legislative determination that condemnation was for a public purpose. As the Court concluded:

> Given the comprehensive character of the plan, the thorough deliberation that preceded its adoption, and the limited scope of our review, it is appropriate for us, as it was in Berman, to resolve the challenges of the individual owners, not on a piecemeal basis, but rather in light of the entire plan. Because that plan unquestionably serves a public purpose, the takings challenged here satisfy the public use requirement of the Fifth Amendment.

The dissenters took a very different view. A dissent by Justice O'Connor warned that the majority's decision left all property at risk of eminent domain. "Nothing is to prevent the State from replacing any Motel 6 with a Ritz–Carlton, any home with a shopping mall, or any farm with a factory."[211] And she blamed the conclusion on "errant language" from *Berman* and *Midkiff*—curious, perhaps, since Justice O'Connor herself wrote the opinion in *Midkiff*. Nevertheless, the dissenters argued for more searching review of public use, and for an end to the deference traditionally afforded to legislatures.

In a separate and interesting dissent, Justice Thomas traced the history of eminent domain and ultimately warned that the majority's opinion would have a disproportionate impact on minority communities and the poor. It is such communities, after all, that have traditionally borne the brunt of takings for economic redevelopment. According to Justice Thomas, economic redevelopment tends to displace, not help, the neediest members of society, and the majority's ruling merely cleared the way for more blight removal.

The public and political backlash against the *Kelo* decision was swift and strong, resulting in a variety of legal reforms described below. But as a matter of federal constitutional law, *Kelo* reaffirmed the Supreme Court's traditional deference to legislative determinations of public use.

Stepping back even more, the real question is whether and when individual property rights stand as a bar to state action, even with compensation. Answering that question requires understanding the underlying justifications for eminent domain.

B. Justifications for Eminent Domain

As described in this Chapter's introductory paragraphs, eminent domain is not a recent invention. It is said to be an inherent

---

211. Id.

right of the sovereign. The government—whether the crown or the people—has a kind of transcendent power over the land within its jurisdiction. Eminent domain, like the power to levy taxes, is a power the government naturally possesses. But this does not provide any explanation for how broad the power should be. For that, a different kind of account is required.

There is, in fact, a relatively straightforward functional justification for governments' eminent domain power: It is necessary to facilitate land assembly by overcoming holdouts. Imagine any effort to assemble fractionated ownership into a larger bundle of property for some higher-valued use, such as connecting land for railroads, combining many parcels for an airport expansion, assembling land on a city block for a new high-rise, and so forth. In each case, many people may be willing to sell at or near their reservation price plus some reasonable surplus, and voluntary transactions are adequate and appropriate. But as the fact and value of the land assembly become clear, each property owner has an incentive to demand something extra to try to capture some of the value of the land assembly. To take the most extreme example, imagine that a railroad company has only one small gap left to fill to connect the East Coast with the West Coast. How much will that last property owner demand? In theory, she could hold out for almost the full value of the railroad regardless of what her property is actually worth to her. Without her consent, the railroad connection will not happen, and so she can demand as much as she wants, up to the value of her property *to the railroad*. If, instead of one person, it is the last three, or thirty, or three hundred people who all want a slice of the ultimate value of the project, they may well demand more in aggregate than the project is worth. As a result, welfare-maximizing deals do not happen, the project does not happen, and everyone is worse off.

Opponents of eminent domain might respond by pointing out that private land assemblies happen all the time in the absence of eminent domain. But private developers are not in the same position as the government for several important reasons. First, private developers are capable of using buying agents, and other secretive arrangements, that hide the nature of the ultimate project from the various property owners.[212] If the sellers do not detect that their parcels are part of a broader land assembly, then they will not try to hold out for part of the assembled value of their land. Governments, though, must act transparently and deliberatively, and so property owners know whether and to what extent the government needs their property. Property owners can therefore enjoy a sub-

---

212. *See* Daniel B. Kelly, *The Public Use Requirement in Eminent Domain Law: A Rationale Based on Secret Purchases and Private Influence*, 92 CORNELL L. REV. 1 (2006).

stantial bargaining advantage when the counterparty is a government as opposed to a developer.

Perhaps more importantly, strategic holdouts for surplus value are less appropriate when the costs are borne by the public instead of private developers. If a property owner seeking to extract holdout value increases the costs of a commercial development, those costs are borne by the developer. It is hard, in the abstract, to find a reason for favoring developers over individual landowners. Whatever bargain they strike—or do not!—mostly implicates the distribution of money between private parties. But when the government is on the other side, increased costs will be borne by the public through increased taxes. And, if the deal doesn't happen at all, the public bears the costs of foregone public benefits—a park, a school, or even economic development.

Of course, eminent domain raises troubling concerns, too. Some worry that the power to compel sales allows the government to buy property for less than owners would genuinely demand for their property in a consensual market transaction. Not only is this unfair to property owners, it amounts to buying property on the cheap and may incentivize too much acquisition by the government. Worse, developers may partner with the government to acquire property for less than they would have to pay in the open market. They may prefer to acquire property "through" the government, which may distort development pressures and preferences.[213] This, however, depends on the compensation the government is required to pay when it takes property by eminent domain.

C. Compensation

Courts have sometimes observed that the ideal form of compensation would leave condemnees indifferent to government takings. That is, compensation would make property owners *subjectively whole*. However, courts have almost universally acknowledged that such a standard is impractical to achieve, and so have applied instead an objective fair market value standard for compensation. The potential gap between property's objective and subjective value accounts for much of the opposition to eminent domain.

There is no quick fix for this problem, however. Subjective value is, by its very nature, subjective. Courts cannot measure it *ex post* with any precision. And ask property owners to self-assess the value of their property *to them* and they will predictably exaggerate

---

213. Thomas W. Merrill, *The Economics of Public Use*, 72 Cornell L. Rev. 61 (1986).

to secure some extra value from the government. Primarily for reasons of administrability, then, courts have consistently held that "just compensation" requires the government to pay only the fair market value of the property.

A number of factors drive the objective fair market value standard. Formally, this is the price a willing buyer would pay to a willing seller. In any consensual transaction, the buyer must, by definition, value the property more than the seller or they would not be able to agree on a price. Somewhere between the seller's reservation price and the buyer's best offer is a bargaining range that consists of the surplus value created by the deal. However, the objective measure of just compensation ignores idiosyncratic reasons that the actual seller might value the property more than a hypothetical "objective" seller. Fair market value can therefore result in compensation that is lower than the actual seller might have demanded for the property, making the seller worse off.

Scholars have proposed a number of responses to this possibility, and many are important and provocative. Professor Saul Levmore, for example, has proposed instituting *ex ante* self-valuation, where the value that people assign to their property is used both for eminent domain compensation and for purposes of property taxes.[214] That way, people will not overstate how much they value their property because it would drive up their property taxes. However, for this proposal to generate the "right" price (meaning owners' actual subjective value for their property) there must be a complex balance between anticipated property taxes and anticipated compensation in eminent domain. Because the former are a certainty—property taxes will be paid!—but the latter is a probability affected by the likelihood of eminent domain, the two are unlikely to offset in a way that will generate "accurate" values. The proposal might even turn out to be quite regressive, forcing people who face the greatest risk of eminent domain to declare the highest value, while allowing property owners with the most confidence in their political power to declare the lowest value and pay the least in property taxes.

Professors Michael Heller and Roderick Hills offered an entirely different kind of solution, proposing a collective bargaining mechanism that they dubbed "Land Assembly Districts"[215] In their view, a central problem with eminent domain is that individual property owners have no good way of bargaining for a share of the

---

214. Saul Levmore, *Self-Assessed Valuation Systems for Tort and Other Law*, 68 VA. L. REV. 771 (1982).

215. Michael Heller & Rick Hills, *Land Assembly Districts*, 121 HARV. L. REV. 1465 (2008).

surplus being generated by a land assembly. Giving individual owners that power runs the risk of creating strategic holdouts and blocking projects altogether. The Heller and Hills solution is to create a kind of governance mechanism for property owners to come together to bargain collectively, with the proceeds of any sale then being divided among the constituent property owners. This, too, requires some degree of coercion, however, and the details of the voting rules and the allocation of the proceeds turns out to be difficult indeed.

Others—notably Richard Epstein—have proposed simply adding a flat percentage increase over fair market value in order to approximate owners' subjective values.[216] After all, the only thing we know for sure is that property owners value their property at more than its fair market value; otherwise, they would already have sold. A variation on this theme includes a proposal to adjust compensation depending on how "public" the public use actually is, awarding more compensation as the public benefits decrease.[217] But this, too, is no silver bullet. Indeed, over-compensation creates its own problems. Property owners might actually seek condemnation because they would receive more money from the government than from a market transaction. And, of course, increasing the costs of acquiring property will either increase taxes or decrease government projects requiring land. In other words, raising the costs to the government of acquiring land is not free; it simply shifts the costs elsewhere, either in the form of higher taxes or foregone projects. Whether this is good or bad depends a lot on your view of government and government incentives, a point taken up below.

Stepping back from the details of these various proposals, they reveal three different but related problems with compensation for eminent domain: accuracy, transaction costs, and fairness. Proposals to generate more "accurate" measures of subjective value seek to overcome administrability constrains that have driven the selection of fair market value as the appropriate standard for compensation. Other proposals, like Heller and Hills', seek to lower the transaction costs associated with land assembly in order to facilitate market transactions and minimize the need for eminent domain in the first place. And proposals to adjust compensation upward are based on the claim that fair market value is fundamentally inadequate to make property owners whole.

---

216. Richard Epstein, Takings: Private Property and the Power of Eminent Domain 184 (1985).

217. James E. Krier & Christopher Serkin, *Public Ruses*, 2004 Mich. St. L. Rev. 859.

But why should the goal be to make property owners whole? Why is that even the standard for eminent domain compensation? One justification is economic. The difference between fair market value and condemnees' subjective harm is a kind of externality. If the government can act without internalizing the full costs of its actions, then it is reasonable to worry that the government will "over act," i.e., take too much property through eminent domain. The purpose of compensation in this account is to force the government to internalize the costs of its actions, and ideally the *full* costs of its actions.

By now, this should be a familiar explanation from a number of property doctrines. But this justification plays out somewhat differently for governments because forcing a government to pay compensation does not necessarily have the same effect as forcing a private party to pay. Government actors are not, after all, spending their own money. They are merely agents for taxpayers. To understand government incentives it is therefore necessary to focus on the political costs and benefits—the "political economy"—of their actions, and not the financial ones.

It may well be, for example, that a government project involving eminent domain will benefit a particular and powerful political backer, as when Detroit condemned property for General Motors. But condemnees are often well situated to exact a substantial political price. They are typically a discrete group—property owners in the footprint of a project—with high stakes in the outcome. Perversely, compensation may function to buy off the political opposition of the people best situated to resist a government project.[218] Compensation, in this view, allows the government to avoid at least some of the political costs of its actions. And while it does so by forcing taxpayers to pay, those taxpayers may be a relatively diffuse and apathetic group, insufficiently organized to monitor government spending except at the margins. A worry, then, in addition to governments underpaying and imposing costs on property owners, is the risk of overpaying and imposing costs on taxpayers. At the very least, the effect of compensation on government incentives is complex, and it is not at all clear that forcing the government to pay will actually lead to efficient incentives.

Fundamental to arguments about eminent domain, then, are competing views about government. People who mistrust government decisionmaking may worry about the over-use of eminent

---

218. Louis Kaplow, *An Economic Analysis of Legal Transitions*, 99 Harv. L. Rev. 509, 571 (1986). For a close look at the political economy of eminent domain, see Merrill, *supra*.

domain. If the government can acquire property more cheaply than private actors in the market, they may take too much property. Relatedly, people may worry that governments are imperfect agents for public preferences. Government actors may be motivated by political interests not financial ones, and they will use eminent domain to serve the interests of mobilized special interest groups— like developers—at the expense of the apathetic majority of voters. And finally, opponents of eminent domain focus on the costs. Eminent domain threatens the security of private property, and imposes costs on individual property owners.

Proponents of broad eminent domain powers, in contrast, worry about the possibility of individual private property owners to stand in the way of important public projects—whether infrastructure or economic development. And they generally support broad government power to pursue objectives that the government determines to be in the public's interest. Increasing compensation will therefore interfere with the government's ability to promote the public good.

D.   Legal Reforms

The eminent domain tide has been shifting since *Kelo.* While the Supreme Court and lower federal courts have continued to defer to legislative determinations about public use, many states have adopted sweeping reforms. These have taken a number of forms, and they are now at the leading edge of the fight over eminent domain.

In some states, eminent domain reform has come from the courts. Some state courts have narrowed their interpretation of the "public use" requirement in state constitutions, providing additional protection to property owners.[219]

Many states have adopted new legislation curtailing the use of eminent domain. Some have adopted definitions of "public use" that explicitly exclude expanding the tax base.[220] That is, taking property purely for purposes of economic development does not satisfy the "public use" requirement. Even in those states, though, many still permit eminent domain to remedy blight, and so the vagueness of the "public use" test has been replaced by the vagueness of the blight standard. After all, if a government can declare just about any property "blighted," then it can always

---

219.   See, e.g., County of Wayne v. Hathcock, 684 N.W.2d 765 (Mich. 2004) [M & S, p. 1223]; [S, p. 1089, 1091].

220.   See, e.g., Fla. Stat. § 163.35 (2006).

justify its taking of the property as blight remediation instead of economic development.[221]

Whatever the institutional source of reform, the basic problem remains the same: identifying a principled basis for distinguishing permissible and impermissible uses of eminent domain. Consider, for example, a rule prohibiting eminent domain to benefit private parties. The problem is that many government actions have the incidental effect of benefitting private parties. When a government uses eminent domain to construct a highway exit ramp, it will often confer a substantial benefit on adjacent property owners who are likely to see their land values increase dramatically. And yet few people would argue against that use of eminent domain. Roads, after all, are quintessential public uses.

Other alternatives are also problematic. Some might argue for a rule prohibiting eminent domain when the government *purpose* was to benefit a private party (instead of condemnations merely having that incidental effect). But how are courts to decide governmental purpose? Conceptually, it is difficult to assign a single purpose to a legislature or government agency, which consists of several if not many people. And, even if that conceptual problem is set aside, this rule simply kicks the can down the road. Must courts defer to legislative declarations of purpose? If so, this rule—prohibiting takings for the purpose of benefiting private parties—becomes little more than a trap for the unwary government that is not sophisticated enough to find and articulate some valid public purpose.

Even a rule prohibiting eminent domain to transfer property to another private party is problematic. After all, building the railroads involved just such transfers. The government took property from individual property owners and transferred that property to private railroad companies. And yet few people think that such transfers were inappropriate, because the railroads created such a substantial public benefit. If eminent domain was appropriate to build the railroads, is there a principled basis for arguing that it cannot be used to build the local economy?

And that is the crux of the problem. If governments could condemn property for the railroads because of the substantial economic benefit, why not also allow them to condemn property for industry more generally—such as Pfizer, in New London? True, the economic benefits in New London never came to pass, but it is not at all clear that courts are in a better position than legislatures to

---

221. See Ilya Somin, *The Limits of Backlash: Assessing the Political Response to Kelo*, 93 MINN. L. REV. 2100 (2009).

evaluate the likelihood of success ahead of time. Moreover, many of the communities that used eminent domain to try to attract railroads also failed; not everyone was a winner even in the land assemblies for the railroads.

Despite these line-drawing problems, some courts and legislatures have prohibited eminent domain for purposes of economic development, or where the sole justification is to improve the tax base. These are lines that courts may be able to police. The effect of these laws is difficult to predict, however. It is possible that they will create important stability in property rights and substantial public benefits in the form of increased security against the government. But it is also possible that they will make land assemblies prohibitively difficult, and drive larger developments to other states.

Moreover, statewide eminent domain reform is likely to have distributive consequences between local governments. Eminent domain is most important for the developed urban core where property is fragmented into many small lots and holdouts are more likely. In suburbs and rural settings, land assembly is generally easier and eminent domain is therefore less valuable. To put it differently, limiting the power of eminent domain statewide will disproportionately burden municipalities where undeveloped land is scarce.

While the law is still evolving, and post-*Kelo* eminent domain reforms are still being adopted and litigated, this much, at least, is clear: the government's power of eminent domain is broad, and potentially as broad as its police power. But some limits in some jurisdictions are emerging. How effective they are, and what costs they will impose on the government and the public, remain to be seen as of this writing.

* * *

Broadly speaking, private property is owned subject to the government's power of eminent domain. That power is extremely broad, but is subject to two constitutional limits: (1) that the government can only take property for public use, and (2) that it must pay just compensation. The content of those limits remains hotly contested, but at stake is the balance between government power and private property rights.

Chapter 14

REGULATORY TAKINGS

As the previous chapter made clear, the government has broad powers to take private property so long as it pays compensation. Limits on eminent domain remain contested, but the basic power is conceptually straightforward. The Takings Clause raises an additional and considerably more complex problem, however: when has the government acted in a way that requires it to pay compensation?

Where the government actually takes title to property, explicitly exercising its power of eminent domain, there is no question that the government must pay. But what of regulations having a similar effect? For example, imagine that a state enacts a new regulation prohibiting developing wetlands, and someone owns property consisting entirely of wetlands. Even though the state is not purporting to take title, has it nevertheless taken the property in a way that requires compensation? That question—deciding when the government has taken property within the meaning of the Fifth Amendment Takings Clause—is the topic of this final chapter.

Regulatory takings—and the idea that a mere regulation could amount to an unconstitutional taking of property—trace their origins to the famous case of *Pennsylvania Coal Co. v. Mahon*.[222] That case remains the best place to begin any discussion of the Takings Clause, not because it provides answers but because it usefully tees up the most difficult questions.

In *Penn Coal*, the state of Pennsylvania had enacted the Kohler Act, which forbade coal companies from mining anthracite coal in a way that would cause the subsidence (settling down or sinking) of buildings on the surface. In other words, the law prevented the coal companies from removing coal in a way that would destroy people's homes.

Importantly, at least for the majority, the plaintiff homeowners had originally purchased their land from the Pennsylvania Coal Company, which had retained the subsurface right to the property. The coal company, in other words, had contracted for the right to mine under the plaintiffs' homes. The Supreme Court, in an opinion by Justice Holmes, held that the Kohler Act was an

---

222. 260 U.S. 393 (1922) [DKA & S, p. 1103]; [M & S, p. 1268]; [S, p. 1098].

unconstitutional taking of the coal companies' subsurface rights. The logic is compelling. Before the Kohler Act, the coal companies had the right to mine certain columns of coal (the so-called "support estate"), and after the Act they did not. The coal companies were deprived of their right to mine the coal as surely as if the government had seized it outright.

Justice Holmes recognized, however, that there were limits to this category of regulatory takings. Indeed, he noted, "[g]overnment hardly could go on if to some extent values incident to property could not be diminished without paying for every such change...." But—and this is the important if vague language—"if regulation goes too far it will be recognized as a taking."

Justice Brandeis saw the case very differently and authored an important dissent, raising two principal objections to the majority opinion. According to Justice Brandeis, the Kohler Act was nothing more than a permissible exercise of the state's police power to prevent a noxious use of property. If mining coal released deadly gases, there is no doubt that the state could have stopped the mining without paying compensation. It is inconceivable, in other words, that the state should have to pay when it prevents someone from killing someone else. And Brandeis urged the same principle to apply where the harm being prevented was not death, but the still-serious subsidence of people's homes.

Moreover, Brandeis argued that the regulation did not "go too far" because it burdened only the coal companies' subsurface rights. True, that is all the coal companies had retained, but that had been their choice. As Brandeis put it, "The rights of an owner as against the public are not increased by dividing the interests in his property into subsurface and soil." Yes, the Kohler Act eliminated coal companies' right to mine coal in certain places, but this amounted to a relatively minor restriction on the property when viewed as a whole.

Penn Coal ultimately won, and the Supreme Court ushered in a new category of constitutional protection for property. But the Court's opinion raised more questions than it answered. When does a regulation go too far? How should the property be defined? And, to what extent can a government regulate to prevent a harm without triggering the Takings Clause? The Supreme Court did not revisit these questions for 50 years, and when it did, the category of regulatory takings exploded as an important but deeply confusing source of constitutional protection for private property.

A.   The *Penn Central* Test

In *Penn Coal,* as noted above, the Supreme Court held that the government could permissibly reduce the value of people's property. However, if the law or regulation "goes too far" then it amounts to an unconstitutional taking of property—a so-called regulatory taking. But what counts as going too far?

The Supreme Court offered its most comprehensive answer in *Penn Central Transportation Co. v. City of New York.*[223] There, a new historic preservation law in New York City resulted in the denial of a permit for the Penn Central Authority to build a new skyscraper atop Grand Central Terminal. The Penn Central Authority (confusingly for New Yorkers, the owner of Grand Central) sued, alleging that denial of the permit was a taking of their air rights.

In rejecting the claim, the Supreme Court articulated a three-part balancing test, focusing on: (1) the character of the regulation; (2) the extent of the law's interference with distinct investment-backed expectations; and (3) the diminution in value of the property resulting from the regulation. *Penn Central's* "multi-factored, *ad hoc* balancing test" remains the touchstone for takings analysis in almost all cases. Moreover, the Court held that the factors were to be applied to the "parcel as a whole" and not to any distinct subunit of property—not, in other words, to the air rights alone.

Applying the factors, the Court reasoned that New York's landmarking law did not amount to a physical invasion or occupation of the property, and so the character of the regulation was relatively benign. Nor did it interfere with Grand Central's ongoing use as a railroad station, which comprised Penn Central's principle investment-backed expectation for the property. While the regulation did impose a substantial economic burden on Penn Central—and did substantially reduce the value of the property—the landmarks law offset some of those losses with transferable development rights. The law allowed Penn Central to transfer or sell some of its now-unusable air rights over Grand Central to adjacent parcels, allowing buildings higher than the zoning ordinance would otherwise permit. According to the Court, the net result was an economic burden that did not go too far. Subsequent case law, however, has clarified but more often problematized the application of each of these factors.

---

223.   438 U.S. 104 (1978) [DKA & S, p. 1113]; [M & S, p. 1285]; [S, p. 1108].

The Character of the Regulation

The "character" prong is perhaps the most straightforward, but also has its complexities. In *Penn Central,* the Court wrote: "A taking may more readily be found when the interference with property can be characterized as a physical invasion by government." And, indeed, the Court in *Loretto v. Teleprompter Manhattan CATV Corp.,*[224] just four years later, reaffirmed that conclusion. New York had passed a law requiring landlords to permit cable television companies to install cable television equipment on their buildings. A landlord sued, claiming a taking of her property, and the Supreme Court agreed. Interpreting *Penn Central,* and the "character" prong in particular, the Court in *Loretto* held that a regulation amounting to a permanent physical occupation is a *per se* taking of private property.

That may seem perfectly sensible. After all, if the government—or someone acting under authority of the government—actually enters and then continues to occupy property permanently, it feels qualitatively different than a regulatory restriction on the use of property, or even a regulatory obligation. On closer inspection, however, the focus on physical occupation is less obvious.

Return to the facts of *Loretto.* There, New York adopted its cable access law in order to facilitate development of a cable network. Government involvement was deemed important to overcome holdouts. But the government could perhaps have adopted a different approach. Instead of requiring property owners to permit cable equipment on their property, the government could perhaps have required property owners to install such equipment themselves and then connect it to neighbors' property. If this seems farfetched, think about smoke detectors or carbon monoxide detectors. Governments often require landlords to install these, and at their own expense. Requiring smoke and carbon dioxide detectors is not obviously more burdensome than the obligation to allow cable companies to install their own equipment on private property. And yet the former appear constitutionally permissible while the "permanent physical occupation" of the cable equipment is not.

Doctrinally, courts may justify the distinction by focusing on the right to exclude. After all, the right to exclude is one of the most important sticks in the bundle of property rights, and requiring access to cable companies amounts to an abrogation of that right. But then what of mail carriers? Governments frequently require landlords to install mailboxes for tenants, and to give mail carriers a way of accessing those mailboxes. And mail carriers

---

224. 458 U.S. 419 (1982) [DKA & S, p. 1082]; [M & S, p. 1302]; [S, p. 1131].

arrive almost every day! True, the cable equipment itself resides on the private property permanently, but which is actually more burdensome, and which infringes more on the right to exclude? Probably the mail carriers.

Regardless of these conceptual problems, the law is by now relatively clear that a permanent physical occupation by the government is a taking of property, and that this rule derives from *Penn Central's* "character" prong. What remains unclear, however, is whether there is anything else to that character prong. It is possible to interpret *Loretto* as merely one application of the character prong; but it is also possible to interpret *Loretto* as constituting the entire inquiry.[225] The conventional understanding, though, is that "character" now simply refers to government regulations that create permanent physical occupations.

Investment–Backed Expectations

The second *Penn Central* factor is the extent to which the regulation interferes with owners' investment-backed expectations. Under this factor, a regulation is not a taking of property if it interferes with abstract or merely hypothetical expectations. Instead, *Penn Central* demands that the expectation be supported by actual investments. A dream of some day building an office park on a site is not enough; actual investment in architectural renderings and site preparation work may be. And, importantly, the principal expectation that most people have regarding their property is the use that is already there. Accordingly, a regulation that interferes with an existing use of property is going to be viewed differently and more suspiciously than a regulation restricting or prohibiting a future use.[226] Under *Penn Central*, then, an investment-backed expectation is a protectable property interest, and a regulation interfering with it can amount to a taking.

Interestingly, though, application of this second *Penn Central* factor has changed over time. In *Kaiser Aetna v. United States*,[227] the Supreme Court subtly but profoundly changed the Penn Central language from "distinct investment-backed expectations" to "reasonable investment backed expectations." Without even acknowledging the difference in language, *Kaiser Aetna* transformed the prong from a sword for property owners into a shield for the government. After *Kaiser Aetna*, it is no longer enough for a

---

225. Thomas W. Merrill, *The Character of the Government Action*, 36 Vᴛ. L. Rᴇᴠ. 649 (2012).

226. See Christopher Serkin, *Existing Uses and the Limits of Land Use Regulations,* 84 N.Y.U. L. Rᴇᴠ. 1222 (2009) (criticizing this distinction).

227. 444 U.S. 164 (1979) [DKA & S, p. 1095]; [M & S, p. 1300]; [S, 1179].

property owner to demonstrate interference with an investment-backed expectation to support a takings claim. Now, that expectation also must be reasonable. Therefore, the prong is now frequently raised by governments defending themselves from takings liability. Yes, the property owner invested money developing the site for a new shopping center, but if it was unreasonable for the owner to think that such a use was appropriate for the property in the first place then no takings liability will attach.

Diminution in Value

The last prong in the *Penn Central* test is the extent of diminution in the value of the property resulting from the regulation. The idea is simple enough: compare the pre-regulation and post-regulation value of the property. The greater the diminution, the more likely the regulation is to be a taking.

There is no hard-and-fast rule about the extent of diminution required for a regulatory taking. One commentator, reviewing cases, has concluded that the diminution in value must "substantially exceed 50%, and should be closer to 90%"[228] before it is likely to result in a taking. Line drawing, of course, is always messy. But there are even deeper conceptual problems lurking behind the diminution in value test.

The first and most profound is the denominator problem. When evaluating the extent of diminution in value, what is the relevant denominator to use? The smaller the denominator, the greater the diminution in value, at least as measured by a percentage of the property's value. If this seems opaque, imagine a developer who owns 100 acres of land, including one acre of wetlands. If the state enacts a new regulation prohibiting any development on wetlands, it has reduced the value of his property by approximately 1% (assuming there is no other economic value to be gained from the wetland). That 1% diminution in value is insufficient to trigger takings liability. But now imagine that the developer subdivides his property into 100 separate one-acre lots, one of which is entirely wetlands. That same regulation is now a 100% wipeout of the affected one-acre parcel. Which is the relevant denominator?

The Supreme Court attempted to answer this question in *Penn Central*. Refusing to focus only on the air rights above Grand Central, the Supreme Court held that the extent of the taking must be judged against the "parcel as a whole." That language remains the touchstone for takings purposes, but despite its rhetorical simplicity it does not resolve the denominator problem. What

---

228. Mark W. Cordes, *Takings Jurisprudence as Three–Tiered Review*, 20 J. Nat. Resources & Envtl. L. 1, 39 (2005).

counts as the parcel as a whole? If the property owner (or her predecessor) divides property up into small "parcels," should each be treated as its own "whole?" This question continues to bedevil both courts and theorists. The doctrine, in other words, is clear enough: diminution in value should be judged against the parcel as a whole. But courts, lawyers, and students of property law retain tremendous discretion in defining the parcel in the first place, with many applying a kind of impressionistic "I know it when I see it" standard, focusing on "natural" divisions in property.

Penn Central highlights another complexity in the diminution in value test, too. The Court, recall, upheld the landmarking ordinance in part because of the system of transferable development rights (TDRs). But why? Is that because the TDRs were compensation for the taking, or because the TDRs prevented the regulation from being a taking in the first place? Notice the conundrum. If viewed as compensation, the TDRs were clearly inadequate under the fair market value standard the Court has traditionally required. While the TDRs were valuable, they were by no means equivalent to the value of the development rights over Grand Central itself. But if viewed as part of the Court's substantive determination of liability, they suggest a peculiar feature of the diminution in value test.

Diminution in value is often conceptualized as a threshold test. If the diminution in value is not too extreme—something less than 50%, say—then no compensation is due. But once the regulation goes too far and reduces the value of property by too much, suddenly full compensation is due (measured by the difference in the value of the property pre- and post-regulation). Therefore, the government can escape liability altogether by providing benefits that blunt the impact of a regulation just enough to fall below that threshold line, wherever it is drawn. The TDRs appeared to serve just this purpose in the *Penn Central* analysis. On their own, they were inadequate compensation. But by including them in the diminution in value calculus, the Court found no takings liability at all. Of course, it is difficult for a government to anticipate in advance how much of a benefit it must offer to avoid takings liability, but the dynamic is important and easy enough to see: by taking steps to mitigate regulatory harms, governments may be able to avoid any obligation to pay compensation.

Despite the profound theoretical problems at the heart of the doctrine, the *Penn Central* test provides the framework for evaluating most regulatory takings claims, unless one of the *per se* rules apply.

B.   The Per Se Takings Rules

While *Penn Central's ad hoc* balancing test governs most takings analysis, the Supreme Court has also identified three *per se* takings rules that supplement or even supplant *Penn Central*. The first has already been described above. It is the permanent physical occupation rule from *Loretto*. Whether principled or not, permanent physical occupations are *per se* takings that are unconstitutional in the absence of compensation. The other two *per se* rules require more introduction.

The Harm Exception Defense

Instead of identifying regulations that are *per se* takings, the harm exception provides a *per se* defense to takings liability. As Justice Brandeis argued in his dissent in *Penn Coal*, the government surely should not have to pay compensation for a regulation preventing coal companies from releasing a deadly gas. This is part of a more general point: regulations consistent with the state's police power, protecting the public's health, safety and welfare, have traditionally not been viewed as takings of property.

There are a number of important cases reaffirming that basic principle. In *Hadacheck v. Sebastian,*[229] for example, Los Angeles had criminalized the operation of brickworks within the city limits. Plaintiff had owned and operated a brickworks within Los Angeles that pre-dated the law. He was ultimately charged with violating the law, and challenged the law's constitutionality as a defense to his prosecution. The Court held that the law was a valid exercise of the City's police power to protect people from a noxious land use and so sustained the ordinance. Likewise, in *Mugler v. Kansas,*[230] the owner of a brewery sued to challenge a law prohibiting the manufacture and sale of alcoholic beverages. The Supreme Court rejected the claim. Even though the brewery was not a common law nuisance, the government acted permissibly within its police powers when it illegalized alcohol, and so there could be no taking.

At the time of these early cases, it may not have been particularly controversial to distinguish between legitimate exercises of the police power, on the one hand, and takings on the other. The police power was narrowly circumscribed, and it provided a principled and relatively limited sphere of government power immune from takings liability. A more serious problem arose, however, with the expansion of the police power in the post-*Lochner* era. As the police

---

229.   239 U.S. 394 (1915) [DKA & S, p. 1096]; [MS p. 1281]; [S, p. 1097].

230.   123 U.S. 623 (1887) [M & S, p. 1281]; [S, p. 1118, 1120–21].

power grew—and as conceptions of public welfare developed into a much more general conception of public benefit—this takings defense lost its limits. If every state regulation could be justified under the state's police power, then no regulation could be a taking.[231] Now that is a conundrum!

Courts have sometimes tried to cabin this defense by distinguishing between regulations that are preventing a harm and those that are conferring a benefit. Only the former are subject to the harm-prevention defense. But it is often impossible to distinguish between the two. On the one hand, *Hadacheck* may be preventing the harm of noise and air pollution near people's homes. On the other, it may be conferring a benefit to those neighbors at the expense of the brickworks. Is it preventing a harm or conferring a benefit? The difference is really only a matter of perspective and of baseline.

If courts defer to legislative determinations about what counts as a harm, governments can simply define their way out of takings liability. This is a particularly pressing issue in the context of environmental regulations. If a government seeks to stop the depletion of wetlands, is it preventing a harm (the destruction of wetlands), or conferring a benefit (stopping erosion and flooding of others' property)? A government might well make legislative findings that protecting wetlands is preventing a harm. But should courts defer? If they do: no taking. But if they do not, courts would have to second-guess legislative determinations about harms and benefits, an enterprise that looks uncomfortably like the kind of economic substantive due process review that courts rejected post *Lochner*.

It may be that community standards are able to distinguish between preventing a harm and conferring a benefit.[232] Or it may be possible to link up to a particular historical account of harm-prevention—an approach considered immediately below. But this much is clear: without a principled basis for distinguishing between harms and benefits, the *per se* harm-prevention defense is an exception that threatens to subsume the entire takings inquiry.

Total Wipeouts

The last *per se* rule comes from *Lucas v. South Carolina Coastal Council*.[233] There, a new beachfront management act prevented David Lucas from building any permanent habitable struc-

---

231. See Bradley C. Karkkainen, *The Police Power Revisited: Phantom Incorporation and the Roots of the Takings "Muddle,"* 90 Minn. L. Rev. 826 (2006).

232. See Bruce A. Ackerman, Private Property and the Constitution (1977).

233. 505 U.S. 1003 (1992) [DKA & S, p. 1131]; [M & S, p. 1314]; [S, p. 1161].

tures on his South Carolina beachfront property. He sued, and instead of simply applying the *Penn Central* test, Justice Scalia, writing for the majority, crafted a new rule that a total wipeout of all economically valuable uses of property is a *per se* taking. On the one hand, this hardly seems surprising. After all, if a regulation that goes too far can be a taking, then a regulation that goes all the way is definitely a taking. But doctrinally, the case heralded a potentially important expansion of *Penn Central* because, where the total wipeout rule applies, courts need not consider the other elements of the *Penn Central* test. That is, a total wipeout is a taking regardless of the extent and reasonableness of the property owner's expectations.

The majority crafted one important exception, however. After criticizing the traditional "harm-prevention defense" discussed above, it held that a regulation effecting a total wipeout was not a taking only if it was consistent with background principles of property and nuisance law. Often dubbed the "common law nuisance defense," it means that regulations of land uses traditionally considered nuisances are not takings, nor are regulations that merely codify background principles of property law. In other words, the government is not taking your property if it is prohibiting activities in which you had no right to engage in the first place.

Both aspects of the *Lucas* test—the total wipeout rule and the common law nuisance defense—are considerably more complex than they might appear at first glance.

At the time it was decided, *Lucas* was seen as an incredibly important case. It appeared to mark a turn to *per se* rules, and therefore a ramping up of constitutional protection for private property rights. Advocates of strong regulatory authority were deeply concerned that stronger protection of property rights would mark the erosion of the regulatory state. After all, many government activities impact property rights, and—as Justice Holmes recognized in *Penn Coal*—government could hardly go on if its incidental impacts on private property are unconstitutional. The *Lucas* test itself promised to curtail a lot of government regulation depending on how narrowly courts were willing to define the property at issue. After all, as the denominator problem demonstrates, it is easy to find a total wipeout if the relevant property is sufficiently small.

In fact, the *Lucas* test has turned out to have very little bite. Total wipeouts are vanishingly rare. In *Lucas* itself, the Court found a total wipeout only because the parties stipulated that David Lucas' land had been made valueless. Although no permanent habitable structures could be placed on the property, it was not literally valueless—a point made by Justice Blackmun in dissent. Someone else might well have been willing to pay to use the property for camping or picnicking. Neighbors might have bought it for some amount of money simply to own more property. In short, the regulation may have dramatically reduced the property's value, but would almost certainly not have been a *total* wipeout if the parties had not stipulated to the fact.

Moreover, the Court subsequently refused to define property as narrowly as property rights advocates had hoped. The case that most limited *Lucas'* impact was *Tahoe–Sierra Preservation Council, Inc. v. Tahoe Regional Planning Agency.*[234] Lake Tahoe presented (and continues to present) complex regulatory challenges. The lake itself is extraordinarily beautiful, and there have been tremendous development pressures in the area. That development, however, has threatened the quality of the water in the lake—one of its most distinctive features. To address those development pressures, Nevada and California (both of which claim some portion of the lake) formed a regional planning agency with jurisdiction over the lake and its environs. That agency adopted successive building moratoria, in place for almost three years, to stop development while undertaking a more comprehensive planning process. Property owners sued, alleging a total wipeout of their property for that three-year period.

The Supreme Court rejected the takings claim, holding that "property is defined by the metes and bounds that describe its geographic dimensions and the term of years that describes the temporal aspect of the owner's interest." While the regulation may have been a total wipeout for the duration of the moratorium, it was not a total wipeout of the value of the property viewed over its economic life. And it therefore was not a total wipeout of *all* economically valuable use of the property. The Court held that *Penn Central* analysis was appropriate instead.

The outcome may seem straightforward, but imagine if the case had come out differently—if a regulation for a discrete period could amount to a total wipeout under *Lucas.* Then, *Lucas* would have applied much more broadly. Property can be divided in many different ways, after all. If a government eliminated the right to lease property, or the right to dispose of it at death, both could be considered total wipeouts of those particular rights. Dividing property in this way is often referred to as "conceptual severance,"

---

234. 535 U.S. 302 (2002) [DKA & S, p. 1158]; [M & S, p. 1330; 1337]; [S, p. 1161].

referring to subdividing property into discrete conceptual parts, each of which can then be treated individually for takings purposes.[235] But by rejecting the total wipeout rule in *Tahoe–Sierra*, the Court also rejected this aggressive form of conceptual severance and rendered *Lucas* largely toothless.

Perhaps ironically, the *Lucas* "common law nuisance defense" has proven to be the more influential aspect of the opinion. While application of the harm-prevention defense remains difficult and contested, *Lucas* has clarified at least this much: if the government is regulating a common law nuisance, or regulating consistently with background principles of property law, it is not a taking. As a result, *Lucas* created a more effective shield for governments than a sword for property owners.

Even so, the common law nuisance defense remains controversial. As Justice Blackmun wrote in his *Lucas* dissent: "There is nothing magical in the reasoning of judges long dead.... If judges in the 18th and 19th centuries can distinguish a harm from a benefit, why not judges in the 20th century, and if judges can, why not legislators?" The point is a powerful one. In an effort to prohibit legislatures defining away takings liability by declaring a regulation to be "harm prevention," Justice Scalia tried to tie the defense to traditional or common law nuisances. But what is so magical about common law nuisances? They simply reflect the determination of common law judges about the reasonable use of property. Justice Blackmun's reasoning suggests that the harm-prevention defense should remain robust, and should not be limited to common law nuisances.

There is another problem, too. What counts as a "background principle of property law?" *Lucas* established that a regulation is not a taking if it is prohibiting you from doing something you had no right to do in the first place (e.g. exclude aid workers from entering your property to meet with migrant workers[236]). But should background principles include only common law property doctrines—the product of decisions by long-dead judges—or should it include legislative enactments, too? And, if so, which ones? Those difficult questions were at the crux of the Supreme Court's decision in *Palazzolo v. Rhode Island*.[237] In that case, a company owned property consisting mostly of wetlands (The company had, in fact, been formed for purposes of acquiring the property.) At the time of

---

235. See Margaret Jane Radin, *The Liberal Conception of Property: Cross Currents in the Jurisprudence of Takings*, 88 COLUM. L. REV. 1667 (1988).

236. See *State v. Shack, supra* Chapter 1.

237. 533 U.S. 606 (2001) [DKA & S, p. 1152]; [M & S, p. 1332]; [S, p. 1162].

that original acquisition, wetlands were largely unregulated and the company anticipated being able to fill them and develop the property. Subsequently, two important events occurred. First, Rhode Island adopted new wetlands protection, making it all but impossible to develop the bulk of the property. And, second, the company owning the property dissolved for non-payment of corporate income taxes. At that point, ownership of the underlying property transferred by operation of law to the company's sole shareholder, Anthony Palazzolo. Prevented from developing the property by the new wetlands regulations, Palazzolo sued, alleging a taking.

The Court first refused to apply the *Lucas* total wipeout rule. Although the regulation had reduced the commercial value of Palazzolo's property from approximately $3.2 million to a mere $200,000, the Court held that this did not effect a total wipeout, and instead applied the *Penn Central* factors.

The critical issue for the Supreme Court was whether the wetlands regulations should be viewed as background principles of state property law. If so—if Palazzolo took title to the property subject to those pre-existing regulations—then he could have no takings claim. Of course, the regulations had not existed when the company originally acquired the property—the regulations were not pre-existing at that time. But when the company dissolved, and title to the property passed to Palazzolo by operation of law, that amounted to a change in ownership. Therefore, the regulations were pre-existing as of that date.

The majority opinion held that a takings claim can survive transfer of the property. Otherwise, the availability of takings claims would turn on idiosyncratic questions about whether specific property had or had not changed hands. As the Court cryptically put it, "The State may not put so potent a Hobbesian stick into the Lockean bundle." In other words, the state does not have limitless power to change property rights. The Court did not provide any particularly clear guidance about how and when pre-existing regulations do become part of the background principles of property law. Other opinions in the case, however, offered three different competing approaches.

According to Justice O'Connor, concurring in the decision, existing regulations are not automatically part of the background principles of property law. They are a factor for courts to consider when examining the extent of a property owner's reasonable expectations. Justice Scalia, also concurring, favored a more bright-line rule that pre-existing regulations are irrelevant to a property owner's reasonable expectations. If a regulation is a taking as applied to owner X, then it is a taking if owner X sells his property to owner Z. A taking is a taking, and a takings claim transfers with the property.

Justice Stevens, however, favored the opposite rule. He believed that the presence of pre-existing regulations was dispositive. In other words, a property owner who takes title to property knowing of pre-existing regulations cannot then challenge those regulations.

These separate opinions are often excluded from property casebooks but nevertheless highlight the important question at the heart of *Palazzolo*. If someone buys property with pre-existing regulations limiting the use of that property, do those regulations constitute the buyer's reasonable expectations with regard to the property? If "background principles of property and nuisance law" from *Lucas* include any legislative or regulatory restrictions on property in place at the time of acquisition, then property owners take title subject to existing regulations and have no takings claims. If not, a buyer is not only acquiring the property itself, but is also acquiring the seller's potential takings claims. The majority opinion in *Palazzolo* only rejected the *per se* rules in either direction, leaving the content of "background principles of property and nuisance law" still up for grabs.

* * *

By now, it should be clear that takings law is in relative disarray. There are any number of important issues—from the denominator problem, to harm-prevention, to background principles of property and nuisance law—that have resisted any neat resolution. If there is one thing that draws consensus from commentators it is that takings law is a conceptual muddle. Indeed, the doctrinal challenges go far beyond those addressed in the standard introduction to property. They involve complicated questions of remedy (injunction versus damages); of justiciability (ripeness and *res judicata*); of unconstitutional conditions (what a government can demand for regulatory approval); and the complicated relationship between the Takings Clause and the Due Process Clause. All of these are topics for further advanced study, and all are deeply contentious.

In an introductory study of the Takings Clause, then, the goal should not be certain answers. The goal, instead, should simply be to apply the appropriate analysis, even as the outcomes remain unsettled. Fortunately, the broad outlines of takings doctrine are surprisingly clear. First, ask whether any of the *per se* takings rules apply. Does the regulation amount to a permanent physical occupation of property? Is it a total wipeout of all economically beneficial use? Is it regulating a common law nuisance (or, at least, consistently with background principles of property and nuisance law)? If not—and usually none of the *per se* takings rules apply, at least not with any degree of certainty—then apply the *Penn Central* test. That test requires balancing: the character of the regulation; the extent of its interference with distinct (or reasonable) investment-backed expectations, and the resulting diminution in value.

If the regulation *goes too far* under that three-factor test, and none of the defenses are applicable, then it is a taking and requires compensation.

C. Scholarly Accounts

The Takings Clause has generally resisted consistent application by courts. Its animating principles remain contested, and the law is in a state of perpetual confusion. Many important scholarly accounts have sought to untangle takings law and a select few are worth considering specifically, both because of their perspective on the Takings Clause, but also for what they reveal about the relationship between the Takings Clause and the rest of the property curriculum. Here, the discussion returns explicitly to the opening chapter's focus on history, law and economics, and more philosophical considerations.

History

Dean William Treanor has provided the most thorough history of the Takings Clause in the legal literature.[238] He points out that the Takings Clause was the only provision in the Bill of Rights that was not demanded during the state ratifying conventions. Accordingly, there are almost no recorded discussions about the meaning or purpose of the Clause. James Madison was primarily responsible for adding the Takings Clause to the constitution. He evidently believed it was necessary to protect landowners from a tyranny of the majority. According to Dean Treanor, Madison anticipated massive population growth that would put landowners at risk of having their property expropriated through majoritarian redistribution. The concern seems somewhat outlandish in retrospect. Yes, we have had a massive population explosion, but we are not particularly worried about systematic exploitation of property owners. Nevertheless, Dean Treanor argues that the history of the takings clause, while murky, reveals that Madison intended it to

---

238. William Michael Treanor, *The Original Understanding of the Takings Clause and the Political Process*, 95 COLUM. L. REV. 782 (1995).

protect only against physical expropriations in the context of political exploitation. Madison never envisioned the Takings Clause applying to mere regulations.

That historical account unfortunately does little to illuminate the takings problem today. After all, modern governments regulate in ways that would have been unimaginable in the founding era, and the capacity of governments to affect property rights has expanded accordingly. Perhaps the most we can safely say is that the history of the Takings Clause is sparse, and something more is needed to make sense of it.

Law and Economics

There are several competing law and economics accounts of the Takings Clause that provide helpful insights. On one view, government actions imposing costs on property owners are a form of regulatory externality. Governments, if allowed to act for free, will discount or ignore the costs of their actions (a phenomenon called "fiscal illusion"). The Takings Clause and its compensation requirement are therefore best seen as constitutional mechanisms to ensure that government actors internalize the costs of their actions. Making governments pay will induce efficient regulatory incentives.

The claim here is familiar and powerful. If a government is unwilling to pay for the costs it is imposing on burdened property owners, then—on this view—the regulation is probably not enhancing societal welfare. For example, if environmental regulations, or historic preservation laws, were really valuable to the public, then the public should be willing to compensate the property owners who bear the costs of those regulatory regimes. And if the public is unwilling to pay—specifically, if the government is unwilling to raise taxes to pay compensation for such programs—then the regulations are probably generating more harm than gain and should not have been enacted in the first place.

In this vision, the Takings Clause can be seen as a mechanism for keeping the government honest. Requiring the government to pay ensures that its regulations are net beneficial from society's perspective. And, therefore, the Takings Clause should apply to any regulatory harm. The Takings Clause should not be limited to instances of extreme regulatory burdens, as in *Penn Central,* but should apply much more broadly than it does now. The underlying intuition is that if the government were forced to pay for all or even most of its regulatory burdens, it would enact far fewer regulations than it does today.

One response to this economic argument focuses on the nature of governments. Public choice theory (sometimes called rational choice theory) posits that government actors are motivated primarily by political pressures and not fiscal ones.[239] Politicians want to maximize their political capital and not government funds. Therefore, forcing governments to pay compensation will not actually force government actors to internalize the cost of their actions, at least not in the relevant currency.

It is possible that fiscal costs will translate into political costs. If voters and taxpayers are extremely attentive to government spending, then incurring takings liability might translate into political costs. But this requires a heroic assumption about the nature of taxpayers, at least in larger jurisdictions.[240] In fact, the effect of compensation may be to buy off the one group of people—affected property owners—well situated to resist inefficient or burdensome government regulations. The effect of compensation may simply be to distribute money from a relatively apathetic and inattentive tax base to affected property owners. In this view, compensation will not force the government to internalize the costs of its actions. It will not deter or meaningfully limit inefficient government regulations. It might even have the opposite effect.

The truth is probably somewhere in the middle. Compensation may well have some meaningful effect on regulatory incentives. As a general matter, government actors often appear quite concerned about incurring costs. But takings liability may not translate into political pressure in any clear or direct way. That is, government actors may be attentive to the fact of liability, but relatively inattentive to the actual cost. In this view, then, the Takings Clause does not create a good mechanism for pricing government regulations, and compensating for the costs of government actions will not ensure efficiency. But all of this depends on competing views of governments: how they act, what motivates government actors, and how responsive they will be to budget outflows. All of this remains contested.

A different kind of economic account, then, focuses on property owners' investment incentives. In the view of some theorists, the risk of regulatory harm is no different from the risk of a fire or natural disaster.[241] All are risks that can reduce the value of people's investment in property. Insurance is the typical response.

---

239. See, e.g., Daryl Levinson Daryl J. Levinson, *Making Government Pay: Markets, Politics, and the Allocation of Constitutional Costs*, 67 U. CHI. L. REV. 345 (2000); Daniel A. Farber & Philip P. Frickey, *Public Choice Revisited*, 96 MICH. L. REV. 1715 (1998).

240. For an account of the political dynamic in smaller jurisdictions, see Christopher Serkin, *Big Differences for Small Governments: Local Governments and the Takings Clause*, 81 N.Y.U. L. REV. 1624 (2006).

241. See, e.g., Louis Kaplow, *An Economic Analysis of Legal Transitions*, 99 HARV. L. REV. 509 (1986).

And a robust private insurance market for risks like fires and floods is critical to prevent under-investment by risk-averse property owners. If people had no way to insure against the risk of fire, for example, they would probably under-invest in their property. Regulatory harms are no different in their effect on owner investment incentives, except that there is no private insurance market to protect against government regulation. In this view, the Takings Clause should be seen as a kind of mandatory public insurance, designed to protect people at least against catastrophic loss at the hands of the government.

But this account, too, comes with countervailing concerns. Takings "insurance" is free to property owners. It is, after all, constitutionally mandated. The availability of free public insurance can therefore induce a kind of moral hazard, allowing people to discount the risk of adverse regulatory changes. Society might actually benefit if people have an incentive to investigate and anticipate at least some new regulations. If new scientific information reveals the importance of wetlands in many ecosystems, we might want property owners to include the risk of new wetlands regulations when making their investment decisions. On the margin, compensation through the Takings Clause allows people to discount if not ignore those risks, and that might lead to inefficient over-investment in property.

Step back for a moment and think about these various competing economic accounts. On the one hand, compensation may be important to force government actors to internalize the costs of their actions. On the other, compensation may actually allow government actors to minimize political costs even for inefficient actions. Alternatively, compensation for government regulations might be important to induce risk-averse property owners to invest in property. But compensation might actually induce property owners to over-invest. Again, there is no consensus on these difficult issues. For the property student, it is enough to recognize these competing accounts, and to understand how different views about the motivations of government actors and property owners generate very different prescriptions for the reach of takings liability.

Michelman's Utilitarian Formula

Professor Frank Michelman offered a different kind of overarching economic framework for the Takings Clause in a seminal article from the late 1960s.[242] According to Professor Michelman, when a government action creates more harm than benefit, it is

---

242. Frank I. Michelman, *Property, Utility, and Fairness: Comments on the Ethical Foundations of "Just Compensation" Law*, 80 HARV. L. REV. 1165 (1967).

inefficient and should not be allowed. It is not rendered constitutionally benign through payment of compensation.

Instead, a takings problem arises only when the regulation is efficient—when, in other words, it is creating more benefit to society than it is harming affected property owners. But in this category of efficient and therefore desirable regulations, when should the government have to pay? In other words, the test for compensation under the Takings Clause should not be whether the regulation is generating a net benefit to society; that should be a precondition for the government to act in the first place. Instead, a different kind of analysis is required.

For Professor Michelman, the appropriate takings inquiry requires comparing three different values: efficiency gains, settlement costs, and demoralization costs. Efficiency gains are simply the net societal gains from the regulations (the benefits minus the costs to the impacted property owners). Settlement and demoralization costs are more complicated.

Settlement costs, in this calculation, include the costs of identifying the property owners who are harmed by a regulation, and then valuing the extent of their damages. Settlement costs can be small, as when a regulation affects a small number of people. Or settlement costs can be huge, as when a regulation has a small and diffuse impact on a large number of people.

Demoralization costs are the most abstract, and also the most innovative. They include the costs of *not* compensating. They are, in other words, the costs suffered by society if government harms go uncompensated. They include real economic costs, like foregone investments, and also psychological costs resulting from the perception of unfairness.

For Michelman, then, the compensation question boils down to this: if settlement costs are higher than demoralization costs, the government should not pay. If demoralization costs are higher than settlement costs, the government should pay. And, if both are higher than efficiency gains, the government simply should not act. To put this in more colloquial terms, takings liability should attach if the costs of compensating are lower than the costs of not compensating.

Obviously, measuring settlement and demoralization costs with any precision is a difficult if not impossible undertaking. Professor Michelman was well aware of the practical difficulties of his calculation. So instead of arguing for some fine-grained application in every case, he suggested some categories of cases in which demoralization costs would almost certainly exceed settlement costs. First, where the government actually invades property, settlement costs are likely to be very low and demoralization costs very high. It is easy to know whose property was physically invaded, especially if the government establishes a permanent physical presence. It is therefore not costly to identify affected property owners. At the same time, demoralization costs are likely to be high if compensation is not paid because of the seriousness of losing the right to exclude. The government is creating a substantial burden, and people are likely to feel that the government should pay.

Likewise, if regulatory burdens are so high that they significantly decrease the value of property then settlement costs are again likely to be low and demoralization costs high. While it can be prohibitively difficult to identify all of the people affected by a government regulation, it is relatively easy to find the people who suffer a dramatic decrease in the value of their property. Settlement costs associated with finding and paying only them will be relatively low. Simultaneously, the demoralization costs associated with failing to compensate people who suffered a significant economic harm will be quite high. So here, again, this combination of low settlement costs and high demoralization costs means that the government should pay.

Finally, if a government interferes with property owners' expectations that are crystallized in the actual use of the property, then takings liability again should attach. As Michelman explained, an interference with an ongoing use of property as opposed to a prospective future use is easier to detect (meaning lower settlement costs) and is generally more demoralizing if uncompensated.

If this analysis sounds familiar, it is. The Supreme Court largely adopted Professor Michelman's conclusions in the *Penn Central* test. The Court's focus on the character of the regulation, investment-backed expectations, and diminution in value track neatly onto Michelman's identification of the categories of cases most likely to be associated with low settlement costs and high demoralization costs. His article, then, provides an important blueprint for understanding the principles animating the *Penn Central* test.

Fairness

An entirely different kind of takings theory focuses on the fairness of the distribution of societal benefits and burdens. As the Supreme Court once held, the purpose of the Takings Clause is to "bar Government from forcing some people alone to bear public burdens which, in all fairness and justice, should be borne by the public as a whole.''[243] Known as the *Armstrong* principle, its focus is on the just distribution of burdens and benefits. It implicates deep questions about the nature of property and the community obligations property entails.

The *Armstrong* principle calls on courts to address directly what counts as a fair and just distribution of burdens and benefits. When it comes to property regulation, this means asking what a community can reasonably expect property owners to give up for the sake of others. And this depends, at least in part, on the fairness of the initial distribution of property. Here, the discussion returns full circle to the concepts and insights from the opening chapters.

Under one account, today's owners can trace their claims back to some mythologized original acquisition. People removed property from the state of nature, invented and fabricated new forms of property, and injected it all into the stream of commerce. Transaction after transaction, always from lower-valued to higher-valued users in a chain of voluntary transfers, has resulted in the current distribution of property. Owners today have a kind of inherited moral claim to their property, acquired through the chain of title all the way back to original acquisition and the principle of first-in-time. And so, in this view, the status quo comes with moral significance and defines the baseline for deciding the fair and just allocation of property. Readjustments by the government are incursions into the status quo, and the Takings Clause should provide a remedy for adversely affected property owners.

Alternatively, the current distribution of property rights may be inextricably bound up with the history of the state. It is the product of political policies, many of which were demonstrably unjust. For example, systematic racial discrimination and the imposition of regulatory and environmental burdens on racial minorities and the poor have created profoundly unfair distributions of property. In this view, the current distribution is not the result of a chain of voluntary transfers, but is instead the product of more or less explicit expropriation by the rich and powerful over the decades and centuries. Owners today inherit property that is tainted by this history, and the current distribution is not entitled to great moral authority. Therefore, the state can make redistributive claims to property, at least for remedial purposes, without interfering in some inherently just and natural ordering.

---

243. Armstrong v. United States, 364 U.S. 40 (1960) [M & S, p. 1282]; [S, p. 1104; 1116].

There is no right answer, only recognition of the complex and contested moral weight given to the current distribution of property. The greater that weight, the less power the government should have to adjust property rights. But the more contingent the allocation of property rights seems—and, worse, the more it results from systemic discrimination and imbalances in power—the more the government should be able to make readjustments without implicating the Takings Clause.

Finally, it may be that the value of property today is at least partly if not largely attributable to the state. Development rights are valuable because the government has made specific investments in infrastructure, and often has created favorable tax treatment or offered other financial rewards for investments in certain kinds of property. At least where this is true, the state may make substantial claims to property without violating the Takings Clause. But notice that this requires a commitment to a particular vision of fairness. It takes as the relevant baseline the value of property in the absence of the governments' programs and incentives. It does not ensure horizontal equity—that all similarly situated property owners are treated alike. If the government makes mortgage interest deductible for all homeowners, that valuable benefit may not justify a regulatory burden on a subset of homeowners.

The goal here is not to resolve these disputes, but is instead to highlight how the Takings Clause implicates the deepest questions about the nature of property. And that, ultimately, is the purpose of studying the Takings Clause in an introductory property course. This material belongs here, instead of in an introduction to Constitutional Law, because of what it tells us about the nature of property.

D.   Judicial Takings and the Public Trust

A final topic—newly ascendant in takings doctrine—ties many of these issues together and is therefore a useful capstone for this chapter and for the book. Can a state *court* take property by changing the content of state property rights? That question was the subject of a recent Supreme Court decision, *Stop the Beach Renourishment, Inc. v. Florida Dep't of Envtl. Protection.*[244]

In *Stop the Beach*, Florida had adopted new beach management regulations that, among other things, redefined the boundary between public and private property. That boundary has its origins in

---

244. 130 S.Ct. 2592 (2010) [M & S, p. 1357].

the complicated public trust doctrine, which requires a detour to put the controversy in its property context.

Traditionally, the mean high water mark—the mean high tide line, in other words—defines the boundary between public and private property. The dry sand to the landward side of the line belongs to the littoral owner (i.e., the owner of the property adjacent to the ocean). The wet sand on the ocean side of the line, however, is public, and is typically held as part of the public trust.

The public trust doctrine comes originally from Roman law, which held the sea to be owned collectively by all mankind for fishing and navigation. That principle migrated to England and then to America, which has traditionally viewed the foreshore—the land submerged by tidal waters between the high and low water marks—as publicly owned.[245]

States take very different approaches to public trust land, and their various definitions are not at all static.[246] Among the most frequently contested questions is whether public ownership of the foreshore also includes a public right of access, and perhaps even use of the dry sand above the foreshore for purposes of recreation. New Jersey has been at the forefront of these issues, and in *Matthews v. Bay Head Improvement Assoc.*,[247] the New Jersey Supreme Court held that the public trust doctrine required the public to have reasonable public access to the beach.[248] Moreover, once people are on the beach, their use is not necessarily restricted to the foreshore itself. As the *Bay Head* court recognized, the ocean's importance to people in New Jersey has changed over the years and is no longer primarily for fishing but instead for recreation, and that recreation requires a dry place to set one's towel. So this right, too, is protected by the public trust doctrine.

Stepping back from these details, however, the public trust cases illustrate how judicial opinions can limit or even abrogate private owners' right to exclude, and can shift the boundary between public and private land. The overarching question, then, is

---

245. The leading case is *Illinois Cent. R.R. Co. v. Illinois*, 146 U.S. 387 (1892) [M & S, p. 296] (invalidating sale of Chicago lakefront for violating public trust).

246. For a comparison, see Robin Kundis Craig, *A Comparative Guide to the Western States' Public Trust Doctrines: Public Values, Private Rights, and the Evolution Toward an Ecological Public Trust*, 37 ECOLOGY LAW QUARTERLY 53 (2010); Robin Kundis Craig, *A Comparative Guide to the Eastern Public Trust Doctrines: Classification of States, Property Rights, and State Summaries*, 16 PENN ST. ENVTL. L. REV. 1, 113 (2007).

247. 95 N.J. 306, 471 A.2d 355 (1984).

248. *See also* Raleigh Ave. Beach Assoc. v. Atlantis Beach Club, 879 A.2d 112 (N.J. 2005) [DKA & S, p. 800]; [S, p. 63]; State of Oregon ex rel. Thornton v. Hay, 462 P.2d 671 (Or. 1969) [M & S, p. 308]; [S, p. 65].

whether a judicial opinion limiting private property rights can violate the Fifth Amendment Takings Clause.

Under the public trust doctrine, the boundary of littoral owners' property has traditionally changed as the actual mean high water mark shifts over time. The line fluctuates with erosion and accretion, and so the property boundary is not traditionally fixed. In *Stop the Beach,* new Florida regulations changed that rule, establishing an "erosion control line" to replace the actual mean high water mark. This would allow the Florida Department of Environmental Protection to engage in beach renourishment, increasing the size of the beach, without actually shifting the boundary between public and private property. This, in turn, raised the possibility that littoral owners would no longer own all the way to the water's edge, but would instead have their property end at the erosion control line, which might be landward of the new mean high water mark.

A number of beachfront owners sued in state court, alleging that the regulation's new definition of the erosion control line was an unconstitutional taking of their property. They litigated all the way up through the Florida court system until the Florida Supreme Court rejected their claims finding, in essence, that the property rights of littoral owners did not include the right to own all the way to the water's edge. In other words, the Florida Supreme Court held that the new regulations were not a taking because the property owners did not actually possess the rights that they claimed had been taken.

Plaintiffs then petitioned for certiorari to the United States Supreme Court, but now alleging that the Florida Supreme Court had taken their property by defining away their property rights. Their claim, in other words, was for a judicial taking of their property.

The Supreme Court issued a fractured plurality opinion. The justices all agreed that the Florida Supreme Court had not, in fact, taken the plaintiffs' property, but they disagreed about whether a judicial takings claim is even possible. The justices all agreed that pre-existing Florida law did not, in fact, grant the rights that plaintiffs' claimed. Therefore, the Florida Supreme Court had not taken plaintiffs' property. But a plurality of the Court was willing to accept the premise that a state court could run afoul of the Takings Clause on different facts.

Justice Scalia, writing for that plurality, observed that the Takings Clause is phrased in the passive voice. It provides: "[N]or shall private property be taken for public use without just compensation." It leaves the identity of the taker undefined, and so the Takings Clause, by its terms, applies equally to all branches of government. Moreover, Justice Scalia argued that it would be inappropriate to allow a state to do by judicial fiat what it could not accomplish through legislative action. After all, if the State enacted legislation expanding the public trust doctrine, or requiring property owners to allow the public to access their property, this could very well be a taking under *Loretto*. The result should be the same if the source of the legal change is a court.

There is a compelling logic to the plurality opinion, but it runs into a profound conceptual problem. After *Erie R.R. Co. v. Tompkins*,[249] there is no federal common law of property. When federal courts apply the Takings Clause, they therefore must look to state law for the content of property rights. How, then, could a state supreme court take property? When the Florida Supreme Court held that Florida law did not give littoral owners the right to own all the way to the water, it could not be wrong, in the same way that the United States Supreme Court cannot be wrong about the federal constitution. There is no higher interpretive authority.

One way to avoid this problem is to find some source for the content of property rights outside of state positive law. But that source cannot be federal common law without overturning *Erie* (a bedrock principle of federal courts). Perhaps, then, there is some natural law backstop to the content of state property rights. State courts are capable of violating natural rights, even if they are definitionally incapable of violating their own state law. But this just begs the question of how those natural rights arise. Federal courts have never committed themselves to a theory of natural law to provide content to property rights, and doing so would be a dramatic step. The problem boils down to this: state courts cannot violate property rights if property rights come from state courts.

There is another doctrinal hurdle, as well. Regulatory takings claims amount to allegations that the government has *de facto* exercised its power of eminent domain. A regulatory takings claim against a government agency is typically styled as an "inverse condemnation" action, and it is effectively an eminent domain action triggered by the property owner instead of by the government. But courts do not have the power of eminent domain. They are incapable of violating the Takings Clause because they lack the power to take private property.

Notice the stakes of the debate. Instead of some narrow issue about the foreshore, the possibility of judicial takings claims raises

---

249. 304 U.S. 64 (1938).

questions about the source and content of property rights, and about the role of courts in shaping private rights. If nothing else, these competing views demonstrate the complexity of the judicial takings problem. While there are strong reasons to extend takings liability to courts, there are equally compelling reasons not to do so. There is no straightforward answer to the judicial takings puzzle, but it both is illuminated by and—as importantly—illuminates some of the different theoretical treatments of the Takings Clause.

For one, the traditional law and economics account of takings liability seems to apply much differently to courts than to legislatures. In this view, the purpose of the Takings Clause is to force the government to internalize the costs of its actions. But that account seems entirely inapplicable to judicial takings. Imposing liability on the state for judicial decisions will not force judges to internalize the costs of their actions. There is no plausible feedback mechanism, or at least no calibrated one, between state liability and judicial decisionmaking.

Nor is it obvious how the threat of judicial decisionmaking will affect property owners' investment incentives. The substance of judicial decisions is harder to anticipate than regulatory changes, which typically come with public notice and participation. And, if people have only limited capacity to anticipate judge-made legal changes, then those changes will have only limited ability to influence property owners' investment incentives one way or another.[250]

In discussing demoralization costs, Professor Michelman posited that regulatory harms can be more demoralizing than other injuries to property because they necessarily involve the government intentionally and strategically imposing burdens. The worry is that government burdens, unlike natural disasters, are not randomly distributed but will be systematically imposed by the political process.[251] This carries less weight where the source of the legal change is a court instead of politics. The case-driven process of common law evolution makes the imposition of systematic burdens much less likely, and people are likely to experience judge-made changes more like natural disasters than strategically imposed governmental burdens. At least where this is true, Professor Michelman's formula will demand compensation less often.

---

250. See Frederic Bloom & Christopher Serkin, *Suing Courts,* 79 U. CHI. L. REV. 553 (2012).

251. Michelman, *supra,* at 1217 ("[O]ne faces the risk of being systematically imposed upon, which seems a risk of a very different order from the risk of occasional, accidental injury.").

However, the property owner presumably does not care about the institutional source of the legal change. Legislatures have no monopoly on the power to interfere with property owners' expectations. And the Supreme Court previously clarified that takings claims—unlike Due Process claims—are based entirely on the extent of the impact on private property rights.[252] Takings claims are indifferent to the purpose of the government action, and are entirely owner-centric. If requiring public access is a taking, it should be a taking whatever the source of the rule.

Judicial takings may well turn out to be a flash in the pan. *Stop the Beach* generated enormous academic attention when it was decided, but its actual reach remains to be seen. Nevertheless, the concept of judicial takings is a useful one for applying takings theories in a new context and for revisiting property concepts that have recurred throughout this book: about the source of property rights, the nature of owners' expectations, and the relative institutional competence of courts and legislatures.

---

252. Lingle v. Chevron U.S.A., Inc., 544 U.S. 528 (2005) [DKA & S, p. 1161n.]; [M & S, p. 1338].

CONCLUSION

Why have property? Hopefully, the answer to that question is now clearer. The doctrines at the heart of property law cover an enormous expanse of people's interactions with each other and with the state. Property law gives us rights against the world, creates a sphere of protected liberty, and encourages the efficient use of resources. It gives us the tools to divide and reconfigure property in valuable ways, and minimizes transaction costs to facilitate transfers to higher-valued users.

But property law is also fundamentally about human interactions. Property rules provide governance mechanisms for neighbors and spouses. It cabins the negotiations between landlords and tenants. And it is one crucial point of intersection between public and private rights.

Property also casts long shadows in time. Property arrangements can apply beyond the parties to an agreement and can bind successors far into the future. And decisions today—about how to bundle or unbundle property, about covenants, about trusts and future interests—can substantially shape that future.

Ultimately, then, property law is not about specific resources in the world. It is, instead, the central building block for private law. Advanced topics, from family law to secured transactions, depend fundamentally on the content of property rights. So, in a sense, the introductory study of property is a kind of smorgasbord; a tasting menu of topics available for further study in the law.

But of this, at least, there can be no doubt: property is one of the most essential sticks in the bundle of the law.

TABLE OF CASES

References are to Pages.

INDEX

References are to Pages

M

N

O

P

†